Information graphics
a survey of typographic, diagrammatic and cartographic communication

U.S. edition published in 1989 by
Van Nostrand Reinhold Company
Inc.
115 Fifth Avenue
New York, New York 10003

Van Nostrand Reinhold Company
Limited
Molly Millars Lane
Wokingham, Berkshire RG11 2PY,
England

Van Nostrand Reinhold
480 La Trobe Street
Melbourne, Victoria 300, Australia

Macmillan of Canada
Division of Canada Publishing
Corporation
164 Commander Boulevard
Agincourt, Ontario M1S 3C7,
Canada

Information graphics

a survey of typographic, diagrammatic and cartographic communication

Peter Wildbur

VNR VAN NOSTRAND REINHOLD COMPANY
_____ New York

Acknowledgements

First published in Great Britain by Trefoil Publications Ltd

Origination of illustrations by Data Base Resources Plc Ltd, Singapore Set in Helvetica Light by Goodfellow and Egan Ltd, Cambridge, England Printed in Italy by Graphicom

Book/cover design by Peter Wildbur

Access Press Ltd, 63. Akademische Verlagsanstalt, 83, 89. Ariston Domestic Appliances Ltd, 32. Austrian State Railways, 97.
BBC TV, 70, 107, 109. Bollman-Bildkarten-Verlag, 95. Braun AG, 31, 35. British Airways, 102. British Library, 50. British Rail, 14. Buckminster Fuller Institute, Los Angeles, 82, 85. Burmah Oil Co Ltd, 65.
Department of Health and Social Security, 13.
Esso Petroleum Co Ltd, 104. Etak Inc, 94.
Falk Verlag, 94. Ford Motor Co Ltd, UK, 36.
German Federal Railways, 100-1. Group for Environmental Education Inc (GEE!), 91, 94. Guardian Newspapers Ltd, 71.
Inference Corporation Inc, 111.
Japan Airlines, 102-3.
Kümmerly & Frey, 83.
Laguna Sales Inc, 88. Lefax Maps, The Ram Press, 95. London Transport, 90. Longines of Switzerland, 139-42.
Maiden Ltd, Arthur, 118. Mary Evans Picture Library, 5, 6. Middlesex Cricket Club, 7. MIT Press, 91, 94.
NASA, 6. National Library of Ireland, 78. National Museum of Denmark, Department of Ethnography, 81. Neurath Isotype Collection, Otto & Marie, 51, 52, 84. Newton Magazine, 104.
Oxford Cartographers Ltd, 83, 89.
Pacific Bell, 70, 91.
Reader's Digest Association Ltd, 134-7. Renault UK Ltd, 36. Reuters Holdings PLC, 56. Reuters Ltd, 90. Rowenta (UK) Ltd, 32. Royal Institute of British Architects, *A symbol for disabled people, symbol application manual*, 22. Schweizerische Transport-unternehmungen, 98-9. Science Museum, 63, 67. Scientific American Inc, 49. Ski Enterprise/British Holidays Ltd, 94. Studio Vista, *Identity Kits*, 77.

Times Books Ltd, 78, 79,86-7, 88, 105. Times Newspapers Ltd, 108, 126-7. Tufte, Edward R, *The Visual Display of Quantitative Information*, Graphics Press, Cheshire, Connecticut, USA, 45, 46, 47, 48, 50. TWA, 103.
United States Accounting Office, 120-3. Univac, 103. Victoria and Albert Museum, 92.

My thanks to all of my contributors for images and information and special thanks to those who provided valuable insights into their specialist areas by means of case studies and comparative articles and to John Blandford for creating the production artwork.

I am particularly grateful to my editor, John Latimer Smith, for his encouragement and enthusiasm at all stages and for bullying me into continuing when my energies were flagging.

introduction

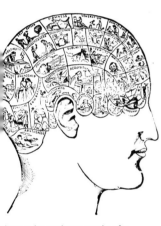

above: An early example of a phrenologist's head, a graphic representation of the areas of the brain.

Many of the precursors of information graphics are to be found in the work produced during the latter part of the 19th century and closely linked with the rise of the industrial revolution. As the means of transportation became mechanised there was an increasing need for map making, sign posting and time tables and due to the changing nature of much of the information type began to take over from traditional sign writing.

Map making was closely associated with the early presentation of statistics and some of the earlier forms of trade diagrams made use of the map as a basis for presenting the information. It was to be some time before the diagram broke free of its geographical basis and to exist in its own right. More recently the increase in world travel and speed of travel has been responsible for the development of network diagrams, a more abstract form of map making and the use of pictograms, a non-verbal form of communication overcoming many of the barriers of language.

Map making has perhaps the longest history and maps have evolved through a form of natural selection in which the survivors could claim greater accuracy and ease of use. We may still delight in the mythological associations of the earlier maps, particularly the star maps, but the all important functional requirement of accuracy, at first meaning compass accuracy, but later embracing accuracy of shape and area, have left little room for the imagination or fantasy. Even that important require-

ment of portability and accessibility perfected in the printed folding map has never been ideal for the car driver since the map can seldom be orientated to the direction in which the vehicle is travelling *and* the annotation read the right way round. The printed map is now under attack from the computerised map which can reconcile both these characteristics as well as providing a zoom facility. This is not to say that there are no losses in the quality of the computerised presentation given that the printed map has over a hundred years of visual development and refinement. To today's user the important qualities are still accuracy but combined with rapid accessibility.

Generally speaking, each technological advance in communication has presented new challenges to the information designer and today we are seeing an unprecedented number of new forms of technology which require new thought and new design formats. In the past, and sometimes even today, the technical advances have been presented using the visual forms of a preceeding generation. The information graphics designer is in a unique position to produce innovative solutions providing he has a grounding in the electronic and technological fields. The ubiquitous mechnical instrument with a circular dial has given way to a variety of display shapes and formats ranging from alphanumeric and pictorial through to synthesised speech. Equally varied are the display technologies from LED's and fluorescent displays to liquid crystal.

Below: The first interstellar graphic message engraved on a 6×9 inch (152×229mm) gold anodised plaque and attached to the pair of Pioneer space probes launched in 1971 and 1972. These 'visual greeting cards', the first attempts to communicate with other intelligences, were later followed by the Voyager 'messages' containing images, sounds and music from our planet. Although not a distinguished example of terrestrial graphics the plaque contains some concentrated information about the origin of the spacecraft. The diagrams show (top) a drawing of the hydrogen atom from which can be deduced a basic time scale, a pulsar 'map' showing the location of our sun in relation to 14 pulsars whose precise frequencies are shown in binary code and (bottom) a drawing of the solar system with relative distances of the planets and the Pioneer's trajectory.

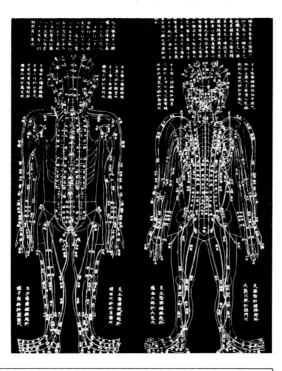

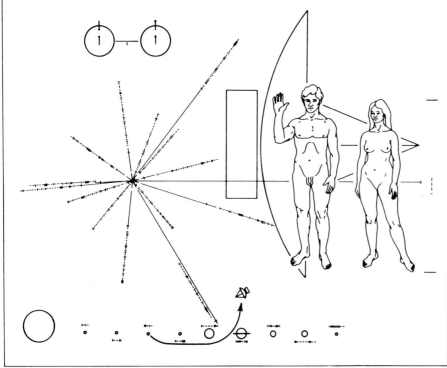

Some of the techniques used in conveying information about skills and operating procedures and especially those used in do-it-yourself manuals derive from an earlier printed tradition, that of the comic strip which has always had a large audience, particularly among the young. The comic strip divided the story into regular 'frames' which, at first sight, appeared to restrict the flow of visual narrative but from which developed one of the key elements of the comic strips' success. The break between the frames allowed a change of time or setting so that the story could be divided into as many changes of scene as required and the pace could be tightly controlled. The framing device also allowed another important development, the viewpoint could be changed from close up to long shot as often as necessary, an important requirement where text was kept to the minimum. These developments influenced film makers and the story-board technique remains the basic structuring/creative device for film and television planning. As George Perry and Alan Aldridge say in their history of the Comics[1], 'In aesthetic terms the strips' achievement is the development of a form of narrative art using its own unique conventions and techniques'. Images on their own, however, do have severe limitations of meaning and so the strip evolved two minimal forms of text; the character's speech was enclosed in speech 'balloons' issuing from the speaker's mouth and the characters' thoughts usually enclosed in a dotted 'bubble'. Various other forms of exclamation or reaction were 'coded' into onomatopoeic words or letters such as 'pow', zap, z-z-z, &c.

While operating at a very simple story telling level they were rivetting experiences to children and proved addictive to adults. As a technique for the rapid communication of a story or a sequence of events using the greatest economy of line, tone and wording they were ready made for application to educational and instructional situations where complex actions and processes required simplifying for the user and with the added bonus that the user accepted them as a 'pleasurable' form of learning.

In preparing this book it soon became evident that the title *Information Graphics* conveyed different

[1] *The Penguin Book of Comics, a slight history,* Penguin Books 1967.

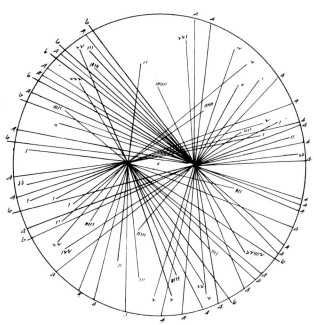

Left: An early Chinese chart of meridians and acupuncture points in the human body. Classically there were 59 meridians and 365 pressure points all requiring exact delineation. More recent diagrams have been printed onto white porcelain models of the human figure.

Right: Cricket graphics: the batting analysis of W R Hammond's score of 336 runs in the England v New Zealand match in 1933.

meanings to different people. To those with a background in computing it was associated with an aspect of information technology while to many designers it suggested a certain category of typographical work such as the design of forms and timetables. To television designers it was synonymous with those forms of presentation which persuade the viewer to assimilate facts and figures, particularly statistical information.

For a number of years many design colleges have included information graphics in their courses but this subject area has often been confined to the design aspects of statistical information and diagrams.

What I have tried to survey in this book is a rather wider field of information graphics, some aspects of which have been neglected by designers and more particularly by those who commission design. The subject areas chosen are not intended to be exclusive, in fact there is no complete cut-off from other types of design, but they are intended to be representative of a spectrum of design which is mainly concerned with conveying essential information to the user with the least distraction and ambiguity. Information graphics may not be the most appropriate term for this subject area but as it is already well established there is no point in trying to make a change but I hope to persuade the reader to enlarge his conception of it and in the case of students to consider it as an interesting and worthwhile field of study.

In each section I have tried to show the problems associated with designing in that area and how the constraints often determine the final result. With the advent of computers and microprocessors many of these constraints have been reduced or have disappeared altogether but often they are replaced by a different type of problem such as the presentation of a multitude of choices or increased information at the expense of legibility.

One of the spin-offs from the mass media is the increased exposure of the reader and viewer to a variety of sophisticated graphic treatments such as pictograms and diagrammatic techniques which means that the designer can assume a familiarity with certain forms and treatments, – a form of graphic literacy, which was not the case even a few years ago. It is interesting that some of these new types of presentation are now appearing in the displays fitted to commercial and domestic appliances and particularly to vehicle consoles. Information graphics is still seen by many designers as the 'green' area of design by which they usually mean that it is free of those connections usually associated with advertising design and which can be summed up by the word 'persuasion'. Persuasion can take many forms in both verbal and visual rhetoric not to mention the more sinister subliminal techniques of film and video where the 'message' is incorporated into an ultra short time space on the film so that it is not consciously picked up by the viewer. Similar effects are possible on sound tracks by introducing spoken words just above the normal frequency of perceived sound.

Advertising techniques used to be based on the well tried street traders' formula of raising one's voice, drawing attention to the virtues of one's product and making extravagent claims for its properties. Legislation has had some effect on the latter but a whole battery of techniques have been perfected to 'influence' the potential buyer, many of which operate below the level of consciousness. It is this subliminal approach which has alienated many designers and caused them to turn to the 'purer' forms of design which they associate with information graphics. There is obviously a large element of truth in this attitude although, as I hope to show, information

by Gui Bonsiepe in 1965[2] that, 'information without rhetoric is a pipe-dream which ends up in the break-down of communication and total silence. "Pure" information exists for the designer only in arid abstraction. As soon as he begins to give it concrete shape, to bring it within the range of experience, the process of rhetorical infiltration begins.' Kinross examines this statement in some historical detail from the 1920's to the present day and reaches a similiar conclusion, '. . . that nothing is free of rhetoric, that visual manifestations emerge from particular historical circumstances, that ideological vacuums do not exist.' Even within such apparently neutral examples of information graphics as the timetable and directory the decision to emphasise and order certain elements is a means of persuading a reader or user to a course of action.

The Concise Oxford Dictionary defines rhetoric as *the art of the persuasive or impressive speaking or writing; language designed to persuade or impress* . . . We are all familiar with the rhetorical devices freely employed by politicians, religious conversionists and street traders which include carefully modulated control of the volume and pitch of the voice coupled with a non-stop delivery. The rhetorical visual devices of graphics may seem somewhat muted by comparison but can encompass close control of the sizes and weights of type matter, repetition and the choice and size of paper. Above all, the choice of colours and, in the case of electronic displays, the pace of movement and the use of flashing images.

My own view concerning visual rhetoric is that although it may be impossible to completely eliminate it from a design, it should be carefully and consciously controlled so that it does not compete with the basic communication process – there is a fine line between emphasis and rhetoric. In general it can be said that when time and attention spans of the user are limited then some visual rhetorical devices may be necessary and this is certainly the case with a time-based medium such as television where the viewer needs to be held if the communication of the information is not to be lost.

Right: Step by step graphics for obtaining prepaid Royal Mail postage labels from a machine. The labels are printed on phosphor coated paper within the machine and the value can be varied to suit the customer's needs. From a Royal Mail First Day Cover.
Designer: Ken Briggs & Associates.

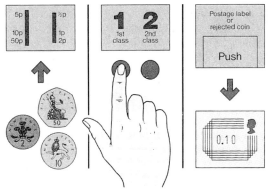

graphics is not completely free of visual rhetoric and it is doubtful if information and its communication can be considered competely neutral.

Information graphics is generally thought to be fulfilling a need in the community by helping people to gain information and knowledge and supplying a need rather than influencing them to buy something. Such designs also have a longer life than the 'throw-away' products of many forms of advertising and contributes to a designer's satisfaction.

'Visual rhetoric' is not a term that many information designer's use about their work and most would disclaim any use of it at all as it has the same associations as E numbers in food, – the less the better. Robin Kinross in a perceptive article 'The Rhetoric of Neutrality'[1] quotes a statement made

[1] *Design Issues* volume 2, no 2.

[2] Visual/Verbal Rhetoric, *Ulm* 14/15/16, December 1965.

1 alphanumeric

Because of the almost unlimited range of information which makes use of letterforms I have deliberately chosen the term 'alpha-numeric' instead of the more conventional term 'typographic' with its emphasis on type based letterforms and printing terminology. This is not in any sense to suggest that new technological alphabets are going to make the conventional printed forms obsolete but to try and see what criteria for legibility and ease of reading can be applied to all lettering systems irrespective of whether they are type derived or machine generated.

In terms of the applications of verbal and numerical information I have concentrated on just a few formats which cover both hand held or screen viewed information and those which are generally viewed at a much greater distance such as signs. The applications include the design of forms, timetables and directional signs, each designed for a specific purpose but each requiring a clear and unambiguous type of treatment.

Type design has dominated western printed information of all varieties for the past 400 years and, even though there was an explosion in the design of type faces during the 19th and early 20th centuries, the basic letterforms of the alphabet and numerals have remained remarkably constant. Even when we compare the serifed and non-serifed families of type faces the structure of the characters shows little variation. Admittedly there were 'dialects' such as the German black letter which

developed a northern 'geometric' quality both in 15th century manuscript form and later in type cut forms as opposed to the more flowing cursive forms of southern Europe. Both were based on the use of slanted nibs but the Gothic black letter or textura evolved into a heavily stressed vertical letter with even spacing between strokes and letter spaces and, in its later Fraktur versions, remained in general use until the middle of this century.

It is interesting to see this same geometric impulse at work in the numeral system created for liquid crystal displays (LCDs) of the type commonly found on calculator and digital watch faces. In their simplest forms these LCD characters are made up from a set of seven even width segments arranged in a double square. The outer corners of each segment are rounded but otherwise they are of identical construction. All of the numerals from 0 to 9 are made up from this simple grid and, not surprisingly, certain letters can be confused such as the 5 and 6. The numeral 7 leaves a large gap if flanked by other numerals and this can give rise to a mistaken decimal point.

In both cases the regular geometric spacing of letters and numerals is achieved at the expense of some legibility.

The history of type design was generally one of slow evolutionary progress in response to cultural influences and technical improvements in die cutting and metal casting. One of the results of this slow evolution was the refinement that could be

An international
journal of
typography.
Eight issues
to be published
at intervals
of six months

Editors
Simon Johnston
Mark Holt
Michael Burke
Hamish Muir

Copies available
by post from
Octavo
PO Box 319
London WC2H 9RW

Single copies
UK £5
Overseas £8/US $12
Full subscription
UK £40
Overseas £64/US $96

Payment by cheque
or money order
(payable to Octavo),
or by credit card:
Access/Mastercard,
Visa or American
Express.
Credit card orders
must include name
and address,
card type, number
and expiry date

Published by
Eight Five Zero.
3000 copies printed
by CTD, London
Typesetting by
Optic, London

Octavo 87.4
will be published
winter 87

The editors
welcome suggestions
for articles.
All correspondence
should be sent to
the above address

02
Ian Hamilton Finlay. Terror and Virtue.
Lindsay Fulcher examines duality and
paradox in Finlay's work

87.3
**The power of typographic communication, its ability to
both inform clearly and excite visually, will often be
determined by the way in which structure is employed;
order is fundamental to understanding. The ability
to exploit typographic structure to its full potential**

07
Where is the School of Thought? Peter Rea
argues the case for a reappraisal of aims
and values in design education

10
Architectural Typography: Willi Kunz
at Columbia. Kenneth Frampton discusses
Kunz's posters for the Graduate
School of Architecture, Planning and
Preservation, Columbia University,
New York

16
ISO 7000/No. 0623. Deviations from the
International Standards Organisation
symbol used to indicate the correct upright
position of packages in transit

requires both a sense of formal spatial relationships -

proportion, scale, optical balance - as well as a

knowledge of the microstructure inherent in letterforms,

the individual units of communication out of which any

typographic design must grow. Physical structure must

be analogous to semantic structure; analysis of the

content of the material will suggest a suitable basis for

typographic formulation. The discipline of structure,

however, must not be regarded as a limitation, but as a

dynamic, expressive tool, a liberating device, used to

animate as well as to order. Extreme uses of structure

and anti-structure are both dangerous; dogmatically

imposed grids can be stultifying, and conversely a lack

of order hinders communication. Between these two

extremes lie infinite possibilities for typographic

experimentation: appropriate order has many forms.

Above: A double spread from issue
three of Octavo, an international
journal of typography. The editorial
statement introduces an issue concerning typographical structure and
communication.
Editors and designers: Simon Johnston, Mark Holt, Michael Burke,
Hamish Muir, London.

brought to bear not only on the letters themselves
but also the spacing between characters and
words. Extra alternative characters were produced
for certain letter combinations which were an
awkward fit when set as individual characters and
modifications were made to many characters in
their smallest sizes to make them appear optically
the same as the larger sizes.

Paper also improved in quality in response to
improved casting techniques; finer strokes and hair
line serifs required a smooth printing surface to
maintain definition.

With the electronic revolution, however, a wide
variety of new communication processes became
available within a short space of time without
apparent contact with any of the traditional type
manufacturing processes or disciplines. All of these
new systems were capable of showing or
displaying letter systems but with widely varying
degrees of definition and legibility.

In many cases this has led to comparatively crude
alphabets and spacing which, over a period of time,
produces eye fatigue and can be the source of
errors in transcription. Very often the alphabets
were modelled on traditional type faces but without
an appreciation of the reasons for their form and
spacing. The constraints of the new medium would
have led to better results if the alphabets had been
designed with the strength of the new medium in
mind rather than by trying to adapt to an existing
format. Most new technologies have always
imitated their predecessors; we only have to think
of early motor cars being modelled on the horse
drawn carriages of the day.

The history of type design is well documented
including the interaction between designers and
changing technology. What we need to do today is
to consider the problem not as type face versus
other forms of letter generation but rather as an
assessment of the common characteristics that
should underlie all lettering systems in order to
make them legible and effortless to read. We
should not totally disregard the element of a
designer's individuality but this quality of style is not
one that we should dwell on for too long as it has a
habit of infiltrating even the most abstract and
impersonal of human artifacts without any.

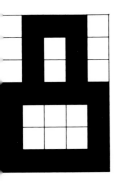

ABCDEFGHI
JKLMNOPQR
STUVWXYZ
0123456789

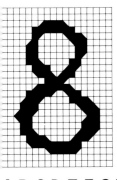

ABCDEFGHI
JKLMNOPQR
STUVWXYZ
0123456789

Above: A comparison between two alphabets designed for machine reading, OCR-A (top) with a coarse grid and OCR-B with a relatively fine grid and diagonal shading. Both enlargements show the numeral 8. Particular attention is required to differentiate the characters for O and D and numeral 0.
Typographical advisor for OCR-B: Adrian Frutiger.

In considering machine produced lettering we can identify several distinct types of system ranging from the typewriter both with fixed and variable letterspacing; type, both foundry, photo and electronically generated; screen displayed systems, (pixel, scanned or liquid crystal) and those point source forms such as dot matrix and LED. Some of these processes use separate printers such as laser (heat fixed powder) or ink jet and these may have more influence on the final form of a letter than the generating process.

Most people would agree that the primary quality in any system is legibility. Without it, the speed of assimilation and concentration breaks down and becomes a source of error and eventually of frustration. Legibility, however, is not a simple quality to quantify. We can approach it by looking at both the macro and micro aspects of the system. The large view would define legibility in terms of scale or the size of the words in relation to the viewing distance whether on the page, screen or sign. Of equal importance is the degree of contrast between letterform and background. For example, black letters on a white background give greater contrast than black on grey (as we often find on LCDs). White letters on a black background are equally contrasted but produce severe eye fatigue if used in large amounts as, for instance, in text setting. Contrast can be enhanced with back lit backgrounds or, in the case of motorway signs, with reflective backing but over intense background lighting has the effect of 'haloing' the image giving rise to an apparently thinner letter form and reducing its legibility.

The question of legibility and contrast is also bound up with that of character definition. A character built up of scan lines or pixels will decrease in apparent density as the scale is increased unless the system compensates for the size change. In systems with a fixed number of lines to the screen (such as television) an enlargement merely means that the lines become wider apart and therefore greyer but the eye does to some extent compensate for this by finding it easier to recognise the shape pattern at larger sizes and so there is likely to be an optimum size for any given level of definition assuming that the same weight is used throughout.

The micro aspect of legibility lies in the clear differentiation of each character and each word in a line. Many of the newer systems are able to close up letter and word spacing so that characters touch each other and in some cases overlap. While these are useful for special effects and, in the past, could only be achieved by handskills they drastically reduce legibility by altering the basic recognition aspects of the letters and complete words.
As soon as we depart from traditional letterforms and use more exotic forms the brain has to work overtime to identify or separate similar characters. This applies to high definition systems as well as the lower definition ones using dot matrix or coarse scanned images.

We often forget that our alphabet is in reality a double alphabet in that all twenty six characters have duplicates in the form of capital letters. The great majority of our reading is from books and newspapers and these are set in what are termed upper (capitals) and lower case characters. For very good reason. The lower case alphabet contains nine characters with strokes rising above the general letter height (ascenders) and five with strokes going below (descenders) and it is this variation which gives each word a specific pattern which the brain has learnt to recognise. When we read text matter we tend to read in terms of word/sentence groups rather than by individual letters. If we try to read the same material set only in capital letters, which all have a common height line, we find that, first of all, our reading speed drops[1] and then, if we persevere, we rapidly develop eye fatigue.

A secondary reason for this difficulty is that some of the capital letters such as F, J, L, P, T and Y leave large gaps in the word line unless they are very carefully spaced and this also hinders steady reading. Lower case letters are much more even in this respect and give an even flow to reading. Traditional type setters expected to individually letterspace words set in caps to optically correct for these gaps and, in fact, many traditional typefaces such as Baskerville, Caslon and Garamond had specially cut sets of small capitals which were the height of a lower case 'x' so that they blended with the lowercase letters instead of jumping out from

[1] Various tests have shown that reading speeds for all-capitals text setting can drop by 10–19 per cent over a ten minute period and that such text occupies about 40–50 per cent more space than text set in lower case.

the line. There are few cases where words have to be set in all capitals for emphasis. Even on a typewriter, which does not possess an italic (sloping) alphabet, words can be underlined for emphasis, but in most lettering systems, italic or a change of height can be used for emphasis.

Capital letters have an important part to play in designating the start of a new sentence or paragraph and identify proper nouns, countries, names of organisations and publications. The general rule should be to ask oneself whether a capital letter is required for any other purpose than the above. Emphasis can normally be achieved by change of weight, size or by spacing. My first typography instructor always insisted that the use of all-capitals was only for tombstones and inscriptions.

There are some lettering systems which only provide capital letters and great care needs to be taken over the number of words set to a line, the interletter spacing, if it is variable, and particularly, the interlinear spacing which should be greater than for upper, lowercase use.

In all uses of lettering the number of words to a line needs considering since by having too few or too many the eye becomes fatigued either by an increased scanning rate for short lines or the inability to pick up the start of the next line for extra wide ones. For book reading the traditional optimum number of words per line is ten which, on the basis of an average of six characters to a word (in English), including a word space, gives a total of sixty characters. The figures for screen displays and signs will vary from these depending on usage.

Closely coupled with the word count is the amount of interline spacing required. It is difficult to generalise on this requirement but lack of sufficient interline spacing also leads to eye fatigue while an increase of spacing leads to greater comfort.

Factors which would require an increase of spacing would be the use of a bold (heavy) letter form, extra long line widths and reversal of the letters from black to white.

Two methods are used for determining the overall look of a block of text (this can be anything from a short paragraph to the text of a book). The first is called unjustified or ragged setting in which the spacing between words is kept constant throughout the text and the right hand edge of each line is therefore variable depending on whether the next word will fit or have to be taken over to the next line (or hyphenated). The text and captions of this book are set in this style.

The second method (justified setting) involves adjusting the spacing between each word so that no space is left at the end of the line and the text has a firm left and right hand edge. Electronic systems make the necessary calculations instantly. Computer programs are available to provide hyphenation at the end of lines where necessary to avoid large word gaps. The overall look of justified setting is of a clean rectangular block of type except for the last short line which makes its own width. In 'good' justified setting one is hardly aware of the variations in word spacing but when badly used, large gaps appear throughout the text and alter the cadence of reading. To the purist the use of even and regular word spacing is more important than a tidy right hand edge. However, unjustified setting can produce some unpleasant patterns on the page and therefore usually requires some adjustment of lines after the first setting.

Assuming that equal word spacing is being used, there is an optimum space to be selected. Too little and the words start joining together and too much and the reading pace is slowed down. For hand held or screeen viewed the optimum seems to be a space equivalent to the lower case 'e' of the alphabet being used. For words to be viewed at a distance or in motion the spacing needs to be slightly larger but should not exceed the width of a lower case 'm'.

Similar considerations apply to the spacing between letters, although, in the case of traditional type systems, the design has built-in spacing so that lower case letters always appear with optically even letterspacing. This is not the case with capitals, as mentioned earlier, which require individual spacing to achieve the same effect.

In lettering systems such as the earlier forms of typewriter, each letter and character is mounted on a striking key of equal width and so the narrow letters such as 'i' and 'l' have much more space on either side of them than the wide letters such as 'm'

Above: Supplementary Benefit claim form for the Department of Health and Social Security. The most recent of a series of versions in which the design has evolved to make its use as simple as possible. Original is A4 and printed in black and one colour.
Design: David Lewis, Document Design Unit, DHSS, London.

and 'w'. By using strong horizontal serifs the designer was able to compensate to some extent for these gaps. More sophisticated typewriters have variable spacing based on the natural width of each letter.

In traditional type systems even the variations in spacing between certain capital and lower case letters (as at the beginning of a new sentence) can be adjusted to avoid large gaps appearing. Combinations such as 'Tv' 'Lo' can be tightened up and the spacing between combinations of narrow letters such as 'ill' extended. This is called a kerning system and can be fine tuned for any alphabet.

Good legibility can be wasted if the organisation of the text material is poor. Information should be logically set out so that sequences are clear, headings written in to assist in assimilating and identifying sections of long text and some indication of the extent of the material. In this respect the printed book or document is immediately informative; we can flick through the pages to gain an immediate impression of length. A VDU has no built-in device to inform the viewer of the length of a particular text or piece of information although a simple screen icon could be used for the same purpose.

Legibility is therefore not a simple formula; it is a combination of a large number of small details working together for a required purpose. Some of these factors can be programmed into a system and more will be possible with 'intelligent' programs but systems are now being designed with so many additional 'extras' such as expansion, contraction and outlining devices that the temptation for the operator is to go for effect rather than legibility.

Form design

Forms can be thought of as a printed equivalent of an interview where the user has to play an active role in answering prepared questions. For the most part the user is an unwilling contributor whether it be withdrawing money from the bank or applying for a passport. The form designer, therefore, has to contend with a user who will take short cuts if possible, leave out information if the question is not clear and, quite often, provide illegible answers.

The administrative time involved in the return of forms and double checking through these omissions is one very good reason for producing clear and easily completable forms.

One of the problems in large organisations is that the writer of the form may never be in contact with the designer and so will not know how the typographical organisation of the material will affect the editorial content or the final appearance. The ideal situation is where both writer and designer (assuming that they are not the same person) work together from the start and interact in order to produce the best result. Both writer and designer may not know of all the various ways that questions can be asked and the graphical formats that can be provided for answers. Some possible treatments are the yes/no, multiple choice (ticks or deletions) and unconstrained answer box. Each of these has advantages in certain situations and for certain types of user. The consistency with which these devices are used is also of importance.

More complex information is often put into a matrix format which is psychologically off-putting for many users as it requires interpreting information read off both a vertical as well as a horizontal axis. In most cases this could be simplified although it would take up more space. Another problem with matrix designs is that keyed information is often used which means consulting footnotes and then having to refind ones place in the form. A series of abbreviations within the body of the matrix can lead to the same type of difficulty. In many cases the matrix seems to have been drawn up before the text was completely formulated or has been adapted from a previous form. Of particular value is the inclusion on the form of example of part of a completed question.

The general organisation of questions needs to be clear and consistent. It is confusing to the user to have some of the question formats running horizontally across the sheet while others run vertically. It may be a good idea to number each question but only if numbering is not employed in the method of answering questions.

The legibility problem of the user's replies has prompted some designers to adopt the series of boxes (known as character separators) which only allow one letter to be entered per box. This has several effects: it slows down the speed of entry producing more legible entries but also slows down the reading and recording of information from the forms by the administrator. If the entries are typed in the problem may be even worse as the box spacers may not match the character spacing of the typewriter. The overall effect is frustration by both user and administrator. The psychological approach of persuading the reader to produce a legible entry, giving guidance for each entry and adequate space is more likely to lead to the desirable result but needs creative copywriting as well as the appropriate design techniques. Also under this heading is the possibility of including some provision for the user to make a contribution beyond that of merely indicating choices. This could take the form of asking the user to comment on any particular question or to add information if the choices given do not cover the particular case. This involvement of the user is more likely to produce an accurate result as well as amplifying the details for the administrators.

Some indication of the need for certain questions and information and the security and retention of the information on file or computer would also do a great deal to reassure the user as to the purpose behind the questions.

Patricia Wright in a perceptive article[2] about the need for better form design ends her article by saying that, 'The fundamental cause of bad forms more probably lies in a failure to appreciate the range of skills required for achieving a satisfactory design in which so many conflicting interests have to be reconciled'.

Timetables

Timetables are one of the most complex examples of information design. They usually include a large amount of numerical information, only a small proportion of which will be used, at any one time, by the user. This information is generally compressed into a small format and requires interpreting by reading off entries from both a horizontal and vertical scale. In using a timetable for the first time the user has to make several selections, for example, the time of year, weekday or weekend, morning or afternoon and then to locate starting places and destination. In addition, there may be coded information in the form of footnotes, asterisks or symbols to denote exceptions and qualifications.

One can point to several design factors which can assist the user, bearing in mind that the user may be consulting the timetable under some pressure in trying to make a connection or flight; under less than ideal reading conditions (the user may be standing) and, often, under less than ideal lighting and noise conditions.

Important factors are that the tabular matter has adequate interline spacing to separate out the horizontal layers of information and the provision of regular breaks at intervals (normally every fifth line) so that the user can come back to the same section of information after consulting footnotes. As an aid to comprehension for first-time users (not to mention the young and elderly) the presentation of an actual example is invaluable so that the user can see how the system operates. This could best be shown in a second colour and at an enlarged scale.

Experiments have been tried using analogue clock faces in place of the 24 hour digital system which many people still have to translate back to clock terms for memorising. It would certainly take up more space but, providing that am and pm confusion can be avoided, would repay further study as an aid to comprehension and it has the added advantage of linking directly to the ubiquitous station and airport clock.

Screen presented information has the advantage over the printed timetable that only a limited amount of information can be shown at any one time but it may be necessary to wait some time for the information to appear again if it is missed at the first showing. A form of visual elapsed time indicator to show how long each frame is held on the screen would be a useful addition to overcome the viewer's mental worry that the screen information may change before it has been read. Screens have one other advantage in that they are usually angled towards the viewer as compared with printed timetables appearing on noticeboards

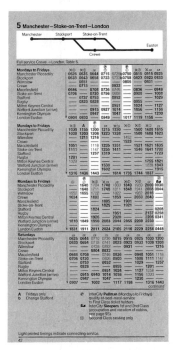

Above: Page from British Rail's InterCity timetable. Main stations shown diagrammatically at top, white vertical panels indicate catering available for all or most of journey.

[2] Informed Design for Forms, *Information Design*, John Wiley & Sons Ltd, Chichester, UK, 1984.

Top row: Signs designed for the Hong Kong and Shanghai Bank. There were two broad user-areas requiring signing: the complex vertical transportation system of lifts and escalators where light boxes were used and the public areas characterised by open planning and glass curtain walls. In these areas transparent, silk screened panels were used with edge lighting so that the text appears to glow.
Architects: Foster Associates, London
Designers: Wim van der Weerd, Wim Verboven, Wim Crouwel, Total Design, Amsterdam.
Execution signage: Erco Leuchte, West Germany.

Right: Signing system for the Barbican Centre for Arts and Conferences. The system also included a series of pictograms for the expected international audiences. A special alphabet was developed based on Akzidenz Grotesk in both light and medium weights. Colours and finishes of the signs were selected to complement the architectural treatment and decor.
Architects: Chamberlain Powell & Bon.
Designers: K B & A Design Consultants, London.

which are usually more difficult to read for a standing reader except for entries close to the natural eyelevel.

Signing

Some of the most successful signing is now seen on motorways chiefly as a result of the pressures for quickly accessible information which has to be taken in at a single glance. Size, contrast and consistency have led to national and international formats plus a great many hours of experimentation and testing. Many of these lessons can be applied to other forms of signing both outdoors and indoors.

Siting must be the first consideration. A sign, to be really effective, must be placed in such a position that it can be seen while still approaching, even before the information on it can be clearly read. The viewer is therefore alerted and is ready to read it in good time. This preliminary sign may not give any direct information but prepares the viewer by announcing that information is coming and aquaints him with the style and scale of the system, for example, the signing may be suspended overhead, project from a side wall or be painted on the road or corridor surface. It may be necessary to provide 'repeats' at intervals to maintain the user's confidence that he is still going in the correct direction. Nothing is worse than a system that disappears before the user has reached his destination.

Complex information appearing at one point or intersection should be avoided. The information should be broken down onto several separate signs each dealing with one aspect of the information. For example, a hospital sign could show on separate panels information relating to visitors, emergency treatment and staff facilities. Another lesson from motorway signs is the separation of the signs from surrounding visual 'noise'. This is often easier said than done, but large background borders will be required to separate lettering from the sign's background.

Legibility, as already discussed, is a measure of the degree of contrast between letterforms and background tone or colour; the degree of natural or artificial lighting and the size of letterforms related to the viewing distance. These are all interactive requirements and any necessary reduction in one will require compensation in the others. The advantages of upper lower case characters and the question of letterspacing, word spacing and interline spacing are equally as important as for the previously mentioned 'close reading' information. In general, the legibility requirements of signs require a slightly greater amount of interword and interline spacing than for printed material and a reduction in the number of words to a line, particularly in the case of multi-line signs.

Computer generated signs which are capable of showing verbal information as an apparently continuous band of moving lettering or a constantly updatable amount of information, as on many dot matrix signs, are able to overcome many of the limitations of static signs. They have the disadvantage that in the case of a power failure they present a blank screen and therefore usually require some form of backup sign or an indication as to where information can be obtained in the event of a failure.

The simple illuminated, moving message sign is capable of providing extended news coverage, weather information or general items of tourist information in a form which is readily accessible to the viewer. Only a few words or a sentence is visible at any one time but the moving letters hold the attention of the viewer regardless of other visual or aural 'noise' and the whole message can be repeated at intervals. In fact, several of these signs in conjunction can give multi-language translations either continuously or in sequence.

Dot matrix signs which can provide up-to-the minute information of train and bus arrival times have removed one of the greatest sources of frustration to the regular traveller. Now he knows how long he will have to wait and can decide whether to do something else in the interval or make other arrangements. The present limited letterforms, the poor spacing and the lack of a legible lower case letterform are things which should be capable of improvement but the faults may not be only technological but lack design research. (See page 17).

Above: Part of a signing system for the Muziektheater, Amsterdam (opera and ballet centre). Designers: Gijsbert Dijker, Wim van der Weerd, Total Design, Amsterdam.

case study

Designing a dot matrix alphabet for an electronic display system
An investigation by Michael Burke and Christopher Bentley

Michael Burke ICTA was a member of the '72 Munich Olympics design team (1969–73). Senior Lecturer at Ravensbourne College of Design and Communication and currently Professor for Design at Fachhochschule, Swäbasche Gmund, West Germany. He is an Associate of 8vo and co-editor of the international typographic magazine *Octavo*.

This project was carried out by Christopher Bentley as part of a third year option programme in information graphics at Ravensbourne. The project was initiated by Michael Burke.

Above: Part of an alphabet designed for a 7×5 matrix showing the limited scope for subtlety of letterform and the difficulty in producing a legible lower case alphabet.

One of the results of the micro-chip revolution in the field of information technology has been the electronic display that conveys instantly programmable messages using words whose individual letters are made up from illuminated dots. These dot matrix systems have been developed for both commercial and public use and appear extensively in the presentation of transport information at rail and air terminals. However, present systems can only be described as being adequate and it was considered an area with great potential for development and refinement in design terms.

The project therefore began as an investigation into the present 'state of the art', to examine the use and capability of dot matrix letterforms, probing into the limitations caused by manufacturing constraints and to see what possibilities there were for design development.

British Rail are currently using a number of dot matrix display systems at their stations and although impressive in size, with two colours, the letterforms are based on a limited 7×5 matrix of square unit cells which carry with them the legibility and inflexibility problems that accompany such constraints.

Initial research soon revealed that the present design of the letterforms is limited by the size of the underlying matrix, the most common of which is the 7×5 system. This automatically limits most of the forms to single lines, inhibits the subtlety of curves

and diagonals and even restricts the size of the letters themselves. There are also 9×6 systems in use but this relatively small increase in grid size offers little more scope and flexibility. The main reason for such small grids is due to the limited memory capability of the electronics that store the character information. Such systems run on an eight-bit memory, seven for each row and one spare for any additional codes.

We decided that a completely new approach to the problem was needed, with whole new character sets and an updated presentation method. The formal constraints presented by the 7×5 grid had to be broken, with both the nature and size of the matrix reviewed to reduce the obstacles created by the physical and electronic limitations, without, at the same time, ignoring production requirements. The decision to increase the grid formation was taken with some evidence to show that the memory capacity of micro-chips was rapidly increasing together with lower unit costs. It was decided that the advantages of an enlarged grid could lead to a considerably more effective solution than working within the present constraints.

With the size of the grid open to review so therefore was the nature and arrangement of the dots or elements themselves. The main consideration was to develop a grid and accompanying system, with the ultimate aim of being able to improve the overall appearance and legibility of each individual

Left: A 7 × 5 matrix and the international test word 'hazbergiwyos' which is a combination of the most frequently used letters together with some problem letters as regard spacing, curves and descenders. shows the weak areas of spacing and legibility, especially in the lower case alphabet which lacks continuity and style and provides no space for descending strokes (g and y).

Left: one of several alternative 7 × 5 matrix experiments, in this case an alternatively staggered dot formation. At first this appeared to be promising in dealing with curves and diagonals but, as can be seen, it reduced formations of dot clusters at some junctions and large gaps at other points within the strokes of certain letters.

Left: Part of a comparison chart using a 14 × 10 matrix. The top three rows show stages in the development of alphabets (only the capitals are shown here) using this grid. The third row shows experiments in using some discontinuous strokes and developed further in the bottom row which formed the basis for the final design shown on page 20.

Above: Experiments were carried out with a transparent diffuser screen which effectively merged the illuminated dots of the matrix.

character within a complete set of similarly formed characters. This should also promote development and more extensive use of a lower case alphabet, presently crude and infrequently used in 7 × 5 systems.

A grid with 10 × 5 horizontal lozenge shaped units was tried but this created a flattened elongated feeling to the characters, along with varying stroke widths and staggered diagonals and curves.

A further grid with an alternate staggered dot formation at first appeared promising in showing curves and diagonals. However, there was very little consistency in the solutions with each letter presenting a different problem and difficulties in establishing a common base line and x-height. The worst occurrence being the formation of dot clusters at certain junctions and large gaps at other sections within the strokes of certain letters.

A combination of the two grids seemed to be the most promising, but turned out to be the least successful. Instead of solving the problems encountered by the others it simply magnified them. Gaps were created at certain points and while one set of curves and diagonals succeed, those against the flow of the grid were a complete disaster. Some of the grid formations quite obviously worked far better than others and their sympathy towards curves and diagonals varied from average to poor. The problem continued to point towards enlarging the original matrix of dots.

The basic aim was to develop and compile a character set based on traditional typographic letterforms and find out how an extended grid would respond to their curves and diagonals. It was found that a 14 × 10 matrix would enable the establishment of an x-height and allow separate space for ascenders and descenders. Varying stroke widths were possible with the opportunity of designing light, medium and bold versions of the same alphabet.

The first attempts based upon more traditional typefaces still encountered some of the problems of the smaller grids with the spacing between the single stroke letters still fairly poor. However, curves and diagonals proved to be far more subtle creating an alphabet with more continuity of style, more attractive and far more legible at a distance.

Visually there was a great improvement to most of the individual characters, although there were problems concerning the overall density of the lower case letters appearing lighter than the upper case and the numerals far bolder. The system of having both single and double line characters created this problem which was only overcome by further development of a single line or light alphabet. Individual character spacing problems diminished but the full flexibility of the grid was not being exploited to the best of its ability.

The next stage, therefore, was to develop an entirely new character set moving away from the conventions of the traditional letterforms towards a more flowing and continuous style ensuring that each character conformed exactly to the new rules. Considerations under the closest examination were the letter spacing, stroke weight and letter density with particular concentration on reducing the number of curves and diagonals wherever possible.

It was realised that major changes to letterforms could not be made without a breakdown of communication but that small changes to detail and continuity of treatment were important factors in overall legibility.

It is interesting to compare the development of each individual letter from the earliest attempts. The search for overall uniformity in size, spacing and density became paramount while not overlooking their general appearance. The major innovation was the movement away from rounded forms and the abolition of serifs together with the desire to maintain a double line width throughout the entire alphabet. Every conceivable combination has been explored along the same theme with great attention to the subtle characteristics of the corners and joints. For a number of the characters a single pair of dots were removed to reduce density and create a more lively alphabet.

Each letter was designed at full display size and sometimes at a larger scale for detailed scrutiny. Words and phrases were rendered in the new letter forms to investigate the success of each letter within their verbal context. Letter and word spacing could be closely examined and general comments invited from colleagues, some of which were incorporated into the final design.

Right: The outcome of the experiments was this alphabet designed to demonstrate the flexibility of the 14×10 system while conforming to the restrictions of a matrix format. It shows the considerably improved legibility, character spacing and consistency of letter form achievable within this enlarged format. Though by no means suggesting that this is the only or even optimum solution, we hope this study will stimulate designers and manufacturers to develop both more legible and 'friendly' systems.

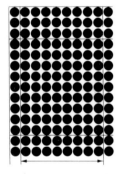

Above: An analysis of the final 14×10 matrix defines the areas of capital height (top rule), X-height (middle rule) and base line. The arrowed dimension shows the width of lower case characters while the capitals use the additional column of dots to the left. Leaving a column of dots each side of the lower case and one column completely free on the right of the capitals creates an inbuilt letterspacing device so that each 14×10 unit can fit flush to the next, the whole unit representing a word space.

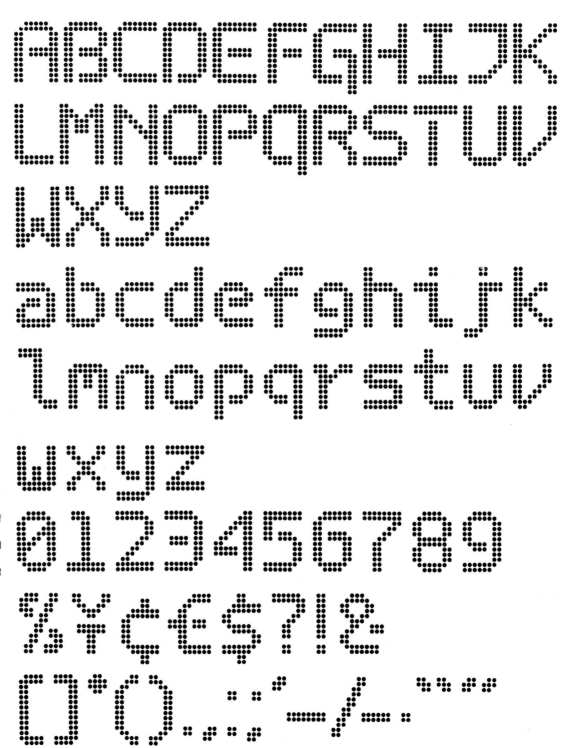

pictogrammic

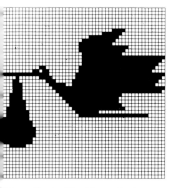

Above: Context is all important. This nursery concept is part of a sign system for departments within a maternity hospital in Buenos Aires. Designer: Shakespear Design Studio, Buenos Aires.

The words symbol, pictorial symbol and pictogram are often used interchangeably to describe a form of non-verbal communication. I have chosen the word 'pictogram' since few applications involve the use of true symbols and most have a direct pictorial equivalence to their subject matter.

Pictograms have one essential value when carefully designed and applied which is that they bypass language barriers. They can therefore be assimilated more rapidly and by a wider audience than verbal signing. They do, however, have a number of constraints which limit their usefulness and it is often the misunderstanding of these constraints that have given rise to criticism of their use in the past.

We are now perhaps less optimistic that, 'world-wide communication through glyphs, an auxiliary language for everyday use, and a scientific abstract script for the scientific interchange of ideas are urgent needs for the world to come', as announced by Margaret Mead and Rudolf Modley in the 1960's. 'With all three', the authors continued, 'we could take full advantage of our new-found mobility, share in the kind of relationship once only available on the "village green", and exchange, rapidly and efficiently . . . the highest developments of human thought with men and women wherever they grew up, wherever they are living, and whatever their mother tongue'.[1] This scenario is nowadays likely to be reserved for electronic mail.

Nevertheless pictograms are now seen, in all their variety of applications, to be powerful means of communicating simple messages within carefully defined areas and computer graphics are extending their applications through animation and colour transformation.

Pictograms for information purposes in signing are most effective when they represent or stand for the objects depicted. They may signify a single object or all tyes of that object, such as a bus or a plane. Pictograms are less successful when they are used to signify some property of the object or the result of interaction with the object. We could take as an example a representation of a wine glass to express the concept 'fragile', a property of the object, but the wine glass can also be used to denote 'a wine bar', interaction with the object. The same image has also been used on packaging to denote 'this way up'. In each of these cases the context will give us the meaning, as in speech, but there are some messages such as 'ticket purchase' where a representation of the object, in this case a ticket, is difficult to render since tickets come in all sizes and formats and the problem is further complicated by the fact that tickets can be issued by hand or by machine. Even conveying the idea of the transaction of money is difficult since notes and credit cards are similar in shape to tickets.

There are a number of pictograms which through long use have a generally recognised meaning beyond their nominal image. 'Restaurant' is one such message where the representation of a knife

[1] Co-founders of Glyphs, Inc. USA 1966, an organisation for the development of universal graphic symbols.

Above: Some early examples in the development of a pictogram for handicapped people. More specifically it is used to show areas of access for wheelchairs although other facilities for the handicapped may be available.
From the top: Italy 1965; Expo 67, Montreal, Canada; Sweden 1968; Australia 1968; and the internationally adopted version.

and fork, sometimes crossed, has a long history of use in travel guides and maps. A coffee cup is used in an analogous way to represent a coffee or snack bar.

Already we can begin to see the ambiguity which can arise with pictograms when a direct visual equivalence is lost.

There are a number of concepts where images can be combined to convey a message. If we take a message such as 'car hire' or 'baggage lockers' the addition of a 'key' image to the object will establish the meaning. We run into difficulties however when we attempt to symbolise more abstract qualities of an object or substance. 'Drinking water' is an important message to convey in many parts of the world but has not given rise to a universal pictogram and 'poison' is still, in many cases, represented by a skull and crossbones – a pirate image from childhood, still effective but archaic. Equally abstract and equally important in any message group are 'no entry', 'information point' and 'first aid' for all of which we have substituted abstract signs which are not self evident and have to be learnt. This category of pictogram is best-avoided unless there is time for a new sign to be learnt.

There are also a number of popular and conventional symbols, as with colours, which have an historical interest and which can be 'activated' when appropriate. These can be of value since the symbolism is firmly established in the viewer's mind and all that is required is an appropriate graphic form. Some typical examples of these would be the lightning flash for electrical danger, the dove for peace, the entwined snake for medicine and, of course, that weapon of war the arrow as a directional imperative.

There are an increasing number of artifacts which are becoming less recognisable by shape alone whether domestic appliances or office equipment. The 'black box' is beginning to iron out those old characteristic silhouettes that objects once possessed. Warning drivers not to use horns except in emergencies poses a problem to the pictogram designer since most motorists are totally unaware of the shape of a modern vehicle horn which is usually hidden from view.

One factor which nowadays limits the effective lifespan of a pictogram system is the rapid technological change in such equipment as cash tills, telephones, ticket machines, vehicles and aircraft. A span of as little as five years may see the need for a review of some pictogram treatments within a system. Newly developed appliances such as answer phones and fax machines present similar problems.

Some account needs to be taken of cultural differences in designing pictograms particularly if they are to be used at international terminals. A pictogram that may be obvious to a western visitor may be meaningless or ambiguous to a visitor from a different culture. Dress and food are two areas where care is needed and colour is also an aspect which can cause problems, There seems to be no reference book that can guide the designer in this area but it does underline the importance of field testing symbols before use.

There are some important message areas where it is difficult to find appropriate visual equivalents. For example, I have yet to see a simple consistent set of pictograms which could be applied to any door guiding the user to either push, pull or slide it or wait for the door to open automatically. The door-frustration-syndrome is all too apparent in any public concourse particularly when the traveller is weighed down with luggage. The ergonomic design of door handles could be used to show the type of movement required but would require national or international standardisation to be effective.

A simple pictogram could be applied to any door regardless of type of opening mechanism. If static doors present a problem then the moving door presents a potential hazard: again I don't know of any pictogram solution to the danger of people opening train doors before the train has come to a stop. The general rule must be that it is better to use a warning or hazard sign in such cases rather than an ambiguous one.

There are three inter-related aspects to designing pictograms for signing. First, the pictograms themselves, then their background shapes and, closely linked with shapes, the use of colour. Starting with colour, this is most often deployed to separate categories of messages such as

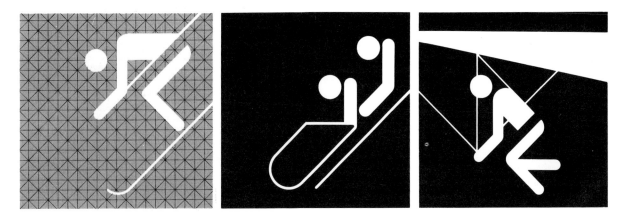

Right: Part of an extensive collection of pictograms designed originally for the Munich Olympic Games in 1972. The collection was taken over by Erco, Lüdenscheid, West Germany and in collaboration with the designer, the collection has been expanded to include subjects for sports, leisure, public buildings, transport, tourism, shops and safety. The first illustration shows the geometric grid used as the basis for the design of all versions. Designer: Otl Aicher and his staff, West Germany.

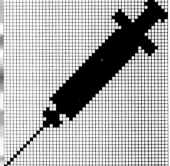

Left and above: Part of a collection of pictograms designed for the Municipal Hospitals of Buenos Aires in 1976. They are used as part of a sign system and include general directional and warning signs as well as images depicting the specialised departments of a large hospital. Carried out with subtety and wit on a closely spaced grid they are screen printed onto metal and glass panels. Designer: Shakespear Design Studio, Buenos Aires, Argentina.

information, public services or warnings. The problem with colour is that the signs may need to appear in applications where colour is not available, such as dot matrix or black and white monitor screens so that it is essential that either colour is always available for key applications or that the sign is always linked with a particular background shape which will reproduce even in monochrome. In general, colour is remembered more easily as a coding medium than shape but it is limited by the small range of easily identifiable and separated hues and has to take into account the safety/ danger colours red and green. Two further factors limit its use: the change in colour values under different types of electric lighting and the fact that a number of people suffer from colour blindness or, the more accurate description, colour deficiency. The most common colour confusion arises over red and green and, according to Richard Gregory,[2] nearly ten per cent of men are markedly deficient in this colour range although it is extremely rare in women. The tonal aspect of colour may also restrict the range since a saturated yellow, for instance, is considerably lighter than most of the other hues in the colour spectrum.

Almost all pictograms are designed as a group or system but it is wise to consider the possibility of later additions since the choice of viewpoints or perspective conventions will need to be considered throughout. Similarly one must decide whether human figures will be included as it will be necessary to consider the scale between human figures and objects. In designing a pictogram group it will be useful to divide the message areas into groups as described above. These will consist of those messages which have direct visual equivalents at one end of the scale and messages with a largely abstract meaning at the other end. Some of the latter may be deemed to be impossible to include and either changed to give an appropriate alternative meaning or dropped from the project.

One is looking for the most characteristic visual quality of the object represented in each case together with the maximum consistency of treatment. Unfortunately, these ideals can sometimes prove to be impossible to reconcile: the

most recognisable viewpoint of a particular object may be in a perspective treatment but this may conflict with an all side view treatment of other items in the group; some objects appear best as a silhouette while others as a linear treatment. A good guideline here is to establish scale relationships and view points at an early planning stage in the design starting from human figures rather than from objects.

The degree of stylisation selected is entirely up to the designer and this forms a spectrum from geometric to free form shapes. Low pixel density in computer generated images will place these images nearer the geometric end of the spectrum. If there is a predominance of 'machine' subject matter a tightly constructed geometrical grid will be more sympathetic than freely shaped forms. Geometrically constructed human figures, surprisingly, have proved to have a universal quality and show no bias to age, race or colour although even minimal attempts at clothing will date the images within a short space of time.

As the pictograms develop and are refined for consistency one must assess the visual 'weight' of each image so that one does not produce a group of images in which some are much darker or lighter than others. Besides affecting legibility under poor lighting conditions, the difference in weighting reduces the overall balance of the design. The variety and limitations of the media through which the pictograms will be shown is often unknown to the designer but one can give three examples where the medium may distort the message or make it illegible: A dot matrix sign or LED equivalent may have such a low definition grid that curves and fine lines may be entirely lost; a back illuminated sign may shrink the apparent size of dark image areas if it is surrounded by too large an area of white illumination; and certain parallel line tints may create annoying moiré patterns when shown on a television screen.

Field testing, as I have suggested above, is an important part of any pictogram project and should be carried out at the full scale of the final signs and if possible under similar visual 'noise' conditions to the final usage. 'Noise' here meaning the typical background of visual clutter and movement within

[2] Eye and Brain, the Psychology of Seeing by R L Gregory. Weidenfeld and Nicolson, London.

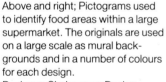

Above and right; Pictograms used to identify food areas within a large supermarket. The originals are used on a large scale as mural backgrounds and in a number of colours for each design.
Designer: Shakespear Design Studio, Buenos Aires, Argentina.

which the pictogram has to be viewed.
It is impossible to cover all the likely uses of pictograms but three further examples can be given to show some of the constraints of their particular applications. Pictograms are increasingly being used on typewriter and computer keys to identify functions or modes and on keyboards as part of a control system for an appliance. When used as part of an alphanumeric key system the pictograms should conform to the weighting or line thickness of the other letter keys unless colour is employed either in the key colour or the image colour. The shape of the key, generally square but on appliances often rectangular, provides the basic constraint, especially difficult when fitting a predominantly horizontal image into a narrow format. The reproduction process for producing the image on the key may limit the amount of detail possible and the thickness of line used. The considerations here come very close to that other exacting discipline, type design, where each character has to be distinctive but work as part of a whole alphabet.

The second example is the creation of a set of laundry pictograms where instructions for washing, drying and ironing have to be used both on cloth labels, washing machines and on driers. The labels may be printed or machine embroidered and the appliances may have the symbols printed or embossed on their controls. The scale of each may be very different and a line thickness suitable for embossing in plastic may be unsuitable for machine stitching. This is a case where two or more line weight versions may be required of each pictogram, the equivalent of the bold and light versions of a type face.

Finally as an example of a well researched and designed set of nationally used passenger pictograms I have included the set produced by the American Institute of Grahic Arts (AIGA) for the United States Department of Transportation. Although designed in 1974 they are still a model of the design process.

The project was set up to produce a set of pictograms for passengers and other users of stations and airport terminals. It was based on the recognition that travellers were already familiar with

Right: A family of transportation related pictograms produced by the American Institute of Graphic Arts (AIGA) for the United States Department of Transportation (see also page 28).
Designers: Cook and Shanosky Associates Inc, Princeton, New Jersey, USA.

Right: Double spread from the AIGA report evaluating a collection of international pictograms based on the theme of 'rail transportation'. The evaluation was scored under four headings: Semantic, the relationship of the visual image to the meaning and how well it represents the message; Syntactic, the relationship of one visual image to another both within the parts of the pictogram and to other pictograms in the system; Pragmatic, relating to factors such as legibility under varying lighting conditions, vulnerability to vandalism and effectiveness in changes of scale and, finally, under the heading 'Group' a rating for each horizontal group as a pictogram concept.

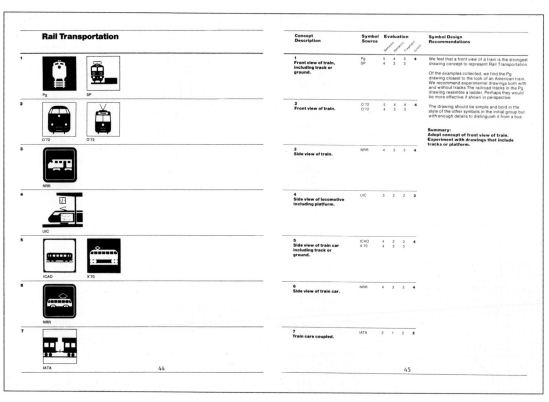

Above: The final version of the pictogram based on the recommendations of the AIGA report.

a wide range of existing pictograms and that what was required was a consistent and inter-related group of pictograms which bridged the language barrier and was capable of communicating a basic set of messages.

The design committee, consisting of five AIGA members under the Chairmanship of Thomas A Geismar drew up a list of the basic message areas required in consultation with the Department of Transportation. At the same time they compiled an inventory of pictogram systems in use around the world. From this information they compared and evaluated all the existing pictograms within each of the proposed message areas and drew up a series of recommendations for the new designs which were produced by Cook and Shanosky Associates, Inc.

This very brief summary is better illustrated by showing one of the double spreads from the committee's report. This represents one of the selected thirty-four message areas, in this case

'Rail transportation' which comes within the general category of Public Services. The 'Rail transport' pictograms on the left hand page are taken from existing pictogram systems each identified with a group of letters. (altogether twenty-four pictogram systems were collected although in this case only ten of them included a 'Rail transportation' pictogram). They are divided into horizontal groups so that pictograms with similar characteristics are grouped together. The committee's evaluation of them is given on the right hand page using a scale of 1 to 5 with 1 representing weakness and 5 representing strength. The last column is a summary of the committee's recommendations which became the brief to the designers and the final design is shown on the left.

As an example of the 'syntactic' treatment of the pictograms the examples shown on page 27 portraying people reveal the consistency of visual treatment between them.

case study

Designing a family of pictograms for the Amsterdam Olympic Games
Andrew Fallon

Andrew Fallon BA, GVN (1947) studied graphic design at Liverpool Polytechnic and the Royal College of Art in London. He started his career at Total Design in Amsterdam. In 1976 he joined Tel Design in The Hague, where he is director and mainly involved in developing house-style projects for commercial, cultural and governmental organisations.

Above: The Amsterdam Bid Book showing the Olympic symbol. Designers: Andrew Fallon, Ronald Meekel, Tel Design, The Hague. Symbol designer: Ad Werner

Pictograms – pictures instead of words – date back before the beginnings of letters and words as we know them today. Ideograms, hieroglyphics and similar symbols have lost ground for centuries as literacy increased but language, spoken and written alike, has become something of an unwelcome barrier in our fast-moving twentieth century where worldwide mobility and international communication have become an ordinary part of our lives.

Pictures have found their way back again, breaking down the word barriers as they gather momentum in international traffic signing, on hi-fi system display panels, on car dashboards, on computer monitors and, of course, in the world of sport. The way we work, rest and play has become increasingly international, in step with a wider understanding of the ways in which we are able to communicate with each other.

Since the 1964 Tokyo Olympics, when, for obvious reasons, Olympic pictograms were first introduced, it has become an Olympic tradition for each host city to provide its own set of pictograms to identify all the sporting events and facilities.

Tel Design was commissioned by the 1992 Amsterdam Olympic Games Foundation to devise a complete house-style, incorporating the previously-designed Amsterdam Olympic symbol by Ad Werner. Part of the brief included the design of the twenty four Olympic sports pictograms and several related ones including one for the Olympic Village.

The Amsterdam identity programme was intended to reflect openness, warmth and hospitality, in combination with the highly-developed cultural, commercial and technological background to everyday Dutch life. The house-style had to overcome the persistent imagery of clogs, tulips and windmills conjured up by the very mention of the word 'Holland'.

A master plan for the house-style was developed by us with Amsterdam's three St Andrew's crosses serving as a focal point for all visualisations. These three red crosses form part of Amsterdam's coat of arms and consequently appear in the city's Olympic symbol. Their digital, diagonal shapes provided a point of departure for the many applications within the Amsterdam Olympic Games corporate identity scheme. Based on one typographical grid system, the applications included cartography and diagrams, illustrations and photography, magazines, brochures, posters, exhibitions, the Amsterdam Bid Book and the Olympic pictograms. The house-style alone was not the only source of inspiration used to create the pictograms. An extensive survey of all existing sport pictograms was carried out, in order to properly analyse each individual sporting event, including the most characteristic view points and movements involved. Scale and detail in each pictogram were then considered separately to achieve a uniform look for the complete pictogram family.

The human figures are all depicted on the same

Above: Olympic poster of sprinters using the same digital, diagonal treatment as in the pictograms. Designers: Andrew Fallon, Gerard van Leyden, John Verkees. Tel Design, The Hague.

Above and top right: a selection from the twenty four Olympic pictograms for Amsterdam.

scale and do not show gender. For the sake of clarity, each pictogram shows only one figure but in exceptional cases, such as judo and wrestling, it was considered better to include two figures per image. The swimming pictogram also includes two figures, or rather two halves of figures, as the swimmers are shown half-submerged in water. All additional information, such as equipment, has been kept to an acceptable minimum to avoid cluttering the total image.

Any movements suggested in the pictograms invariably run from left to right. This is intended to support the overall style of the complete set and they always show a white figure reversed out of a red square background, never the other way round. All roughs and final designs were done by hand, the computer being introduced later for reproduction and presentation purposes. This left plenty of breathing space for pure design work in the opening stages leaving the computer to plot out the final artwork when all the creative thinking had been done.

The digital, diagonal style found in the Amsterdam Olympic pictograms, maps and diagrams was used also effectively in photography. Resolution, colour and contrast could easily be modified to achieve a variety of effects. The characteristic style behind the Amsterdam Olympic pictograms and related house-style applications was designed to leave plenty of room for variation, without the danger of it becoming boring at a later stage.

Unfortunately for Amsterdam, the 1992 Olympic bid failed but maybe the twenty-first century will bring the Games to The Netherlands, so in the meantime we may relish the thought of even more pictures and fewer words when the time arrives.

(The Olympic Games house-style and pictograms were designed by:
Andrew Fallon, Gerard van Leyden, Ronald Meekel and others of Tel Design, The Hague).

product interface

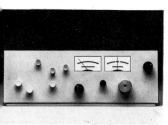

bove: An orderly arrangement of
ontrols (lower photograph) makes
r easier use and shows what
elongs together. It shows which
re similar and which different and
uggests degrees of importance.

In operating any appliance or machine the graphics
and controls are the basic interface with the user.
The graphics identify, inform and, in many cases,
supply a feed-back about the state of the operation
by means of a system of words and symbols. Unfortunately, there are far too many products where the
graphics fail on one or more of these counts, are
inferior in design terms to the engineering qualities
of the product or simply do not survive the useful
life of the product. There are a number of reasons for
this. In some cases the majority of the funding has
been devoted to research and production and ,
little left over for the graphics design or it may be a
lack of a professional graphics designer on the
design team. Other causes are the passing of the
graphics responsibility to the advertising agency
responsible for the marketing of the product and, in
a few cases, the graphics are seen as fulfilling only
a short term need to aquaint the new user with
a working knowledge of the operation of
the product.

Certainly, in simple appliances safety is unlikely to
be affected by poor graphics but as we go up the
scale in terms of complexity and possible number
of users, safety and stress, and these are often
inter-related, can both be markedly affected by a
graphics treatment which has not been clearly
formulated and researched as part of the whole
design process. At the very least, good graphics
contribute a bonus to establishing the overall
quality of the product in the mind of the purchaser.

One of the weaknesses evident in some products
is that the positioning of all the major controls have
obviously been planned in advance of the graphics
involvement. In these cases the graphics designer
can only have a limited effect on the outcome of the
design. The important considerations of
positioning, scale and consistency of treatment
may all be affected.

On the other hand, no matter how good the
graphics, they will only be partially successful
if the overall ergonomic design has not been
carefully thought out. The ease with which the
controls can be used, their positioning and
grouping are the first requirement. In fact the ideal
arrangement is for the ergonomist and designer to
work closely together from the earliest design
stages. The designer's desire for simplicity and
order must be mediated by the ergonomic
requirements for the most efficient shapes of
controls and their positioning.

In those machines with mainly or entirely
mechanical controls the choice of positioning of
the control knobs and switches is usually extremely
limited because the body of each of the components takes up a fixed minimum space behind the
fascia and, apart from cooling and servicing
considerations, limits the closeness and sometimes
the alignment of controls. As some of these
components are not always made by the product
manufacturer there is little possibility of modifying
them. With the advent of electronic controls few of

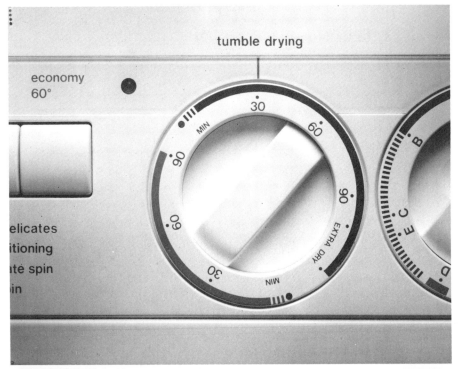

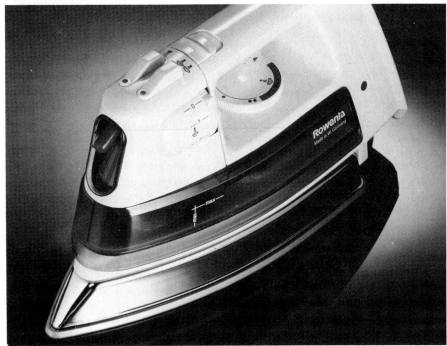

these constraints apply and a near perfect ergonomic approach is possible.

The graphics of the interface normally take three forms: verbal, symbolic or pictogrammic. Both words and pictograms are used to identify controls and functions, words also being used to amplify directions and give warnings and symbols, such as arrows and arcs, to show direction of movement, increases or decreases and sequence of operations.

Grouping of controls

The simplest grouping of controls is in a continuous line either vertically or horizontally and our (western) conditioning is for a top to bottom and left to right scanning. In the simple case of, say, lift controls the buttons follow the logical vertical sequence of lift stops with a separate grouping for door controls. A domestic product such as an electric fan heater could also follow a similar linear sequence in operating order starting with, say, the on/off switch followed by heating/cooling selector, heat intensity, continuous mode or thermostatic mode. Where there is no natural sequence of operations and where some of the controls will be used infrequently it is more logical to group the controls into areas or zones designated by use or function and to define them by colour or background.

A good example of this type of grouping is that found on some car fascias. The zones in this case would relate to controls and instruments associated with distinct phases in driving a car such as the basic pre-start checks, starting, driving, heating and ventilation, night driving and parking. If we take one of these phases as an example such as the starting phase this would show a grouping of the controls for choke (if not automatic), ignition and indicators for seat belt (worn) and doors (closed). When the number of controls increases, particularly where there is no natural association, then grouping is still important so that the eye can easily select the correct one out of a number of, possibly, identical controls. Groupings of five in an horizontal arrangement are ideal as the eye can easily make the choice between the one in the centre, which acts as a datum, those to left or right of it or those

t upper: Clear labelling of rotary
d push buttons on an Ariston
shing machine.

t lower: Pictograms, symbols and
ours used to indicate settings on
ariety of rotary and push button
ntrols on a Rowenta steam iron.

ove: A set of pictograms for a car
shboard and an experimental set
markings for a set of control
obs.
esigner: Giancarlo Illiprandi, Milan,
ly.

on the outer edges. Beyond five repeated units errors of selection increase rapidly, particularly under stress. Groups lying far to left or right of the viewer at an oblique angle should be reduced in numbers. In terms of vertical stacking two to three rows are probably the most that should be combined giving a matrix of ten to fifteen units. Large displays with these groupings are usually reserved for control rooms operated by full time professional staff who are less likely to make mistakes than the wide spectrum of age and experience represented by car drivers.

Simple control systems

These are systems with manual controls which rely entirely on the positioning of the controls to show the settings. There is no illuminated or audio indication that they are switched on or at any particular setting except, perhaps, for an audible click when changed and no feedback to the operator from meters or displays. The simple two-position switch or rotary knob are the commonest examples. The shape of the control should give the user the clue as to the type of movement required and the graphics should indicate the extent of the movement and/or the number of fixed positions that are possible. On/off switch positions should be clearly shown as there are some system conventions, such as on aircraft control panels, which are the opposite to those in general use (the up positioning representing 'on').

With rotary controls a dot or marker on the control and markers on the fascia can immediatley show the extent of rotary movement and this can be supplemented by a linear arc of movement which can be progressively thickened at one end to show an increase of value such as volume or speed. Similar considerations apply to switches where it is important to show if more than the usual two positions are possible. The indication on the control knobs should be sufficiently contrasted to enable the user (or another user) to see quickly where all the controls have been set. Where no other warning devices are used all of the controls should be visible to the user without movement.

[1] The European Community has set up a committee to standardise vehicle dashboard graphics.

The associated graphics problem is to identify the functions of all the controls in such a way that none are masked and that they are all clearly readable, including pictograms, from the users' normal sitting or operating position. It is surprising how often this simple requirement is overlooked, particularly when, as on car fascia layouts for example, controls can be easily masked by the steering wheel or the driver's hands or where the graphics have to be read at an oblique angle to the driver.

The choice of words, symbols or pictograms to label controls and functions depends on several factors. If symbols or pictograms are chosen will they all be intelligible to the anticipated users? A good safety guide is to use words for vital actions where no clear and unambiguous symbol or pictogram exists or can be created. In some cases it may be desirable to add small size verbal descriptions to symbols much in the same way as sub-titles are used but the two systems should not be of equivalent importance and the words should be treated as learning aids to memorising the visual image. A mixture of part language, part image should not be used as this can lead to confusion and a reduction in effectiveness.

Now that so many products are exported world wide we are likely to see an increase in the use and number of symbols and pictograms and the standardisation of symbol systems[1]. The problem with verbal labelling is that each export market may require a separate language edition which in practice usually means a printed form of presentation whereas the most effective technique and one giving the longest life may be to incorporate the message into the production process so that the lettering is integral with the material.

Symbols and pictograms can be designed to fit a standard format such as a square or circle and therefore are more consistent in shape and proportion, especially on such features as keyboard keys, than the varying width of entries if words are used. In the case of translations these may require as much as twice the width of the original language necessitating the use of a condensed letterform or a smaller letter form to fit the available space.

Where letterforms are used, the choice of letterform

must be made in relation to the surfaces on which they are to appear and the nature of the printing process. Very thin letters will not stand up well if screen printed onto relatively coarse textured surfaces; on the other hand fine detail can be reproduced, even in reversal, as part of the anodising process on aluminium. The choice of capitals, lower case or a mixture of the two must be considered. For reasons given in the first section of this book, lower case is the first choice and, since many descriptions giving the function of a control consist of a single word, the use of all lower case will give a more harmonious look to the panel than starting each word with a capital letter.

Lettering position with respect to the controls is a problem that can only be solved by reference to all the captioning on a complete panel or family of panels. A ranged solution is more consistent with most layouts especially if the lettering ranges alongside each control rather than appearing above or below it. Centred lettering, although consistent with individual controls and meters, rarely looks right when viewed as a whole panel. Ranging is even more desirable when descriptions run to two or more lines since the critical left hand edge of each lettering block will be ragged if each line is centred. In general a centred positioning treatment only allows of one choice in each case but a ranged treatment allows of a number of choices without graphic inconsistency.

Controls with visual or audio indicators

These are control systems which give an immediate indication either as to their status or mode. They take a number of forms such as illuminated keys or buttons which light up when pressed, pilot lights (neon or LED's) or illuminated lettering. Audio indicators give a click or bleep to confirm that the electronic contact has been made, particularly important with 'flush' controls concealed beneath a flat membrane surface and the user does not feel any physical movement of a key. The membrane system probably allows the widest range of graphic treatment since the shape and area of the pressure point is not so exactly defined as with a mechanical system. Both illuminated and audio indicators have

very compelling forms of signalling a warning, either immediately or when something becomes critical, in the form of flashes or bleeps of varying intensity or duration.

Controls which have an associated meter or other form of display provide feedback to the user and the main graphic problems are in identifying different scales and which controls activate which meter especially if the meter can be switched between different controls. In grouping meters on a console the variable range of arc of different meters may also present a problem; some meters may extend to a 270 degree sweep while others may only cover 90 degrees. If there is an 'optimum' working position for the indicators of a set of meters showing related functions then they can be arranged so that this optimum indicator position is vertical for all of them with respect to the panel. In this way it is easier to monitor a number of dials to see if any one hand is out of position. This treatment is often found on car dashboards where meters for water temperature, oil pressure and electrical charge give a near constant position reading when the vehicle is warmed up.

Illuminated displays, including the bar type of display being used as a speedometer on some vehicles, present a problem when combined with non-illuminated graphics. Depending on the light source the illuminated displays often dominate and so a balance has to be found between controlling the amount of illumination on the console as a whole and the display lighting. Some form of automatic compensation is the ideal so that under changing lighting situations as, for example, on a car's console where the range may be from direct sunlight to very low levels at dusk, the display retains the same relative contrast.

Pictogram and symbol treatments may be affected by these considerations when backlit since a positive (black) image on a light background may let through too much background light, particularly if several pictograms are grouped together.

A reversal of the image (white on black background) may be more succesful but, if designed for a positive application, may require a strengthening or thickening of line strokes to read clearly.

Where controls are used for a number of separate

Above: Medical equipment for analysis of blood and urine samples. It features a back printed and illuminated control/display panel with a flowchart graphic layout that automatically sequences the operator through a series of call and response interrogations driven by the electronics. The visual result is clearly presented and operator error and response time reduced to a minimum.
Designers: BIB Design Consultants Ltd, London
Client: Corning Medical (UK).

functions, and this is most often the case with keyboard controls, the difficulty is to show which mode the machine is in. The choice is between separate positioning of information and/or colour coding. The ideal solution, and this applies to any multi-function control system, is one in which only the relevant graphics are shown for any one mode selected. This is a solution chosen for some hi-fi equipment (see page 37) where black illuminated lettering shows information for only one selected mode of operation at any one time. This method allows all the appropriate information to be shown without the distraction of, temporarily, irrelevant information. This 'filtered' information can be shown in more detail (fascia space allowing) than would be possible or desirable if it was shown in its totality. Multi-mode operation is less liable to user error when a screen is in use since this can graphically indicate the mode the machine is in although a monochrome screen will not be able to make use of colour codes.

Analogue versus digital

Both analogue and digital presentations have their uses but they should always be chosen for their appropriateness of function rather than for space or cost (or stylistic) reasons. Peter Rea has contributed a study on this subject on page 41 and so I will only briefly mention the limitations of each presentation. Analogue, of which our circular clock and watch dials are by far the commonest forms, indicate the time in as much a graphical form as a numerical one. The two hands make a recognisable pattern against the dial calibrations, in fact we rely on this pattern rather than the numerals to tell us the time.

The clock's great strength is that we can relate the displayed time visually as being before or after the hour, as time gone or time to come and we also get a very good idea of the rate of change, of time which can be further enhanced with a third (seconds) hand. With a digital time presentation we have to read the numerical information, which is time now, and then relate it to the hour or an event. Digital systems require numerical thought rather than analogue pattern recognition and are much

more difficult to appreciate in terms of rate of change.

All-digital presentations were tried out for aircraft altimeters to replace the existing analogue (dial) ones and it was soon found that being able to assess the rate at which height was changing was of vital importance and that a set of rapidly changing counters in a digital system gave no clear indication of this factor. Accidents have been caused in the past by pilots misreading the small hands on analogue altimeters which represent thousands of feet (height is still measured internationally in feet in the aviation world) and so the ideal presentation was found to be an analogue (dial) presentation with a small digital presentation at the base to give an unambiguous 'height now' readout.

Speed indicators for cars also went through a transition phase to all digital presentation with similar results. These displays did have the advantage that conversion from imperial to metric units could be changed immediately but this was of small importance to most drivers. Another type of analogue speed display replacing the conventional dial is in the form of an extended, illuminated bar diagram where segments of a coloured strip are illuminated with the total length varying according to the speed of the vehicle. This can be thought of as an adaptation of the circular band swept by the indicator hand on a conventional speedometer being spread out as a straight line bar. The moving band of light and colour can be more distracting than a conventional moving indicator, particularly after dark, but is extremely effective.

The car has also seen the introduction of another form of audio presentation: the synthesised human voice. This has mainly been used to remind drivers that some action has not been carried out or to give a warning about one of the cars' systems. It has not been well received by most drivers but whether this is because of the irritation with the uses to which it has so far been put or to the accent in which it is delivered is not clear but this is potentially an interesting area for interface communication. Another factor which needs to be taken into consideration is that of reflections from displays which, like changing light levels, can make even the

Above: Analogue clock face and digital display from a Braun hi fi tuner.

best of designs difficult to read. Advances have already been made in this area by the use of non-reflective glass and finishes. Perhaps the ultimate type of display for any situation involving rapid user response such as high speed driving and flying situations is the head-up display. Although still the province of the military, this type of display does overcome the time lag of head movements and eye refocussing necessary with conventional panel displays.

The mixture of different types of presentation on one panel can be difficult to adjust to perceptually and presents greater problems of co-ordination in graphic terms. Whichever system is employed the most sucessful graphics will be those in which there is the greatest consistency of labelling between controls and displays and between linguistic and symbolic presentations of information. As can be seen the problems are often complex and sometimes contradictory and the best examples are usually the result of close collaboration between several disciplines.

Most of the above relates to users with normal sight and vision but a certain proportion of users are partially sighted or have limited hearing. In terms of illuminated or audio indicators it is relatively easy to build in volume adjusters but the size of printed graphics once selected are fixed and research is needed to know what are optimum sizes and contrasts for these users. Computers are able to offer zoom enlargement of text and this feature may soon be available on other types of display thus allowing the user to set the most legible size of lettering. Partially sighted users have a need for controls which are recognisable through their shape or tactile properties as well as by their graphics but we must also accept that special shapes have to be usable by both left and right handed operators.

Technical limitations

The graphics used on the product interface have to be reproduced and although there are a number of processes available each will have its own constraints in terms of durability, quality of definition, setting up costs versus length of run and

other factors. Probably the most important quality is the one of durability because the graphics should be capable of lasting the estimated life of the product or appliance taking into account such factors as the working environment and frequency of use. We have all used products from which the graphics (often in the form of adhesive labels) have peeled off or worn away leaving in doubt the function of the control settings and, in some cases, reducing safety margins.

The commonest reproduction processes are printing either directly onto the product material by ink or foil blocking or by means of a label. Embossing or relief moulding, etching (with or without colour filling) and anodising are other common techniques. There is not space to go into the details of each process and their effect on graphic treatments but we can summarise their desirable properties under several headings. From the point of view of durability, as already mentioned, they should be capable of surviving the life of the product taking into account the probable working environment and frequency of use which means being highly resistant to handling, scuffing, weather and, in some cases, chemicals. If labelling is used the adhesives used should be resistant to both accidental and deliberate removal and this can be helped by mouding or machining recessed areas on the product surface to accept the label. Printing processes, such as screen printing, can have a long life if special resin inks are used matching the type of plastic onto which they are to be printed. The ink bonds itself chemically to the surface and is resistant to most cleaning materials. In terms of definition the chosen reproduction process should be capable of reproducing the finest details required in the graphics. In this respect processes which are based on photo-graphic reproduction are to be preferred and this is particularly important where letter forms have to be matched exactly for style and spacing since some processes have their own alphabets (sometimes only capitals) which are unlikely to match in either respect. If all the reproduction processes employed on one product have a common photographic basis then this will ensure conformity of letter style, size and weight.

Above: Part of the Renault 21 TXE electronic dashboard shows some of the visual problems in fitting together a variety of graphic displays compared with the simplicity and ordered layout of traditional analo-gue dials. Colour is used to good effect in the original and more infor-mation can be shown in the same space but probably requires a longer learning time.

Above: A graphics display which includes a plan view of the vehicle and warns of bulb failures, low air temperature and doors that are not completely closed. From the instru-mentation for the Granada Ghia, Ford Motor Company Ltd, UK.

case study

**Designing the graphics for a Bang & Olufsen music system
Sally Beardsley**

Sally Beardsley, is an American graphic designer who, after receiving a BFA from Rhode Island School of Design, worked in Rome and London for many years before settling in Copenhagen in 1981. She is a freelance designer involved with both product development (consumer products as well as children's toys and games) and information design, with a special interest in operating structures and design and on-screen graphics for electronic products.

Above: a detail of the Beocenter 9000 showing the illuminated graphics.

When you are scanning a newspaper, your eye automatically picks out items of special interest, and everything else recedes into the background. This natural 'selection process' is also present when you operate a piece of electronic equipment. But your senses are often numbed by the amount and kind of extraneous information requiring selective processing.

With a music system, you don't want to make a recording, change the balance, select bass and treble, search for a station, play an auxiliary source turn up the volume, set the Dolby, rearrange CD tracks, make a timer programming, rewind the tape . . . or rather, you want to do all of these and more, but not all at the same time. Ideally, you should only have to look at those 'buttons' and displays that are immediately relevant to the operation you have in mind.

Of course, a music system can't actually read your mind but by carefully structuring each operating sequence so it follows a specific visual path, and by temporarily making all other operation controls invisible, most of the 'hard work' of selective processing can be done for you.

Bang & Olufsen's Beocenter 9000 is designed on the principle that unless you need to use something, it's not there. A complete music system, incorporating a hi-fi amplifier, an FM/AM digital synthesized tuner with twenty station presets, a compact disc player, and a cassette deck, the 9000 is designed for both sensi-touch and remote control operation.

The Beocenter 9000 can also function as the audio unit in a complete audio/video system, datalinked to other Bang & Olufsen units, as well as to the Beolink system, allowing for integrated operations from anywhere in the home.

The basic lead-in functions are constantly visible, discretely printed on the front glass panel, but until you indicate what you want – by lightly touching the name of the source or function – the system remains . . . well, inscrutable.

The instant you make a choice, however, those displays relevant to your choice light up. If you simply want to hear music, and you touch CD, Radio or Tape, your wish is instantly granted, as long as you have loaded a CD or tape cassette.

To load, you touch Load CD or Load Tape, and the small aluminium cover slides inward, revealing the loading section. The CD cover closes automatically in playback; the tape cover closes by touching Load once more; and both covers close automatically when the system is in stand by.

Of course, once you're listening to a source, you want to know everything about it, its full status; and you want every operational possibility related to that source to be at your fingertips. The 9000 has two glass panels: the front panel is for sensi-touch operation and the rear panel is for feed-back and status displays.

When you touch the operating panel, both panels react: the rear panel shows you what is actually happening as a result of your choice, and the front

Right: The Beocenter 9000 in radio-play mode with its aluminium loading covers closed. All operations except loading tape or CD can still be carried out. The 9000 is designed for touch and remote control operation. Dimensions are 760×110×340mm (30×4¾×13⅜in.).

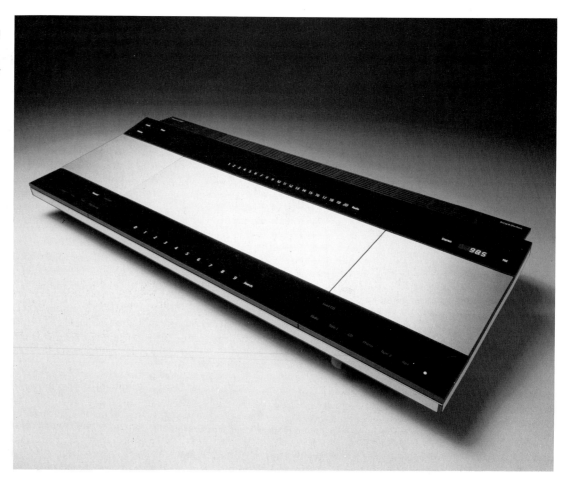

panel offers you the next set of choices you can – or should – make. In that way, you are led through each operation – even ones with several steps, like timer programming – without needing to look at the user's guide.

Which brings us to the original idea behind the 9000 design.

Bang & Olufsen felt that much enjoyment of today's complex electronic products is lost through the user's inability to take full advantage of a product's potential. By ploughing through an often complex guide, a persistent user can eventually get to know the system. But the pleasure of completely effortless enjoyment is postponed, to say the least.

Reasoning that there must be an easier way, and acknowledging the superiority of menu-type operations over a combination of knobs, buttons and user's guides, Bang & Olufsen designed a music system with a built-in guide-cum-operations system. The total absence of buttons makes this music system extremely intriguing, inviting a user to experiment, rather than intimidating him with technology.

In developing the 9000, the advanced technology and versatility required called for some innovative software design, coupled with product, operational and graphic design that would faithfully express the product idea.

Product designer Jakob Jensen interpreted the Beocenter's technical requirements in an ingenious

way. The two glass panels were created naturally, separated as they are by the central sound panel. The display and operating panels are thus two discrete units, visually alike but functionally different.

As graphic designer I worked closely with Bang & Olufsen's engineers to develop an operational structure and design which would be visually clear, despite a number of different display permutations. In a product of such physical simplicity, the graphics no longer play a 'supporting role' – they are central to the total look of the product.

The typeface chosen is Berthold Frutiger. Both elegant and extremely legible, Frutiger is in harmony with the pure lines of the 9000, avoiding the industrial, functional look of many other sans serif faces. The size of the Beocenter's panels allows for the use of upper and lower case letters – increasing the legibility and, equally important, the 'identity' of each word displayed; from a distance, words in caps tend to form blocks, while upper/lower case letters form distinctive, recognisable shapes.

The display text is silk-screened on the back of the glass. It is back-lit by LED's (light emitting diodes). The glass panels appear to be totally black when the system is in stand by, and each text, when activated, appears discrete and luminous against a totally black background.

This apparently simple effect required several

Right: Detail of the 9000 in radio-
search mode with its CD loading
cover shown open.

engineering innovations. In addition, other criteria had to be met by B&O engineers: good legibility, independent of ambient light conditions; homogeneous illumination with no 'hot spots'; and long-life LED's, combined with extremely low power consumption.

There were no standard LED's that could meet the company's unusual requirements, so a special chip (GaAlAs) and casing design (in pocan) were developed. One LED can backlight a 7×10mm text; ($1/4 \times 3/8$in.) a 7×19mm ($1/4 \times 3/4$in.) text requires two. Uneven lighting and 'hot spots' are eliminated by diffusing the glass cover on the diode case as well as the diode itself.

The rich red colour of the displays is in fact the best colour to use for both maximum luminosity through very dark glass and also invisibility when not illuminated.

Green, found lower down the colour spectrum and therefore less ideal for luminosity/invisibility, was chosen as a second colour to clearly distinguish the recording functions and sound/recording measurement bars.

The luminosity/invisibility effect is further enhanced by a red/green filter. This is silk screened directly over the printing of the display text, on the back of the glass panels. Outside, everything is simple, while inside, there is a whole world of extremely intricate engineering, creating the contradictory states of luminosity and invisibility, at the touch of a finger.

comparative study

The perception and presentation of time by analogue and digital formats
Peter Rea

Peter Rea ARCA, FSTD has worked as a designer and educator for twenty five years. Formerly visiting assistant Professor Philadelphia College of Art 1971–72; Head of the Advanced Typographic Design course at London College of Printing 1972–80; Head of Graphic Design Leicester Polytechnic 1980–83. Since 1984 Peter has been in private design practice as Director of Archetype Design and Archetype Visual Studies, London. Appointed Head of the School of Graphic Design, Ravensbourne College of Design and Communication, London in 1988, Peter will also continue in private practice.

This comparative study is based on an article which appeared in Typographic 9, Journal of the Society of Typographic Designers 1976.

Conventional graphic means of representing time are not necessarily the most efficient for all situations and I shall outline other ways of visualising time and our interaction with it. To begin with it may be useful to review the existing graphical formats for representing time.

Analogue time

The digit hour 12, at the apex of the conventional clock dial, conforms with our instinctive feelings. Part of the day is before midday and part after; during the normal morning of work, the hour hand rises up the hill of the day (of the dial), and during the afternoon it runs down, with the evening beginning as of 6 at the foot; it then rises again until, when it approaches 12, we visualise time for rest.
Perceptually, the dial is viewed in segments of halves and quarters. Looking at the middle illustration, the eye easily selects the datum points

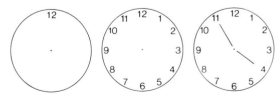

12, 6, 3 and 9 (or *vice versa*), travelling continually over the surface; the smaller wedges, ie, 12-1, 1-2, 2-3, are received as simple sub-divisions of the

quarters, and so on. In the right hand illustration the brain reads the two hands, and also compares the two segments which it groups subconsciously into 'so much time past' and 'so much time before'.
In using the watch dial to tell time, there is normally some perceptual adjustment being made against another factor: for example, in this same illustration there is another hour (segment) and five minutes (segment) before the hypothetical train leaves at 5; I am five minutes early for my appointment at 4.
The watch dial, then, presents a most satisfactory way of showing an analogy of time corresponding to the manner in which we perceive concepts of time units (time past, time present and time future).

Digital time

Digital time, as with many other technological advances, removes the necessity of understanding techniques required to interpret an analogy (reading the hands), and substitutes an instant read-out situation in digits. That of course is an advantage under circumstances where, for example, the relevance of *time now* to some other time or to the segment of the day is immaterial. In circumstances directly involving *time now* (eg, time keeping for speed-against-time; auto-timed actions in activating machinery at specific times); digital time is highly accurate, as there are in essence no perceptual characteristics to interfere with the communication of the digits on the read-out panel.[1]

[1] The design of the ciphers and visual display panels themselves, however, may embody perceptual characteristics which interfere with legibility.

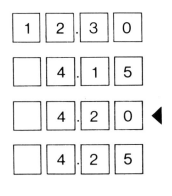

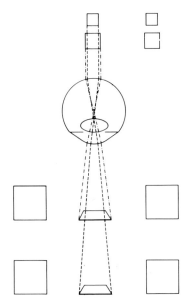

The top illustration gives an absolute time while the next one demonstrates how we have to visualise and mentally calculate (ie, create) an analogous before-or-after situation in order to be able to express the *time now* in terms of how much time is left. By covering up the second and fourth lines of the illustration, you can see how isolated the *time now* 4.20 becomes, when the observer is denied a means of perceptually grasping its relevance to living time; uncover the second line and the *time now*, 4.20, becomes 5 minutes *after* 4.15; uncover the fourth line, and 4.20 is seen to be 5 minutes *before* 4.25. When the means of comparison is revealed, then a *sense* of time as a motivated or moving measurement becomes apparent. This is of course how we normally wish to use 'the time': as a means of perceiving how much more time remains or has passed before our next time-related action.

Thoughts on perception to support the usefulness of graphic linear time

Since it is a necessary basis of my point of view to refer to perceptual characteristics, and the way in which we interpret what we see, I put forward here some relevant thoughts on perception.

If you are unfamiliar with the difference between perception, reality, and retinal image (the image physically received on the retina at the back of the eye when seeing), and with the interference that our perceptual system continuously operates between that which the eye-retina 'sees' and what the eye-brain perceives (or appears to see), then the following simple demonstration is worth study.

In the second illustration, two objects of the same overall size but set at different distances from the eye, are viewed at the same time. The images of the objects on the retina shown at the bottom of the illustration clearly indicate that the receptors at the back of the eye see the objects as different sizes (due to the difference in distance). The images, however, when 'seen' *appear* not to differ in size), but to be the same. Thus one might say, things are not always what they seem.[2]

To test this theoretical statement, use your hands to re-create the demonstrations shown. Place one hand at arm's length, the other at half the distance.

Although the illustration shows that the further hand will be only half the size of the nearer on the retina, what we see is that they are both almost exactly the same size.

Move the nearer hand sideways to overlap the further, and they will now look very different in size. It can be concluded that very strong influences interfere in the act of seeing.[3]

An understanding of perception supports both the forms that graphic linear time can take, and also the usefulness of the approach. Systems used for the measurement of distance demonstrate similar perceptual properties.

Measurements of distance, or time travelled

To understand this, I would like you to think of the measurement of distance as a measurement of *time travelled*. Units of time that we can group together in a manner that allows us to perceptualise a length of time, also represent a length of distance.

With perceptual principles, distance is structured just as time has been.

Measurement can be thought of: as a concept of distance related to time, as time for the body to travel the distance, as time for the eye to travel or comprehend the dimensions of an object to visualise their appropriateness to some function (dinner plate to a dinner, ladder to a wall, seat to a body), as macrocosmic time for the eye to span minimal dimensions, as real time for the eye to be carried as part of the body on a journey (eg, to visualise 60 mph we see ourselves travelling at 60 mph).

Measurement takes account of hills, dales and twisting roads, but presents itself to us in a feasible conceptual form as a length of time, a *linear concept of time*. To this linear concept, we add variable factors such as recalled experience or learned information: viz., over water, by foot, as the crow flies, and so on. The linear concept is perceptualised as units of time travelled, drawn together quickly, intermittently or slowly, according to the particular factors we apply.

A preference could perhaps be made for the measurement of distance to remain in imperial

[2] This phenomenon, now known as size constancy, was first described by Descartes in *Dioptrics* (1637): also that which is now known as shape constancy.

[3] The strangeness of this and other influences on the psychology of seeing are discussed in detail in Richard Gregory, *Eye and Brain*, Weidenfeld and Nicolson.

divisions of measure, rather than metric, on the basis that the former are conceptual and can be grasped in the mind. The advantages and disadvantages of analogual and digital time are mirrored in imperial (analogual) dimensions and digitally based metrifications. Although this is not the place to debate the idea in full, it would be interesting to know whether the classical empire of Rome, the British Empire, the United States of America and the Soviet Union, all of which built their respective achievements around a system of dimensional units of a similar size, did this intuitively or logically on perceptual grounds, or by some chance coincidence.

Imperial dimensions can be grasped in a perceptual sense; fractions, inches, feet and yards are group-able concepts offering many variables. 6.3 cm has to be visualised as either 6 + 3/10 or as less than 6.5; whereas 6½ inches is a specific concept, as is 6¼ in., and so on.[4]

Using the scale above, try to identify 1¾ in. as though you were going to make a mark on a design layout; analyse the manner by which you isolated the 1¾ in. datum point.

Repeat, and identify 1 15/16 in., and again analyse. Finally, seek 15/32 in.; the technique used to identify this last, more refined, subdivision is slower because of the greater complexity of subdivisions, but is still basically the same as in the previous examples and, once found, is held accurately.

It is likely that you made sophisticated use of a simple grouping instinct by dividing the available datum points on the rule into halves, quarters and so on, finally certifying that the eye has locked on the correctly selected datum by checking that it is the centre of a pair of equal divisions – this last still applies even where counting of the units has had to take place. Progressively one isolates the sub-division sought by defining the centre point between equal subdivisions.

Make an analysis of the way in which you isolate the

datum points on the second scale below. It can be seen that this is basically a different technique to that used above.

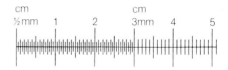

Verification of accuracy in these examples is carried out by mathematical calculus rather than by perceptual proof.

Since the means by which our sensory eye-brain systems interpret imperial and metric measurement systems seem, for the former, to utilise our perceptive system and, for the latter, to be dominantly a mathematical calculus, it is interesting to pursue this a little further.

When visualising quantities of millimetres (mm) we cannot readily break the quantitive figures down into smaller subgroups. Fractional divisions and subdivisions are simple to grasp. A dimension may be comprised of a group of two halves, four quarters, eight eighths. The concept 'foot' gives us an immediate guide to visualise the base unit length, and the secondary divisible unit of 12 inches provides many groupable subdivisions. Subdivisions in fractions give a perceptual notion of a unit of measure continually subdividing, diminishing to infinity.

The metric system, which is based on decimalisation as a mathmatical principle, has advantages in digital calculation, particularly the moving of the decimal point to divide and multiply on a percentage basis. A disadvantage is that it is not analogous to any general dimension less than a metre, nor to any perceptual notion, unless one applies a fractional and thereby groupable concept, eg, 30 cm being nearly one third of a metre, and so on. There is also a practical disadvantage in that, having reduced a metre to centimetres, and then to millimetres, it becomes physically impossible to render a decimal one-tenth of a millimetre. Consequently, since millimetres often seem too

[4] This harmonius relationship to our seeing-thinking visual system provides a quick grasp of subdivisions when (for example) identifying at which point to make a division, before such a mark is actually made on paper.

Right: Sub-divisions of the linear foot. Far right: Sub-divisions of the decimal fraction.

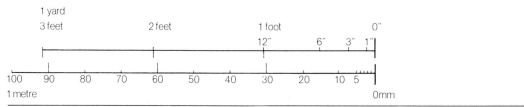

12 units	a whole	1		10 units	a whole	1.
6 units	a half	½		5 units	a half	.5
4 units	a third	⅓		2 units	a fifth	.2
3 units	a quarter	¼		1 unit	a tenth	.1
2 units	a sixth	⅙				
1 unit	a twelfth	1/12				

Right: Comparison of imperial and metric scales. In proportion but not to size.

Le Corbusier's *Modular*, a scale of metric measurements based on the human body.

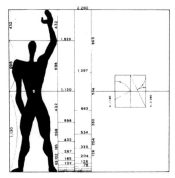

coarse a division, there is a tendency towards half millimetres, compounding the difficulty of perceiving a clear notion of these subdivisions.

Imperial measures allow one to visualise divisions and multiples, by grouping together simple units in the mind: four quarters to make one inch, twelve inches to make one foot, three feet to one yard. The concept of this dimension is readily continued as being approximate to an ordinary human foot.

When using diminishing fractions a similar simplicity of groups exists (see chart above).

Even at the point of illegibility on a normal ruler (1/32 in. approximately) the concept of diminishing dimensions continues. Much the same contra-

diction between analogous and digital advantages applies to the sub-divisions of kilometres and miles, kilograms and pounds.

Possibly le Corbusier's attempts to relate the metre to the human body were manifestations of an unhappiness caused by the dilemma between (his) perceptual grouping instincts and digital simplicity. [The original article from which this excerpt is taken went on to introduce the reader to examples of linear time concepts including flow charts and the grouping tendencies inherent in 'tabular' typography such as timetables.]

Right: This matrix of dots can be read as vertical columns, diagonals, squares, horizontals; sometimes we see the dots, at other times the white space.

Far right: A mathematically correct disposition of tabular matter can be perceptually wrong, causing continual irritation to the sensory system, as the system repeatedly applies a correction factor to enable information to be read logically.

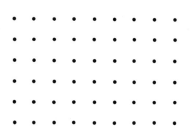

Windsor → Slough → Hayes → Ealing → London
Mondays to Fridays continued

Windsor & Eton Central	Slough	Langley	Iver	West Drayton	Hayes & Harlington	Southall	Hanwell	West Ealing	Ealing Broadway	Acton Main Line	Westbourne Park	Paddington
20 11	20 25	→	→	→	→	→	→	→	20 40	→	→	20 51
20 11	20 31	20 35	20 39	20 43	20 48	20 52	20 56	20 59	21 02	21 06	→	21 15
20 41	20 55	→	→	→	→	→	→	→	21 15	→	→	21 26
20 41	21 01	21 05	21 09	21 13	21 18	21 22	21 26	21 29	21 32	21 36	→	21 45
21 01	21 25	→	→	→	→	→	→	→	21 44	→	→	21 55
21 01	21 31	21 35	21 39	21 43	21 48	21 52	21 56	21 59	22 02	22 06	→	22 15
21 31	22 00	→	→	→	→	→	→	→	22 13	→	→	22 24
21 31	22 04	22 08	22 12	22 16	22 21	22 25	22 29	22 32	22 35	22 39	→	22 48
22 01	22 35	→	→	→	→	→	→	→	22 50	→	→	23 01
22 31	22 41	22 45	22 49	22 53	22 58	23 02	23 06	23 09	23 12	23 16	→	23 25
23 01	23 31	23 35	23 39	23 43	23 48	23 52	23 56	23 59	00 02	→	→	00 13
23 31	00 01	00 05	00 09	00 13	00 18	00 22	00 26	00 29	00 32	→	→	00 43
23 31	00 09	→	→	→	→	→	→	→	00 25s	→	→	00 36

Saturdays

	00 01	00 05	00 09	00 13	00 18	00 22	00 26	00 29	00 32	→	→	00 43
	00 02									→	→	00 13
	00 09	→	→	→	→	→	→	→	00 25s	→	→	00 36
	05 07	05 11	05 15	05 19	05 23	05 27	05 31	05 34	05 37	05 41	05 46	05 51

diagrammatic

ght: A tenth-century diagram of
e inclinations of the planetary
bits as a function of time. The
rliest recorded example of a graph
eatment.

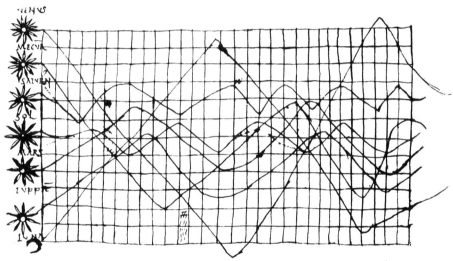

Apart from one medieval example of a time-series diagram, the earliest recorded examples of the graph, bar chart and pie chart date from the end of the 18th century. The basic requirement for any statistical diagram is the recording and compiling of reasonably accurate figures over a period of time. From the middle of the 18th century this type of information became available especially from government sources.

In the early stages statistics were used to record such items as wages, profits, imports and exports and it was not until the mid 19th century that the same techniques were applied to special phenomena. The precursors of the diagram are to be found in the work of the early map makers. Many different types of statistical information could be superimposed on a map: rainfall, trade winds, shipping density and imports and exports between countries but it took a long period of time before the statistical information broke loose from the constraints of the map format. The release from being tied to a geographical base encouraged the use of diagrams for the presentation of a whole range of political, trade and social comparisons. The changeover finally took place when the twin bond of latitude and longtitude was replaced with freely selectable axes such as quantity and time.

Edward R Tufte in his book *The Visual Display of Quantitative Information* gives as the two inventors of modern diagrams, J H Lambert (1728-1777), a

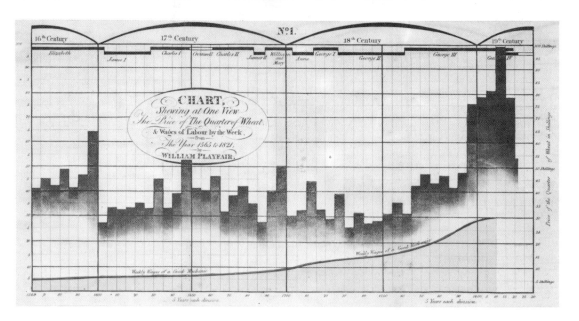

Right: One of William Playfair's most complex diagrams relating to the prices of wheat, bread and labour in Britain over a period of 250 years. Today we would hardly accept the omission of the final 21 years of the wages graph without entertaining bias in its author.

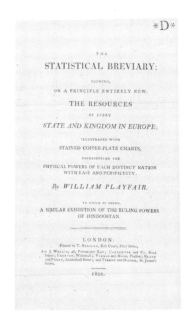

Above: Title page of William Playfair's *The Statistical Breviary* of 1801.

Swiss-German mathematician and William Playfair (1759-1823), an English political economist.

William Playfair

William Playfair's book, *The Commercial and Political Atlas* (London 1786) contains the first time-series graph using economic data in a series of forty-three diagrams (see page 50). In contrasting his new graphic method with the earlier tabular presentation of data Playfair makes a point that is just as valid today as when it was written:

Information, that is imperfectly acquired, is generally as imperfectly retained, and a man who has carefully investigated a printed table, finds, when done, that he has only a very faint and partial idea of what he has read; and that like a figure imprinted on sand, is soon totally erased and defaced. The amount of mercantile transactions in money, and of profit or loss, are capable of being as easily represented in drawing, as any part of space, or as the face of a country; though, till now, it has not been attempted. Upon that principle these Charts were made; and, while they give a simple and distinct idea, they are as near perfect accuracy as is any way useful. On inspecting any one of these Charts attentively, a sufficiently distinct impression will be made, to remain unimpaired for a considerable time, and the idea which does remain will be simple and complete, at once including the duration and the amount.

The only other diagram to appear in the *Atlas* is the first known example of a bar chart 'which playfair invented because year-to-year data were missing and he needed a design to portray the one-year data that were available'. Tufte further comments: 'Fifteen years later in *The Statistical Breviary*, his most theoretical book about graphics, Playfair broke free of analogies to the physical world and drew graphics as designs-in-themselves'. One of the four plates in *The Statistical Breviary* contains a diagram comparing the extent, population and revenues of the principal nations of Europe. The data is expressed both by variable areas to represent quantity and by what appears to be the first use of a pie chart.

Thus by the early 1800's all three of the basic diagrammatic formats had been invented even if their use was confined to books for a specialist audience. The majority of present day diagrams rely on these three treatments either alone or in combination and it is interesting to speculate as to whether there are more formats waiting to be discovered or whether these three will serve us into the next century. Certainly they were evolved in response to a need to interpret and communicate a particular type of information and a particular level of complexity. It seems likely that any new formats will also evolve from a need to interpret new and more complex relationships between data.

Right: William Playfair's *Chart of all the Import and Exports to and from England* from *The Commercial and Political Atlas* of 1786. The crisis in exports is highlighted by the amplification of the grid on the right hand side of the diagram. It is interesting that in nearly all of Playfair's diagrams the vertical scale is annotated on the right hand side unlike modern usage.

Below right: The first known bar chart from William Playfair's, *The Commercial and Political Atlas*. The imports and exports are shown as parallel strips (the import lines are cross hatched on the original line drawing). The diagram also illustrates one of the problems for any designer of bar charts when there is a very large disparity between the longest and the shortest entries. (See section on logarithmic treatments.)

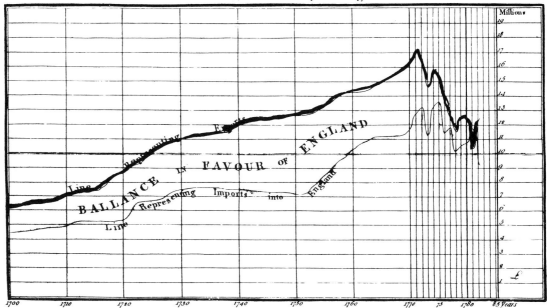

CHART of all the IMPORTS *and* EXPORTS *to and from* ENGLAND *From the Year 1700 to 1782 by W. Playfair*

The Divisions at the Bottom, express YEARS, *& those on the Right hand,* MILLIONS *of* POUNDS

Publish'd as the Act directs, 20.th Aug.st 1784

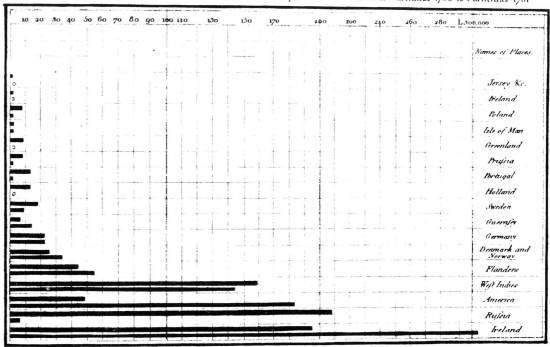

Exports and Imports of SCOTLAND to and from different parts for one Year from Christmas 1780 to Christmas 1781

Below: Napoleon's march to Moscow, a classic diagram designed by Charles Joseph Minard (1781–1870). It combines geographical and statistical information with great economy of means. The thick band shows the size of the army (422,000 men) when it invaded Russia in June 1812 (left hand side) and its reduction to 100,000 when it reached Moscow. The retreat is shown in the black line, which is linked to a temperature scale, and graphically portrays the scale of the disaster ending with only 10,000 men.

The diagram plots several variables: the size of the army, its location geographically, direction of the army's movement and temperature on various dates.

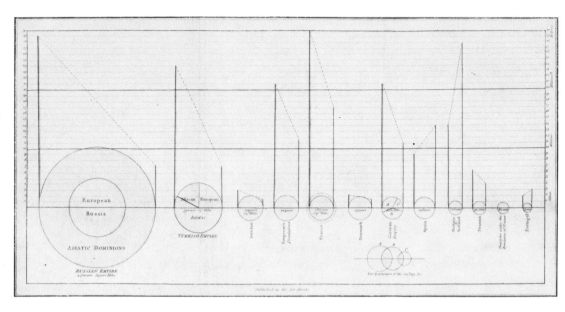

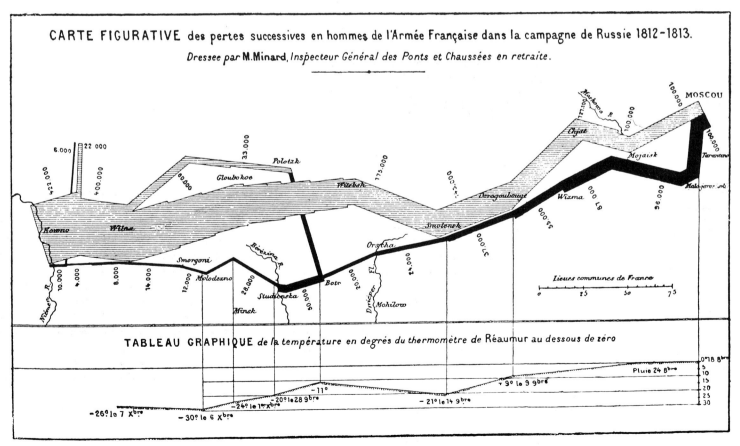

CARTE FIGURATIVE des pertes successives en hommes de l'Armée Française dans la campagne de Russie 1812-1813.

Dressée par M. Minard, Inspecteur Général des Ponts et Chaussées en retraite.

TABLEAU GRAPHIQUE de la température en degrés du thermomètre de Réaumur au dessous de zéro

X^bre = December   9bre = November   8bre = October

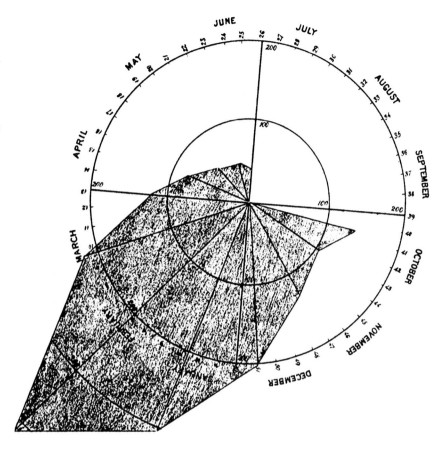

eft: One of four diagrams in Play-
r's *The Statistical Breviary* show-
g the earliest use of the pie chart
id the use of variable area to repre-
nt quantity. The circle represents
e area of each country, the line on
e left, the population in millions on
e vertical scale; the line on the
ght, the revenue (taxes) collected in
illions of pounds sterling and the
otted lines drawn between the
opulation and revenue, are merely
ended to connect together the
es belonging to the same country.
e ascent of these lines being from
ght to left shows whether in pro-
ortion to its population the country
burdened with heavy taxes or
herwise'.

ght: Florence Nightingale's dia-
am of mortality rates at the main
itish Hospital in the Crimean War
iring the winter of 1854–5. The
ctor for March shows the begin-
ig of her sanitary reforms which
ecked the high death rate from
alnutrition, exposure and preven-
ble disease. The diagram is taken
om the report of a Royal Commis-
on set up after the war to investi-
te sanitary conditions in the army.

Florence Nightingale

iove: Florence Nightingale photo-
aphed in later life. She died at the
e of 90 in 1910.

Another significant figure in the history of statistical diagrams, although little known in this context, is Florence Nightingale (1820-1910). She is now remembered as a pioneer of nursing, a reformer of hospitals and a popular heroine of the Crimean War. In an article by Bernard Cohen[1] he describes her use of statistical diagrams as a powerful weapon in trying to persuade the War Office in London to implement basic sanitary standards in military hospitals and barracks in order to reduce the high mortality rates from disease.
'Throughout military history until the 20th century the main cause of death in war was disease rather than wounds sustained in battle, and the Crimean War was no exception. Nightingale's numbers still speak eloquently. During the first months of the Crimean campaign there was "a mortality among the troops at the rate of sixty per cent per annum from *disease* alone", a rate exceeding that of the Great Plague of 1665 in London . . . This means that if mortality had persisted for a full year at the rate that applied in January, and if the dead soldiers had not been replaced, disease alone would have wiped out the entire British army in the Crimea'. The polar-area diagram was invented by Florence Nightingale as one of the means of graphically illustrating these needless deaths by disease. She called these diagrams 'coxcombs' as they were made up from a series of segments each representing, in distance from the centre, the

[1] *Florence Nightingale*, a paper by I Bernard Cohen in *Scientific American*, March 1984.

Right: One of William Playfair's diagrams from *The Commercial and Political Atlas* engraved in 1786.

Below: Florence Nightingale invented the polar-area diagram which she used to great effect to show the needless loss of life from disease during the Crimean War of 1854-6. From a privately printed book, *Notes on Matters affecting the Health, Efficiency and Hospital Administration of the British Army*, London 1857.

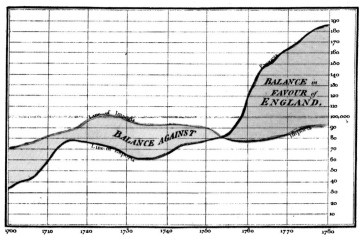

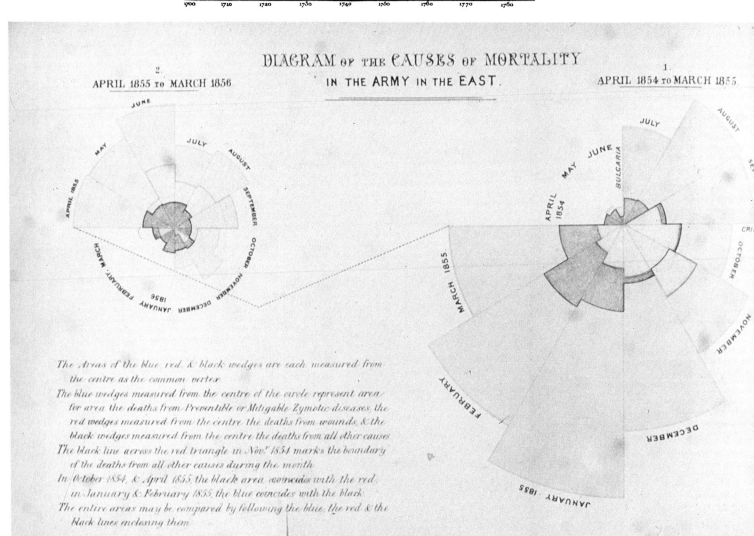

Right: A typical Isotype chart, Vienna 1930.

Below: Isotype charts dating from 1928 and 1929.

All illustrations on this page are taken from originals in the Otto & Marie Neurath Isotype Collection, Department of Typography & Graphic Communication, University of Reading.

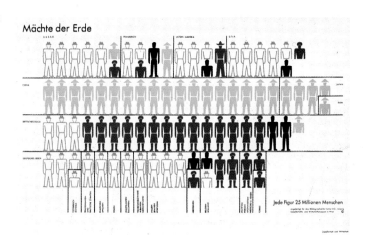

Right: An Isotype chart on the Great War of 1914-18 depicting the casualties on both sides. It departs from the typical Isotype presentation of symbols placed in rows or blocks and deploys its images in a parallel projection. This graphic presentation of statistical material, although not developed further by Isotype, pointed the way ahead in diagram design. It is a model diagram in which all the elements of information, pattern, colour and detailing reinforce each other. This English language version dates from about 1933. Original measures 420 × 630 mm (16½ × 24¾ in.).

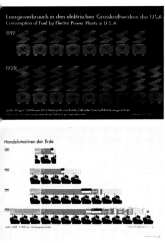

Right: Isotype diagram of car production between 1914 and 1928
comparing the United States with
the rest of the world.

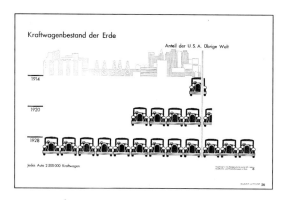

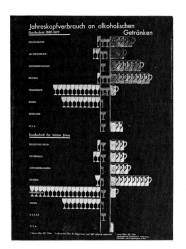

Above: Isotype diagram of alcohol
consumption by country, comparing
wine, spirits and beer. Original in
colour on black background.

monthly total of deaths. Colour coding within the
segments showed the proportion of deaths from
preventable diseases, wounds and all other causes
(see page 50).
Cohen also makes the point that '. . . in addition to
advancing the cause of medical reform itself she
helped to pioneer the revolutionary notion that
social phenomena could be objectively measured
and subjected to mathematical analysis'.

Otto Neurath and Isotype

Otto Neurath was a significant pioneer in the
1930's in presenting statistics in pictorial form. He
was dedicated to the idea of presenting information
in an accurate and visually interesting way based on
underlying principles which could be applied to a
developing body of work.
His approach to an information 'system' was
developed by a team which he led at the Social and
Economic Museum of Vienna in 1925 and which
moved, under the pressure of political events, to
The Hague in 1934 and to Britain after 1940. The
Isotype Institute was founded in 1942 under the
direction of Otto and Marie Neurath. Otto Neurath
died in 1945 and the work of the institute was
carried on by Marie Neurath until her retirement in
1972.
Isotype, an acronym for International System Of
Typographical Picture Education, which, in its
unabbreviated form, hints at the social and edu-

cational outlook which informed all the Institute's
work, was conceived as a method of communication which would be understood by people
irrespective of language or cultural barriers. It is
probably for this reason that it has had a continuing
influence on graphic designers (see page 51).
The word 'system' in the title may be misleading as
has been pointed out by Robin Kinross[2] as it was
not a set of rules which could be applied to any
statistical material but rather an *approach*, and
usually a team approach, with an underlying
philosophical viewpoint of history. In fact, before
the institute was set up in Austria in 1935 it had
become known as the 'Wiener Methode' (the
Vienna *method*).
A general principle which is at the heart of the
Isotype designs is the use of pictorial symbols
which represent fixed amounts of information and
which can be used in repetition with equal spacing
to denote larger quantities. The detailing of these
symbols was quite subtle and included the use of
colour but great care was taken that the details
should not weaken the overall unit effect. A parallel
projection was always used in preference to
perspective so that the symbols maintained their
constant size and an equal-area projection for
geographical maps took preference over those
projections that distort certain areas of the globe.
The strength of the Isotype approach was to give
immediate pictorial interest to statistical material
without overburdening it with verbal captioning and
explanation making it of special value in teaching.
Isotype's main limitation was the limitation of all
symbols to show abstract concepts without
confusing the viewer.
Isotype diagrams also have a problem in showing
fractions of whole units and so it is necessary to
accept the substantial rounding off of quantities.
To be fair, most of the symbols were designed so
that they worked in at least half unit form but the
truncation of the unit, particularly of a human form
was never an ideal or unambiguous design solution.

Contemporary diagrams

The ubiquitous graph, bar chart and pie chart serve
so many purposes that it is difficult to imagine what

---

[2] *On the Influence of Isotype*, a paper by Robin Kinross
published in *Information Design Journal*, volume 2/2, 1981.

ight: The doubling of world popu-
tion. Part of a graphic presentation
n global interdependence exploring
e possibility of using non-verbal
echniques.
esigners: Aaron Marcus and
ssociates, Berkeley, California.

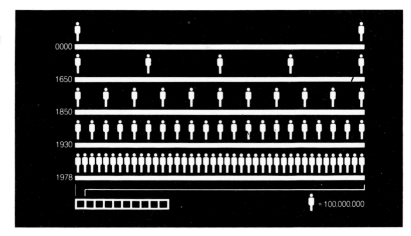

ight: Explosive power compared.
his makes an interesting contrast
the illustration above and makes
s point dramatically through pat-
rn. It appeared in a newspaper in
984, source unknown.

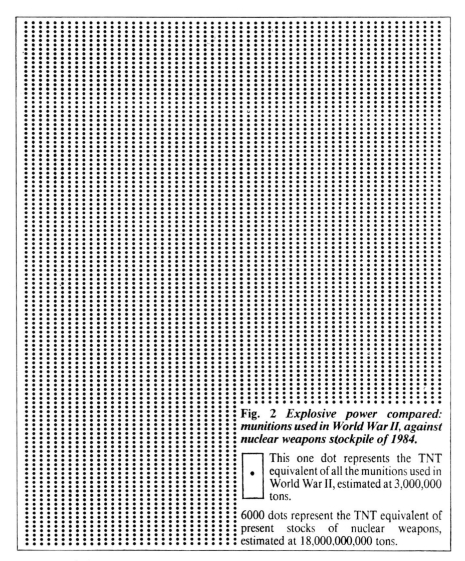

Fig. 2 *Explosive power compared:*
munitions used in World War II, against
nuclear weapons stockpile of 1984.

This one dot represents the TNT
equivalent of all the munitions used in
World War II, estimated at 3,000,000
tons.

6000 dots represent the TNT equivalent of
present stocks of nuclear weapons,
estimated at 18,000,000,000 tons.

Right: Computer generated graph.
Designer: Trevor Bounford.
Programmer: Stephen Silver,
Creative Data Ltd, London.

Opposite page: Three dimensional
diagram for Roche Products Ltd.
Designers: Mervyn Kurlansky and
Maddy Bennett, Pentagram,
London.

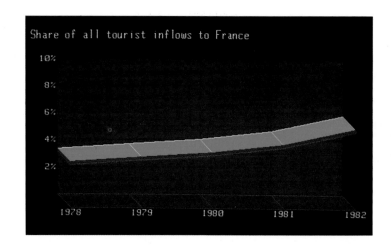

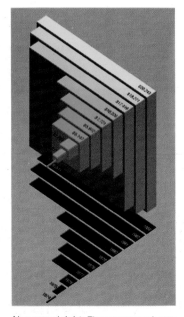

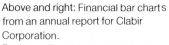

Above and right: Financial bar charts
from an annual report for Clabir
Corporation.
Designer: Tom Morin, Jack Hough
Associates Inc, Connecticut, USA.

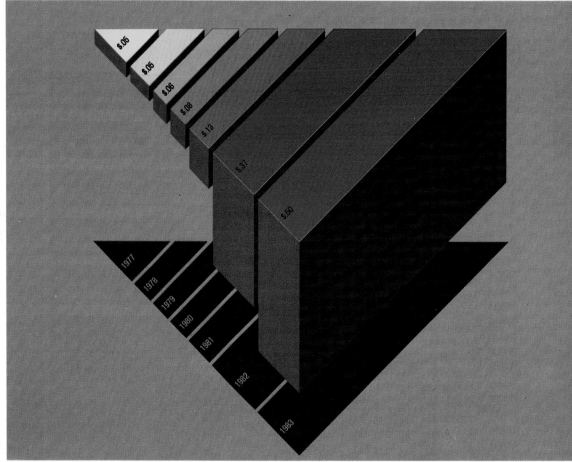

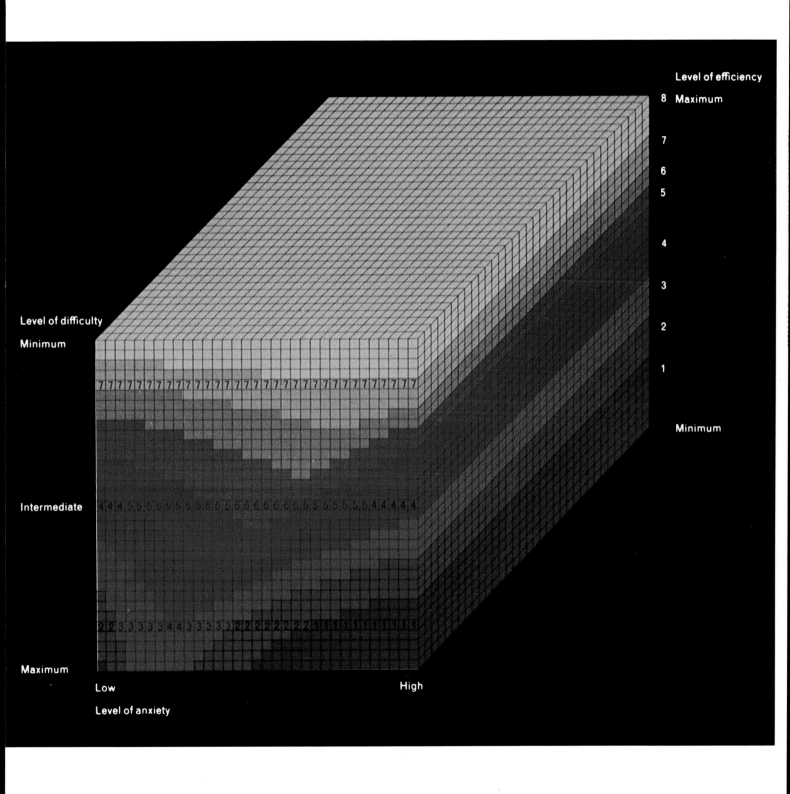

Level of efficiency

8　Maximum

7

6

5

4

3

2

1

Level of difficulty

Minimum

7 7 7 7 7 7 7 7 7 7 7 7 7 7 7 7 7 7 7 7 7 7 7 7 7 7 7 7 7

Minimum

Intermediate

4 4 4 5 5 5 5 5 5 5 5 6 6 6 6 6 6 6 6 6 5 5 5 5 5 4 4 4 4 4

Maximum

2 2 3 3 3 3 3 4 4 3 3 3 3 3 2 2 2 2 2 2 2 2 1 1 1 1 1 1 1 1 1

Low   High

Level of anxiety

Right: Diagram shows the range of propeller power density (MW/m) in relation to the propeller power magnitude (MW) for different types of vessel. From a brochure for Lips, a propeller manufacturer.
Designers: Andrew Fallon and Gerard van Leyden, Tel Design, The Hague.

Below: Reuters' markets and products, a diagram from the 1986 annual report.
Designers: Mervyn Kurlansky and Claire Johnson, Pentagram Design Ltd, London.

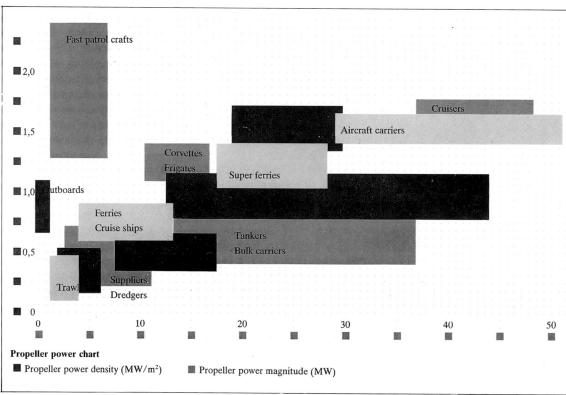

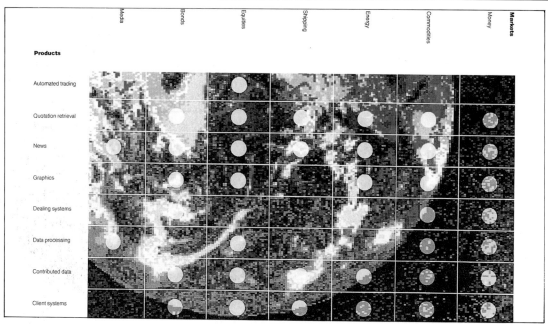

we would do without them, they are as much a part of our lives as the telephone and wrist watch.

In essence, they make sense of complex numerical material by showing us a simple pattern of events. The visual *shape* of this pattern is instantly recognisable and, more importantly, remembered even after the figures are forgotten. Superimposed on the main pattern can be subsidiary patterns so that several layers of information can be combined in one diagram and by the close control of colour or tone the separation of information can be selectively controlled. The added time element of animation allows the pattern to grow or interact with other patterns so that multiple elements can be built up step by step.

Numerical material is only the starting point for a diagram and Nigel Holmes in an introduction to Diagraphics[3] sums this up when he says, 'Unexplained numbers are not information. We mistakenly refer to the "Information Explosion" in the world today. There is no information explosion – it's a numbers explosion, and it falls to designers to turn the numbers into useful information. Unfortunately too few are doing it.'

Just because of the apparent simplicity of a diagram and its visual order we should be aware that significant errors or distortions of the facts can and do take place. These can be accidental in that the designer was not aware that the design was producing an ambiguous or distorted statement or deliberate in that certain factors in constructing the diagram were altered to magnify or obscure the true situation.

One of the most obvious ways that this can be produced is by altering the relationship between the vertical and horizontal scales. By increasing the proportion of the vertical scale in relation to the horizontal, the peaks and troughs of a graph line become steeper and by reducing the scale they become flattened. The omission of a zero on one of the scales can lead to ambiguity unless the diagram is clearly marked and another source of confusion is to leave out the key to the units being employed. The units could be interpreted as, say, dollars or pounds on a financial chart; miles per hour or kilometres per hour on a transportation chart. Where two similar diagrams are shown together the omis-sion of the units on one of them leads the viewer to infer that they are the same on both.

The use of different scales on the left and right hand sides of a graph (where a double graph line is shown) can be misread even with appropriate colour coding. Beware the optimism shown by some 'projection' lines on graphs; the visual power of a heavily dashed line following on from a solid one lends an air of authority to what is probably little more than guess work and, invariably, is only used when the solid graph line is moving upwards.

Some more subtle ways of introducing distortion into diagrams are by means of perspective and bar charts, particularly, lend themselves to this treatment. A receding plane shown in perspective can be used to diminish or increase the apparent size of units. A non-linear, or logarithmic scale, is sometimes used to compress a diagram into a limited space or proportion and it can also be used by designers to avoid large empty areas in a diagram where most of the information fills only a small part of the overall area. These scales are almost always confusing to a non-technical reader and should be used sparingly with suitable annotation drawing attention to their use.

Logarithmic scales do have a specific technical use. Whereas the line graph shows increases or decreases in quantity the logarithmic graph is used to show rates of change as well as amount. It is sad but true that we often only scan the figures at both ends of a diagram and assume that the intervals in between are of equal value.

Apart from these distortions or omissions the designer has to be very careful in using data relating to currency over a longish period of time without making adjustments for inflation or indicating its present day value. The reader should also be aware that a graph shown with finely 'calibrated' axes may only be based on a handful of plotted data points. The frequency of the divisions is no guarantee of the accuracy of the curve of the graph line.

Let us take a look at some of the reasons for selecting one of the three main types of diagram and attempt to show the advantages and disadvantages of each type. In many cases a diagram may use two or more types of chart so as to combine the advantages of both.

[3] *Diagraphics*, published by Japan Creators' Association, Tokyo, Japan, 1986.

Right and below: Bar chart diagrams showing West German export markets. The brief was to present given data in a scientifically exact and graphically attractive poster-oriented form. Originals printed in ten colours, size (each) 970 × 1380 mm (38¼ × 54¼ in.).

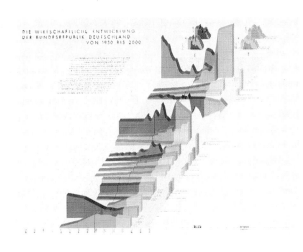

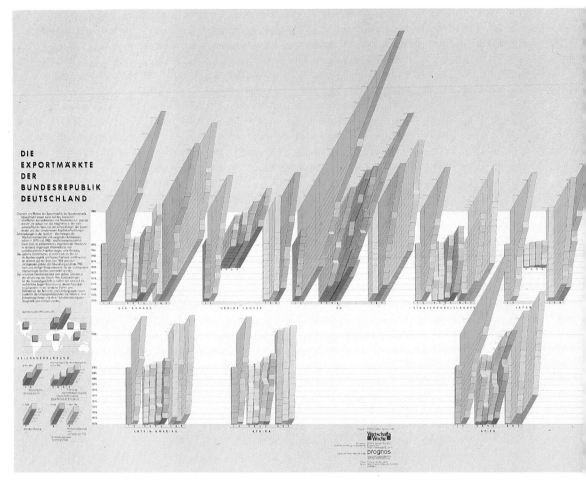

Right and below: Two bar charts
from *A technical guide for BP
Chemicals* aimed at specifying
chemists. Each chart shows the
results of a specific test of the
effects of a range of plasticisers
on a base resin.
Designer: David Lock,
Lock/Pettersen Ltd, London.

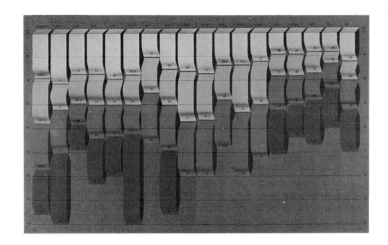

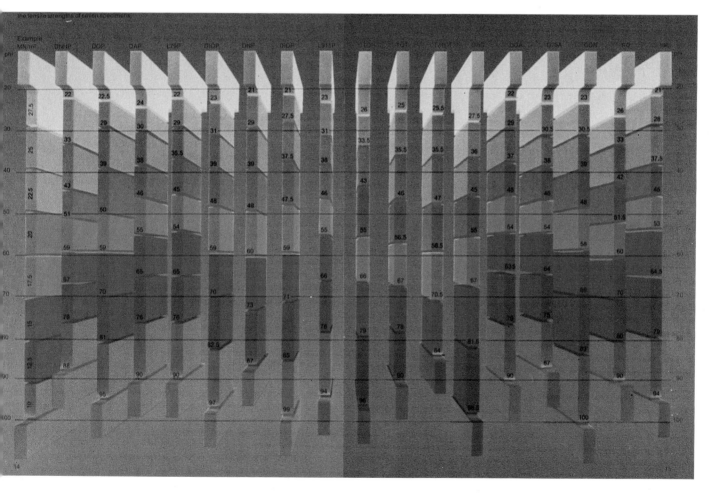

Right: Organisational diagram.
Designer: Rivista Pirelli

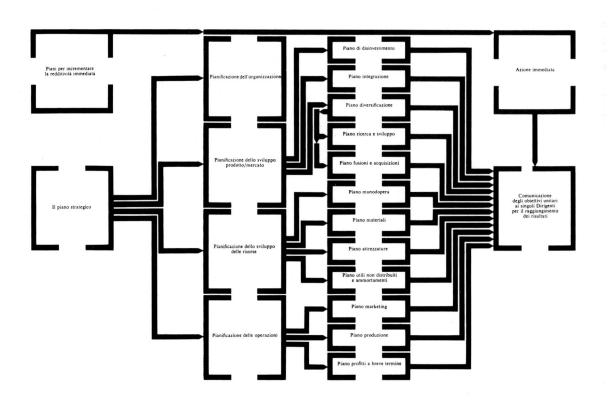

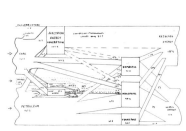

Above and right: Client's sketch and
final flow diagram for UK energy
flows for one year.
Designer: David Muriel, Chainhurst,
Kent, UK.

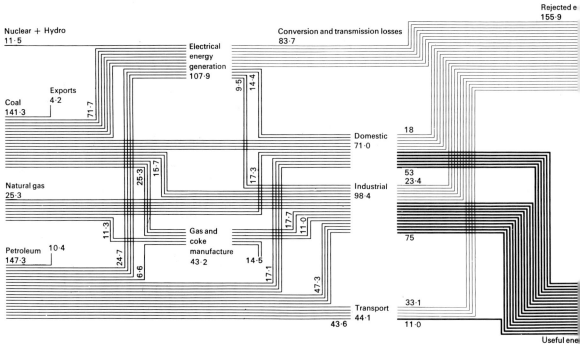

Right: Diagram from a book *The Port of Rotterdam Development Potential*, showing means of transhipment to and from overseas territories via Rotterdam.
Designers: Benno Wissing and John Stegmeyer, The Wissing Gengler Group Inc, USA.

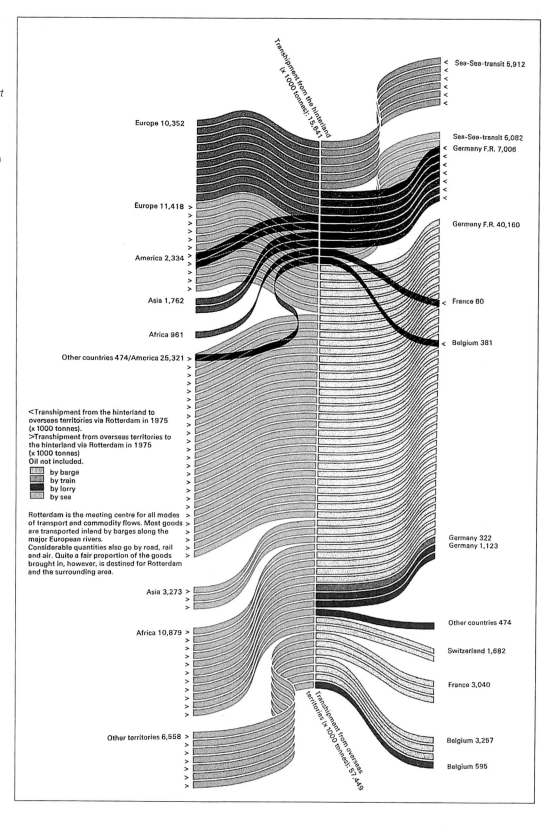

Europe 10,352

Transhipment from the hinterland (x 1000 tonnes): 15,641

Europe 11,418 >

America 2,334 >

Asia 1,762

Africa 961

Other countries 474/America 25,321 >

<Transhipment from the hinterland to overseas territories via Rotterdam in 1975 (x 1000 tonnes).
>Transhipment from overseas territories to the hinterland via Rotterdam in 1975 (x 1000 tonnes)
Oil not included.

▨ by barge
▨ by train
■ by lorry
▨ by sea

Rotterdam is the meeting centre for all modes of transport and commodity flows. Most goods are transported inland by barges along the major European rivers.
Considerable quantities also go by road, rail and air. Quite a fair proportion of the goods brought in, however, is destined for Rotterdam and the surrounding area.

Asia 3,273 >

Africa 10,879 >

Other territories 6,558 >

Sea-Sea-transit 5,912

Sea-Sea-transit 6,082
Germany F.R. 7,006

Germany F.R. 40,160

France 80

Belgium 381

Germany 322
Germany 1,123

Other countries 474

Switzerland 1,682

France 3,040

Belgium 3,257

Belgium 595

Transhipment from overseas territories (x 1000 tonnes): 57,449

1

Right: Diagram, 'How trade barriers affect UK exports.'
Designers: David Lock and David Freeman, Lock/Pettersen Ltd, London.

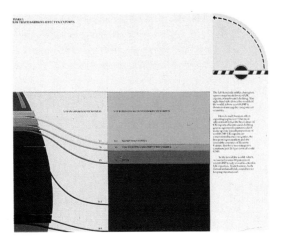

Right: Bar charts of assets and liabilities from a company annual report.
Designer: Peter Skalar, Ljubljana, Yugoslavia.

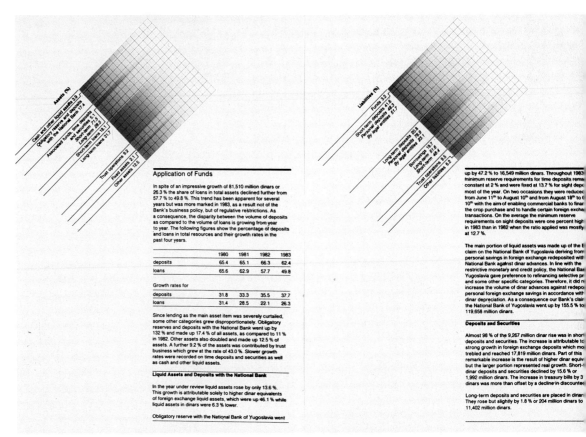

Application of Funds

In spite of an impressive growth of 81,510 million dinars or 26.3 % the share of loans in total assets declined further from 57.7 % to 49.8 %. This trend has been apparent for several years but was more marked in 1983, as a result not of the Bank's business policy, but of regulative restrictions. As a consequence, the disparity between the volume of deposits as compared to the volume of loans is growing from year to year. The following figures show the percentage of deposits and loans in total resources and their growth rates in the past four years.

	1980	1981	1982	1983
deposits	65.4	65.1	66.3	62.4
loans	65.6	62.9	57.7	49.8
Growth rates for				
deposits	31.8	33.3	35.5	37.7
loans	31.4	28.5	22.1	26.3

Since lending as the main asset item was severely curtailed, some other categories grew disproportionately. Obligatory reserves and deposits with the National Bank went up by 132 % and made up 17.4 % of all assets, as compared to 11 % in 1982. Other assets also doubled and made up 12.5 % of assets. A further 9.2 % of the assets was contributed by trust business which grew at the rate of 43.0 %. Slower growth rates were recorded on time deposits and securities as well as cash and other liquid assets.

Liquid Assets and Deposits with the National Bank

In the year under review liquid assets rose by only 13.6 %. This growth is attributable solely to higher dinar equivalents of foreign exchange liquid assets, which were up 46.1 % while liquid assets in dinars were 6.3 % lower.

Obligatory reserve with the National Bank of Yugoslavia went

up by 47.2 % to 16,549 million dinars. Throughout 1983 minimum reserve requirements for time deposits rema constant at 2 % and were fixed at 13.7 % for sight depo most of the year. On two occasions they were reduced from June 11th to August 10th and from August 18th to 10th with the aim of enabling commercial banks to finar the crop purchase and to handle certain foreign exchan transactions. On the average the minimum reserve requirements on sight deposits were one percent high in 1983 than in 1982 when the ratio applied was mostly at 12.7 %.

The main portion of liquid assets was made up of the E claim on the National Bank of Yugoslavia deriving from personal savings in foreign exchange redeposited with National Bank against dinar advances. In line with the restrictive monetary and credit policy, the National Bar Yugoslavia gave preference to refinancing selective pr and some other specific categories. Therefore, it did n increase the volume of dinar advances against redepo personal foreign exchange savings in accordance with dinar depreciation. As a consequence our Bank's clair the National Bank of Yugoslavia went up by 155.5 % to 119,658 million dinars.

Deposits and Securities

Almost 98 % of the 9,267 million dinar rise was in shor deposits and securities. The increase is attributable to strong growth in foreign exchange deposits which mo trebled and reached 17,819 million dinars. Part of this remarkable increase is the result of higher dinar equiv but the larger portion represented real growth. Short-t dinar deposits and securities declined by 15.6 % or 1,992 million dinars. The increase in treasury bills by 3 dinars was more than offset by a decline in discounted

Long-term deposits and securities are placed in dinar They rose but slightly by 1.8 % or 204 million dinars to 11,402 million dinars.

Right: Financial pie chart from an annual report.
Designer: Rosmarie Tissi, Odermatt & Tissi, Zurich, Switzerland.

Below right: Financial pie chart from an annual report for Clabir Corporation.
Designer: Tom Morin, Jack Hough Associates Inc, USA.

Bottom right: Financial pie charts from *Science Museum Review 1987*.
Designer: Ken Garland and Associates, London.

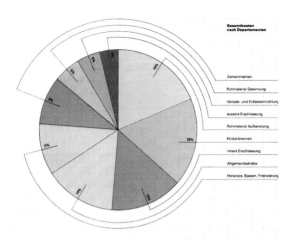

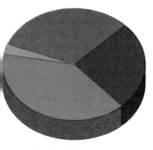

35% *Patients decision*
34% *Joint decision/ doctor & patient*
23% *Doctors decision*
8% *Don't know*

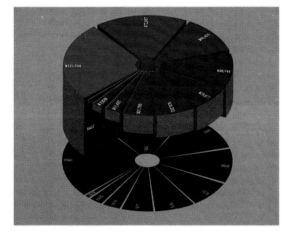

Above and far right: Pie charts, 'Choosing Hospitals – Who decides?' and 'Federal budget outlays by percentage', both from *Medical Access*, a layman's illustrated guide to modern medical tests, surgeries and institutions.
Designer: Richard Saul Wurman, New York City, USA.

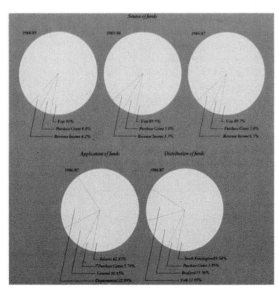

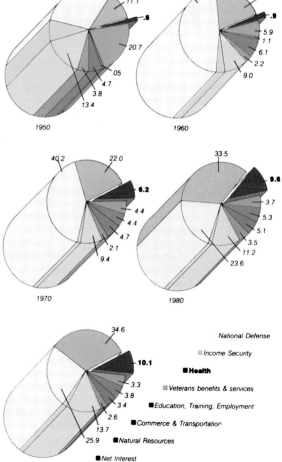

National Defense
■ Income Security
■ **Health**
■ Veterans benefits & services
■ Education, Training, Employment
■ Commerce & Transportation
■ Natural Resources
■ Net Interest
■ Other

Source: U.S. Bureau of Census

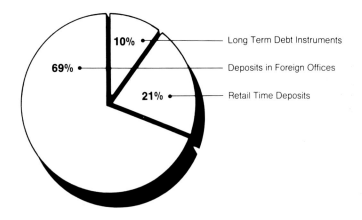

10% — Long Term Debt Instruments

69%

21% — Retail Time Deposits

Deposits in Foreign Offices

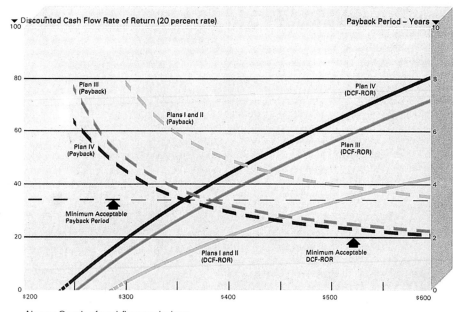

Above: Graph of cashflow analysis; a
tool for evaluating project feasibility.
Designer: Shoji Teraishi, Bill Brown &
Associates, USA.

Graphs

Perhaps the greatest advantage of the graph is that
it is the most familiar of the three forms and one that
most people have had experience of using, if not
constructing, at school or work. Graphs show how
changes in one quantity are related to changes in
another. The patient's temperature graph is a
typical example plotting changes of temperature
against a time base. The graph line when joined to
a number of plotted points on the grid will give a
series of spiky progressions to the graph whereas a
smoothly curving line most often represents a
series of approximations within a scatter of plotted
points. The elegance of the line disguising the
accuracy of the information. Within this latter
limitation the graph is easy to plot by hand or
computer and relatively easy to annotate. The best
graph treatments maintain a visual balance between
indicating adequate information relating to the grid
and prominence of the graph line. There is a point
at which oversimplification drastically reduces the
amount of information that the reader or viewer can
gain from the diagram.
By (western) convention the graph lines progress
from left to right and from base to top but this is not
an inflexible rule provided that direction is
graphically stated or implied. Typographical annotation becomes difficult to read at acute angles to
the base line and one welcomes solutions which
keep to horizontally set annotations.
The disadvantages of graphs are that they are more
difficult to combine with graphic imagery without
damage to the essential features of the graph and
are not easy to treat in a three dimensional manner.

Bar charts

Unlike graphs, bar charts show discrete areas for
each segment of information. Traditionally drawn as
parallel 'bars', arranged either vertically or
horizontally, the technique allows a wide variation of
format. Since the basic statistics are often collected
at fixed intervals rather than continuously the bar
chart can be said to give a more accurate display of
its information than the rounded-off or interpolative
graph. Additional information can be incorporated

eft: Pie chart, 'Fundraising costs as
percentage of contributions'.
esigner: Robert P Gersin Assoc-
tes Inc, New York.
lient: United States Accounting
ffice.

into each bar by sub-dividing it into a number of
divisions relating to the make-up of the total
quantity.

As a graphic device the bar chart lends itself to a
wide variety of graphic treatments. The bar itself
can be transposed into a shape or shapes relating
to the visual content of the diagram but perhaps its
most useful feature is the ability to give a spatial
dimension to the diagram through perspective.
The two conventional axes of a chart can now be
pushed to three or more axes enabling more
complex inter-relationships to be established. For
these reasons the bar chart is a much more flexible
medium for making graphic comparisons than the
graph. The main weakness in the creation of bar
charts is the tendency to overload the amount of
information which most readers can absorb in a
limited time. The same principle applies to the
design of bar charts as for any other diagram: use
two diagrams instead of one if this will improve
the comprehension of the information (see
pages 58–59).

Pie charts

These have a more limited application in showing
the break down of specific amounts or a specific
time scale (usually a year). Within this limitation they
are extremely effective in showing the relative
values of the considerable number of entries that
can be included. They are normally produced as
sub-divisions of a circle although sometimes shown
in perspective. The resulting ellipse can produce
visual distortion of the segments which can mislead
the viewer.

The disadvantages of pie charts are that they are
more difficult to plot, except on a computer, since
the values have to be converted from percentages
to degrees of a circle.

The narrowness of some of the segments on a
completed pie chart present a problem of
annotation in that the segments may be too small to
contain type matter. This often results in one or two
of the annotations taking a different form from the
rest. On the other hand if all the annotation is kept
outside the circle the ease of 'reading' and comparing the information is reduced. Percentages

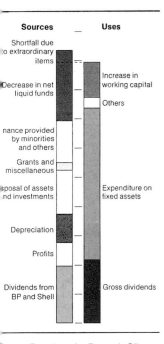

Sources — Uses

Shortfall due
to extraordinary
items

Decrease in net
liquid funds

Increase in
working capital

Others

nance provided
by minorities
and others

Grants and
miscellaneous

sposal of assets
nd investments

Expenditure on
fixed assets

Depreciation

Profits

Dividends from
BP and Shell

Gross dividends

bove: Bar chart for Burmah Oil
howing sources and uses of funds.

ight: Bar chart of earnings and divi-
ends per share for Merincorp (Mer-
hant Investment Corporation)
esigner: Han Kardinata, Indonesia.

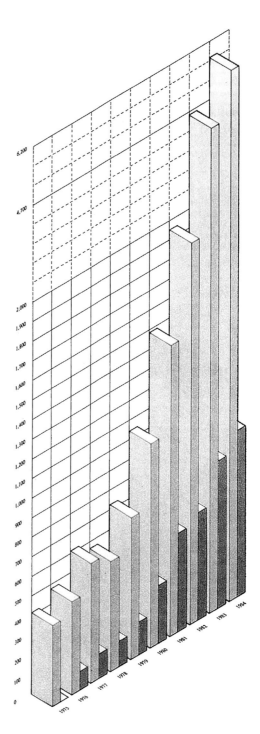

○ Laba Per Saham/*Earning Per Share*
● Dividen Per Saham/*Dividend Per Share*

Right: Flow diagram, 'Information networks and the digital revolution' from *Information Resource Management*.
Designers: David Hillman, Bruce Man, Sarah Pyne and Wolf Spoerl (illustrator), Pentagram Design Ltd, London.

Below: Flowchart, 'The UK textile industry 1968-70'. A flow chart bringing together complex strands of information, quantities and end users in a textile-like pattern.
Designer: David Lock, Lock/Pettersen Ltd, London.

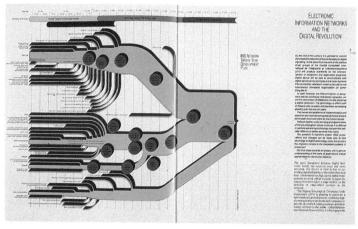

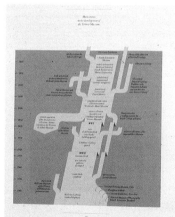

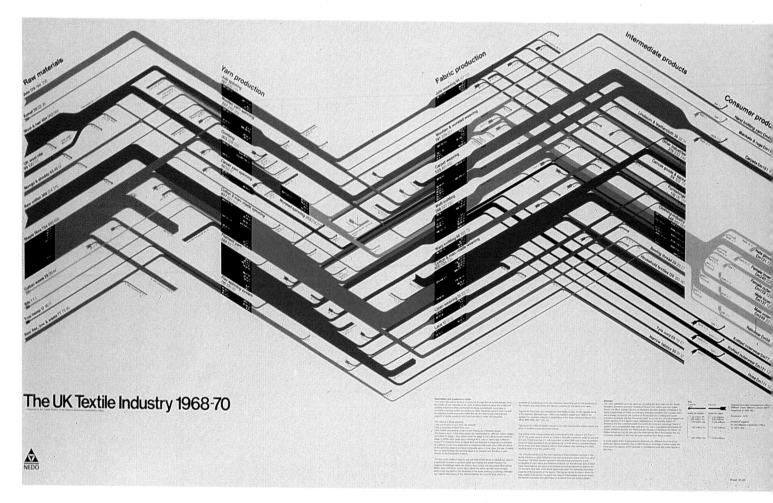

The UK Textile Industry 1968-70

Left: Flow diagram, 'Main events in the development of the Science Museum' from *Science Museum Review 1987*.
Designer: Ken Garland and Associates, London.

Right: Magazine diagram explaining the causes of the winter climate in Japan.
Designers: Ukei Tomori and Kazuo Oriki, Japan.

Below: Flow diagram, 'Dutch ports and intercontinental shipping'.
Designers: Benno Wissing/John Stegmeger, Rhode Island, USA.

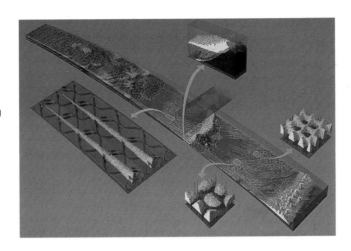

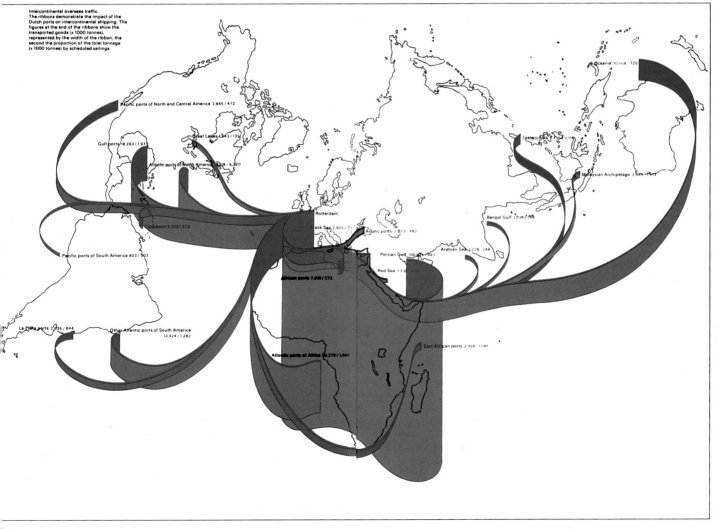

Intercontinental overseas traffic.
The ribbons demonstrate the impact of the Dutch ports on intercontinental shipping. The figures at the end of the ribbons show the transported goods (x 1000 tonnes), represented by the width of the ribbon, the second the proportion of the total tonnage (x 1000 tonnes) by scheduled sailings.

are normally shown for each segment since it is not easy to estimate them in this radial form without an appropriate grid scale (see pages 62–63).

Non statistical diagrams

A time chart compares information over a given time scale. The time covered can be anything from divisions of a second to the time span of the universe. The practical design problems are usually to do with the crowding of information into relatively small areas of the time axis and some quite elegant solutions have been produced by 'folding up' the time scale or using 'zoom' techniques for enlarging certain segments.

Flow charts show the sequence of stages through a process. They are most commonly used to simplify a description of a complex process and are normally not concerned with comparison of quantities (see page 66).

A development of the flow chart is the *logical tree* or *decision tree* which uses the flow chart principle to arrive at a correct decision. It is a sequence of statements or questions, proceeding in a logical hierarchy from the general to the specific. The reader is presented with yes/no headings at each branch and by taking the relevant direction arrives at an appropriate answer.

The logical tree is often referred to as an *algorithm* which in theoretical mathematics and in computer

Right: Flow diagram of cement production for Cementfabrik Holderbank.
Designers: Odermatt & Tissi, Zurich, Switzerland.

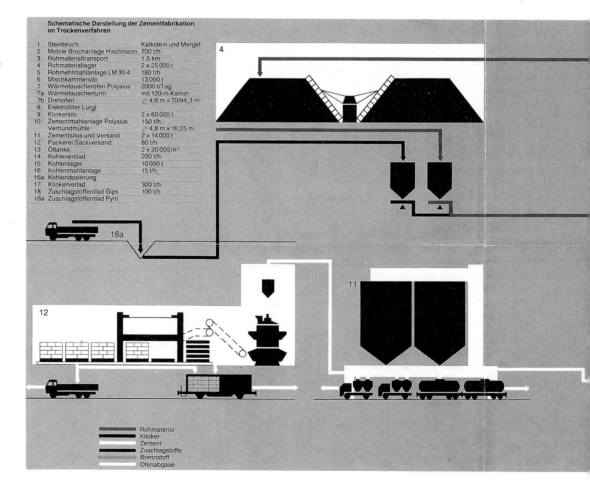

Schematische Darstellung der Zementfabrikation
im Trockenverfahren

1	Steinbruch	Kalkstein und Mergel
2	Mobile Brechanlage Hischmann	700 t/h
3	Rohmaterialtransport	1,5 km
4	Rohmateriallager	2 × 25 000 t
5	Rohmehlmahlanlage LM 30-4	180 t/h
6	Mischkammersilo	13 000 t
7	Wärmetauscherofen Polysius	2000 t/Tag
7a	Wärmetauscherturm	mit 120-m-Kamin
7b	Drehofen	∅ 4,6 m × 70/94,3 m
8	Elektrofilter Lurgi	
9	Klinkersilo	2 × 60 000 t
10	Zementmahlanlage Polysius	150 t/h
	Verbundmühle	∅ 4,8 m × 16,25 m
11	Zementsilos und Versand	2 × 14 000 t
12	Packerei Sackversand	80 t/h
13	Öltanks	2 × 20 000 m³
14	Kohlenentlad	200 t/h
15	Kohlenlager	10 000 t
16	Kohlenmahlanlage	15 t/h
16a	Kohlendosierung	
17	Klinkerverlad	300 t/h
18	Zuschlagstoffentlad Gips	100 t/h
18a	Zuschlagstoffentlad Pyrit	

Rohmaterial
Klinker
Zement
Zuschlagstoffe
Brennstoff
Ofenabgase

programming relates to an exact formula describing a complex process. When used as the basis for a diagram the concept is more loosely defined to cover any verbal or visual treatment that leads the user to a correct answer or decision.[4]

Family trees show genealogical or corporate relationships over a given time span. Scientific publications tend to show the most interesting graphic solutions within this format.

Critical path diagrams, first developed in the 1950's, are intended as working aids rather than a record of completed projects. They are in essence a tool for graphically recording in the form of a network the various processes or actions which have to join together over a fixed time span to achieve a given result. The system has developed its own format, conventions and vocabulary and aims to identify those parts of the process where there is time to spare and those, the really *critical* ones, where any delay means that the whole project is delayed.

Now that the computer can produce the basic diagram formats from given data in a fraction of the time previously taken to plot and construct them manually the designer is freed to concentrate on the graphic treatment. Far from being replaced by a 'program' the designer can concentrate on producing an unique design integrated to the typographical and graphic requirements of the publication.

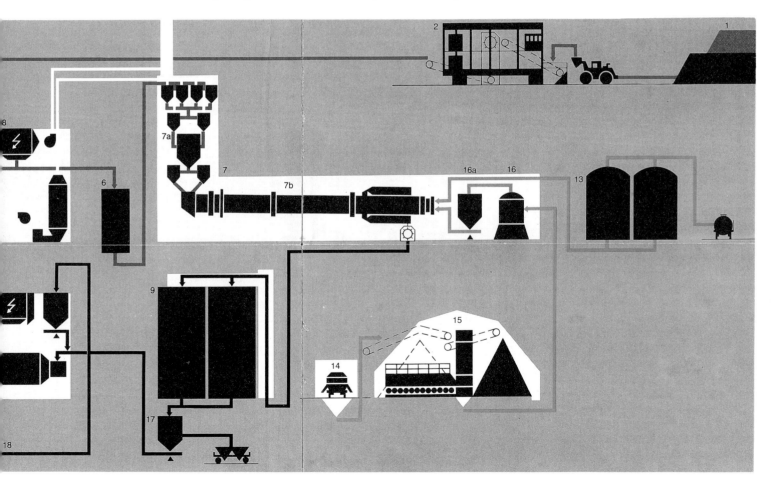

[4] See *Flow charts, logical trees and algorithms for rules and regulations* by B N Lewis, I S Horabin and C P Gane, Civil Service College Occasional Papers. HMSO, London 1975.

Right: Television graphics for a General Election. These two histograms were part of a 'results' sequence which were produced by BBC TV for the General Election coverage of 1987. The first shows the percentage of the vote cast and the second the change of vote from the previous election. Both carry a map identifying the particular constituency area (see page 109).

Below: A 'decision tree' diagram, 'Choosing a doctor' from Pacific Bells' *Smart Yellow Pages Directory*. Designer: Richard Saul Wurman, TUB, USA.

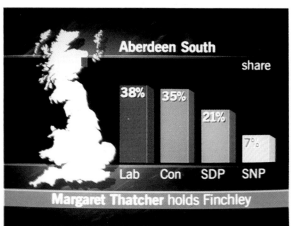

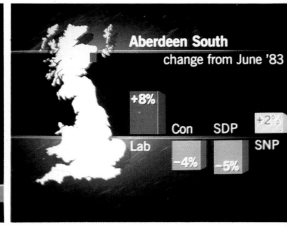

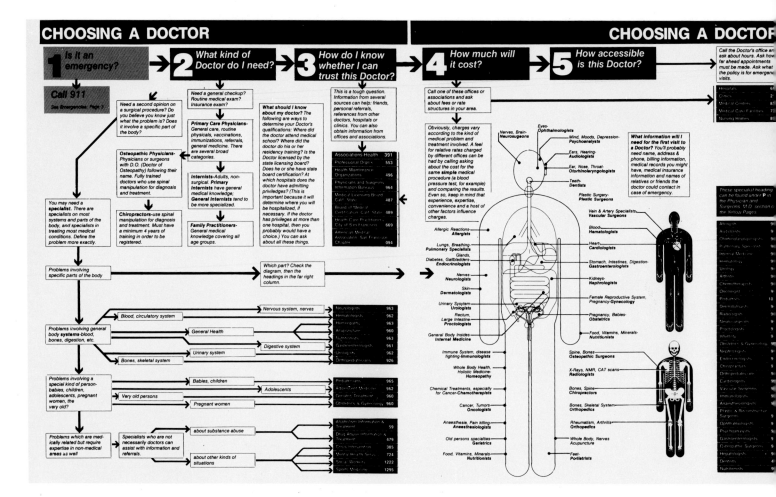

elow: The *Guardian* newspaper
ection chart for 1987. This three-
irectional diagram was devised to
nable its readers to quickly work
ut how many seats the three main
olitical parties would win in the
ouse of Commons on a given
hare of the vote. The example
ight) shows how the percentage
esults of an opinion poll, or of
esults as they came in on election
ght, could be simply plotted to
rrive at a given circle which listed
ne forecast number of seats.
evised by Martin Linton and
esigned by Paul McTurk.

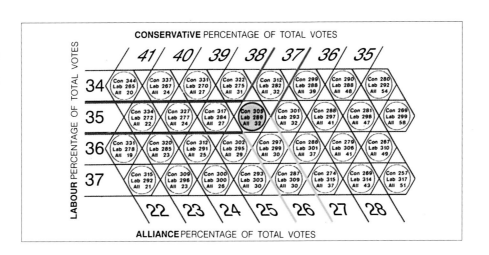

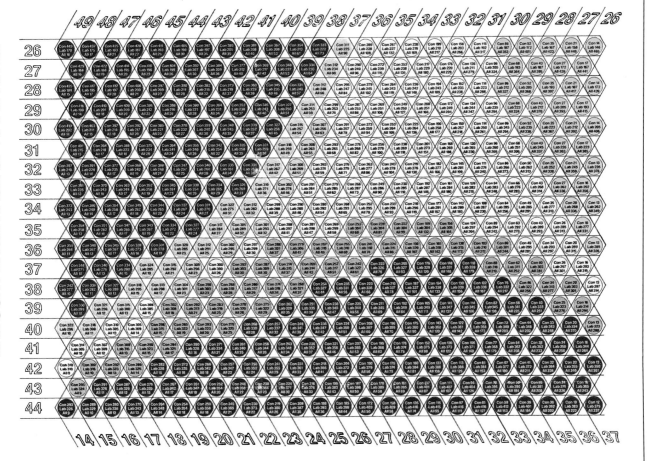

Right: Heller Generale Aspemar Barometer. Table of results of a business poll held regularly in Belgium showing the outcome in percentages.
Designer: Andrew Fallon, Tel Design, The Hague, Holland.

HELLER-GENERALE ASPEMAR BAROMETER 1984/1

	Totaal	Regio			Type bedrijf			Aantal personeelsleden		Bestaanstijd in jaren		Jaaromzet in BF	
		Vlaamse provincies	Waalse provincies	Brabant	Industrie	Groothandel	Dienstverlening e.d.	5-24	25-199	<20	>20	<85 miljoen	>85 miljoen
Aantal respondenten	200	103	44	53	46	74	80	144	56	73	127	118	82
	%	%	%	%	%	%	%	%	%	%	%	%	%
Regio													
Antwerpen	17,5	34,0	–	–	17,4	17,6	17,5	16,7	19,6	20,5	15,7	16,9	18,3
Brabant	26,5	–	–	100,0	17,4	31,1	27,5	25,0	30,4	30,1	24,4	20,3	35,4
West Vlaanderen	13,0	25,2	–	–	13,0	16,2	10,0	13,9	10,7	13,7	12,6	15,3	9,8
Oost Vlaanderen	11,5	22,3	–	–	15,2	6,8	13,8	15,3	1,8	9,6	12,6	14,4	7,3
Henegouwen	8,0	–	36,4	–	13,0	8,1	5,0	7,6	8,9	4,1	10,2	7,6	8,5
Luik	9,5	–	43,2	–	13,0	8,1	8,8	8,3	12,5	5,5	11,8	11,0	7,3
Limburg	9,5	18,4	–	–	6,5	6,8	13,8	9,0	10,7	15,1	6,3	9,3	9,8
Namen	0,5	–	2,3	–	–	–	1,3	0,7	–	–	0,8	0,8	–
Luxemburg	4,0	–	18,2	–	4,3	5,4	2,5	3,5	5,4	1,4	5,5	4,2	3,7
Taalgebied													
Vlaams	59,0	100,0	–	28,3	58,7	55,4	62,5	61,8	51,7	68,5	53,5	63,6	52,4
Waals	41,0	–	100,0	71,7	41,3	44,6	37,5	38,2	48,2	31,5	46,5	36,4	47,6
1 **Aantal personeelsleden in dienst**													
5 - 24	72,0	76,7	65,9	67,9	58,7	71,6	80,0	100,0	–	76,7	69,3	88,1	48,8
25 - 49	16,5	15,5	18,2	17,0	23,9	14,9	13,8	–	58,9	12,3	18,9	8,5	28,0
50 - 99	6,5	4,9	9,1	7,5	8,7	8,1	3,8	–	23,2	8,2	5,5	2,5	12,2
100 - 149	3,0	1,9	4,5	3,8	4,3	2,7	2,5	–	10,7	2,7	3,1	0,8	6,1
150 - 199	2,0	1,0	2,3	3,8	4,3	2,7	–	–	7,1	–	3,1	–	4,9
200 en meer	–	–	–	–	–	–	–	–	–	–	–	–	–
2 **Type bedrijf**													
industrie, fabriek	25,5	25,2	36,4	17,0	100,0	6,8	–	21,5	35,7	24,7	26,0	29,7	19,5
groothandelsbedrijf	41,5	37,9	43,2	47,2	19,6	100,0	–	41,7	41,1	37,0	44,1	33,9	52,4
dienstverlening	34,5	30,1	34,1	43,4	2,2	6,8	78,8	38,2	25,0	39,7	31,5	37,3	30,5
transport, expeditie	10,0	15,5	2,3	5,7	2,2	–	23,8	10,4	8,9	9,6	10,2	10,2	9,8
overige	2,0	2,9	2,3	–	–	4,1	1,3	2,8	–	2,7	1,6	2,5	1,2
3 **Bestaanstijd van het bedrijf in jaren**													
minder dan 1 jaar	–	–	–	–	–	–	–	–	–	–	–	–	–
1 - 4 jaar	3,5	1,9	2,3	7,5	4,3	4,1	2,5	4,2	1,8	9,6	–	2,5	4,9
5 - 9 jaar	11,0	12,7	6,8	11,3	4,3	10,8	15,1	11,8	8,9	30,2	–	12,7	8,5
10 - 19 jaar	22,0	27,2	9,1	22,6	30,4	16,2	22,5	22,9	19,6	60,3	–	22,9	20,7
20 jaar en meer	63,5	58,3	81,8	58,5	60,9	68,9	60,0	61,1	69,6	–	100,0	61,9	65,9
4 Welke verwachtingen heeft u ten aanzien van de **bedrijfsomzet** voor het 2e halfjaar van 1984 in vergelijking met het 2e halfjaar van 1983? Zal deze omzet veel hoger, enigszins hoger, ongeveer gelijk, enigszins lager of veel lager zijn?													
veel hoger	22,5	17,5	22,7	32,1	21,7	21,6	23,8	20,1	28,6	26,0	20,5	16,9	30,5
enigszins hoger	32,0	36,9	20,5	32,1	32,6	32,4	31,3	31,3	33,9	37,0	29,1	33,1	30,5
ongeveer gelijk	27,0	27,2	27,3	26,4	30,4	23,0	28,8	25,7	30,4	26,0	27,6	28,0	25,6
enigszins lager	11,5	12,6	13,6	7,5	10,9	13,5	10,0	14,6	3,6	6,8	14,2	16,1	4,9
veel lager	4,0	3,9	6,8	1,9	2,2	2,7	6,3	5,6	–	1,4	5,5	4,2	3,7
weet niet	1,5	1,9	2,3	–	2,2	2,7	–	0,7	3,6	–	2,4	–	3,7
kan niet vergelijken	1,5	–	6,8	–	–	4,1	–	2,1	–	2,7	0,8	1,7	1,2
Gevraagd aan industrie en handel = 120 bedrijven													
5 Vindt u dat uw **voorraden** momenteel veel groter, enigszins groter, normaal, enigszins kleiner, veel kleiner zijn dan u wenst?													
veel groter	11,7	11,9	13,3	9,7	10,9	12,2	–	12,5	10,0	9,8	12,7	9,1	14,8
enigszins groter	16,7	10,2	23,3	22,6	15,2	17,6	–	11,3	27,5	4,9	22,8	12,1	22,2
normaal	48,3	50,8	46,7	45,2	52,2	45,9	–	50,0	45,0	53,7	45,6	53,0	42,6
enigszins kleiner	14,2	20,3	–	16,1	13,0	14,9	–	13,8	15,0	12,2	15,2	13,6	14,8
veel kleiner	0,8	–	3,3	–	2,2	–	–	1,3	–	–	1,3	1,5	–
weet niet	8,4	6,8	13,3	6,5	6,5	9,5	–	11,3	2,5	19,5	2,6	10,6	5,6
Gevraagd aan alle ondervraagden													
6 Ik wil u nu iets vragen over uw **debiteuren.** Staan uw fakturen of vorderingen veel langer, enigszins langer, ongeveer even lang, enigszins korter, of veel korter uit dan een half jaar geleden?													
veel langer	7,5	7,8	4,5	9,4	6,5	12,2	3,8	8,3	5,4	6,8	7,9	8,5	6,1
enigszins langer	23,0	21,4	31,8	18,9	17,4	23,0	26,3	20,8	28,6	19,2	25,2	22,0	24,4
ongeveer even lang	49,0	47,6	56,8	45,3	56,5	40,5	52,5	53,5	37,5	57,5	44,1	54,2	41,5
enigszins korter	16,5	17,5	6,8	22,6	19,6	18,9	12,5	13,9	23,2	9,6	20,5	11,9	23,2
veel korter	2,5	2,9	–	3,8	–	2,7	3,8	2,1	3,6	5,5	0,8	2,5	2,4
weet niet	1,5	2,9	–	–	–	2,7	1,3	1,4	1,8	1,4	1,6	0,8	2,4
7 Is de in uw bedrijf beschikbare hoeveelheid **liquide middelen** momenteel veel groter, enigszins groter, ongeveer gelijk, enigszins kleiner, of veel kleiner dan een half jaar geleden?													
veel groter	12,0	12,6	6,8	15,1	13,0	10,8	12,5	10,4	16,1	13,7	11,0	11,0	13,4
enigszins groter	22,0	19,4	20,5	28,3	13,0	24,3	25,0	24,3	16,1	24,7	20,5	22,9	20,7
ongeveer gelijk	46,0	46,6	50,0	41,5	47,8	36,5	53,8	45,1	48,2	45,2	46,5	44,9	47,6
enigszins kleiner	14,0	14,6	15,9	11,3	17,4	20,3	6,3	13,2	16,1	11,0	15,7	14,4	13,4
veel kleiner	2,5	1,9	2,3	3,8	4,3	4,1	–	2,8	1,8	1,4	3,1	2,5	2,4
weet niet	1,5	2,9	–	–	4,3	–	1,3	2,1	–	1,4	1,6	2,5	–
kan niet vergelijken	2,0	1,9	4,5	–	–	4,1	1,3	2,1	1,8	2,7	1,6	1,7	2,4
8 Maakt u in deze periode veel meer, enigszins meer, ongeveer even veel, enigszins minder, veel minder gebruik van **bankkredietmogelijkheden** dan een half jaar geleden?													
veel meer	4,0	6,8	2,3	–	2,2	4,1	5,0	4,2	3,6	5,5	3,1	4,2	3,7
enigszins meer	11,0	13,6	9,1	7,5	19,6	13,5	3,8	10,4	12,5	12,3	10,2	11,0	11,0
ongeveer even veel	34,5	38,8	27,3	32,1	34,8	32,4	36,3	31,3	42,9	34,2	34,6	34,7	34,1
enigszins minder	15,0	15,5	13,6	15,1	6,5	24,3	11,3	17,4	8,9	13,7	15,7	14,4	15,9
veel minder	4,0	6,8	–	1,9	4,3	5,4	2,5	4,9	1,8	4,1	3,9	4,2	3,7
weet niet	1,0	1,9	–	–	–	2,7	–	0,7	1,8	1,4	0,8	–	2,4
kan niet vergelijken	1,0	1,0	–	1,9	–	–	2,5	0,7	1,8	1,4	0,8	0,8	1,2
geen bankkrediet	29,5	15,5	47,7	41,5	32,6	17,6	38,8	30,6	26,8	27,4	30,7	30,5	28,0
9 Ik wil u nu een vraag stellen met betrekking tot de **winstontwikkeling.** Verwacht u dat de winst voor de 2e helft van 1984 veel hoger, enigszins hoger, ongeveer gelijk, enigszins lager, of veel lager zal zijn dan in de vergelijkbare periode van één jaar geleden?													
veel hoger	14,5	13,6	9,1	20,8	13,0	13,5	16,3	13,2	17,9	21,9	10,2	12,7	17,1
enigszins hoger	30,5	29,1	29,5	34,0	26,1	28,4	35,0	29,9	32,1	30,1	30,7	25,4	37,8
ongeveer gelijk	24,5	25,2	27,3	20,8	23,9	28,4	21,3	22,9	28,6	20,5	26,8	28,0	19,5
enigszins lager	22,5	25,2	27,3	13,2	32,6	17,6	21,3	25,0	16,1	20,5	23,6	25,4	18,3
veel lager	2,5	4,9	–	–	2,2	4,1	1,3	2,8	1,8	1,4	3,1	2,5	2,4
weet niet	1,5	1,0	2,3	1,9	–	4,1	–	1,4	1,8	2,7	0,8	0,8	2,4
kan niet vergelijken	4,0	1,0	4,5	9,4	2,2	4,1	5,0	4,9	1,8	2,7	4,7	5,1	2,4
10 Bent u momenteel alles bij elkaar genomen zeer tevreden, tevreden, ontevreden of zeer ontevreden over het aantal afnemers of cliënten die u heeft en over de **vooruitzichten** die dit voor uw bedrijf biedt?													
zeer tevreden	18,5	18,4	20,5	17,0	13,0	24,3	16,3	20,1	14,3	24,7	15,0	22,0	13,4
tevreden	60,5	63,1	54,5	60,4	67,4	45,9	70,0	59,0	64,3	60,3	60,6	53,4	70,7
ontevreden	19,5	16,5	22,7	22,7	19,6	27,1	12,5	19,5	19,6	15,1	22,1	22,9	14,7
zeer ontevreden	1,5	1,9	2,3	–	–	2,7	1,3	1,4	1,8	–	2,4	1,7	1,2
11 Bent u van plan het **aantal mensen** dat in uw bedrijf werkt in het lopende halfjaar sterk te vergroten, gelijk te houden, enigszins of sterk in te krimpen?													
sterk vergroten	1,0	–	2,3	1,9	–	2,7	–	1,4	–	2,7	–	0,8	1,2
enigszins vergroten	23,5	28,2	13,6	22,6	17,4	25,7	25,0	18,1	37,5	32,9	18,1	19,5	29,3
ongeveer gelijk	66,5	65,0	68,2	67,9	73,9	55,4	72,5	69,4	58,9	61,6	69,3	68,6	63,4
enigszins inkrimpen	7,0	5,8	11,4	5,7	8,7	12,2	1,3	9,0	1,8	1,4	10,3	8,5	4,9
sterk inkrimpen	2,0	1,0	4,5	1,9	–	4,1	1,3	2,1	1,8	1,4	2,4	2,5	1,2
12 Bent u van mening dat de **houding van de banken** tegenover uw bedrijf in het algemeen zeer positief, tamelijk positief, normaal, tamelijk negatief of zeer negatief is?													
zeer positief	42,5	45,6	34,1	43,4	37,0	50,0	38,8	42,4	42,9	45,3	40,9	37,3	50,0
tamelijk positief	36,0	36,9	36,4	34,0	47,8	21,6	42,5	34,7	39,3	34,2	37,0	39,8	30,5
normaal	10,0	9,7	13,6	7,5	10,9	12,2	7,5	10,4	8,9	4,1	13,4	12,7	6,1
tamelijk negatief	3,0	3,9	–	3,8	2,2	2,7	3,8	4,2	–	5,5	1,6	2,5	3,7
zeer negatief	1,5	1,0	–	3,8	–	2,7	1,3	2,1	–	1,4	1,6	2,5	–
verschilt per bank	3,5	1,9	4,5	5,7	2,2	6,8	1,3	2,8	5,4	5,5	2,4	1,7	6,1
weet niet	3,5	1,0	11,4	1,9	–	4,1	5,0	3,5	3,6	4,1	3,1	3,4	3,7
13 Welke zijn uw indrukken over het ondernemingsklimaat in uw bedrijfstak? Zal volgens u het **aantal faillissementen** in uw bedrijfstak in het komend half jaar sterk afnemen, enigszins afnemen, gelijk blijven, enigszins toenemen, of sterk toenemen?													
sterk afnemen	2,0	3,9	–	–	–	4,1	1,3	2,1	1,8	2,7	1,6	1,7	2,4
enigszins afnemen	12,5	16,5	2,3	13,2	19,6	8,1	12,5	13,2	10,7	23,3	6,3	13,6	11,0
gelijk blijven	37,0	34,0	34,1	45,3	41,3	36,5	35,0	38,2	33,9	41,1	34,6	37,3	36,6
enigszins toenemen	26,0	28,2	22,7	24,5	13,0	29,7	30,0	26,4	25,0	20,5	29,1	28,0	23,2
sterk toenemen	8,5	4,9	13,6	11,3	8,7	6,8	10,0	8,3	8,9	4,1	11,0	6,8	11,0
weet niet	14,0	12,6	27,3	5,7	17,4	14,9	11,3	11,8	19,6	8,2	17,3	12,7	15,9

case study

Designing new maps for the Municipal Transport Company of Amsterdam
Hans van der Kooi

Hans van der Kooi was born in 1952 in Leeuwarden, Holland and studied at the Academy of Art in Arnhem and Groningen. He worked as a designer with Eli Gross Designers in Tel Aviv, Total Design in Amsterdam and Kilkenny Design Workshops in Ireland. From 1982–85 he was in freelance practice and from 1985 has been a partner in the design group Samenwerkende Ontwerpers in Amsterdam.

The new map for public transport in Amsterdam originated from an 'umbrella' committee in the Municipality of Amsterdam under the chairmanship of Wim Wessels, Head of the Department of Traffic and Transportation. This committee is concerned, *inter alia*, with the promotion of public transport, and in particular of trams. We formulated the starting points for a new map in numerous discussions: the new map had to be clear and easy to understand, had not to contain too much information and had to emphasize the simplicity of the system.

Before starting the project we studied at least a hundred maps from all over the world commencing with the existing map of the city. In Amsterdam transport by bus and tram is above ground, so it is easy to visualise: the routes go over bridges, past familiar buildings and round corners. Thus I was forced to stay closer to reality than is necessary, for example, in a map of the London Underground which can be drawn more abstractly because the system is mainly underground.

I did not want to include any elements from the old map, and started completely from scratch. In consultation with the Municipal Transport Company, and in particular with the 'initiator' of the whole plan, Harry van Noord, a number of decisions were made.

The Central Station was used as a starting point because it is the place where approximately twenty five per cent of the passengers get on. In contrast to the old map, the new map was required to place special emphasis on change-over stops so that the passengers could read off more easily the shortest route between two points on the map. In this way the system of the tram network, in particular, would be made clearer. For this purpose research was carried out to find the stops at which most people changed to another line. The map also needed to give a clearer idea of the number of different tram lines that follow a single route.

These principles were first applied to a pocket-sized map, 100,000 of which were distributed and tested on the public. This little map, small enough to put in your pocket, was intended for people travelling to their work and back by tram. The new system took some getting used to, even for the transport company itself, but the response was predominantly positive.

In the first attempt at the new design I tried to impose a visual order on the lines by using a system of forty five degree angles. However, this distorted the structure of the city of Amsterdam too much and would have led to problems later on when combining it with the network of bus routes. To keep the design as simple as possible I finally chose a system of angles of thirty degrees, sixty degrees and ninety degrees, combined with a horizontal lay-out for the text. This coincides fairly well with the actual street map of Amsterdam. As regards the general visual impression, I wanted to emphasise a sense of tranquility. The only background of the city that I have included is the water – no parks or buildings are

Right: Experimental network based on 45° angle construction.

Far right: Network based on 30°, 50° and 90° angles.

Below: The new pocket-sized rail map of Amsterdam shown actual size.

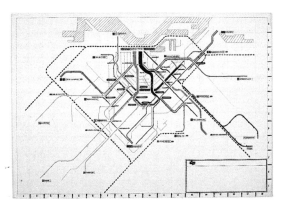

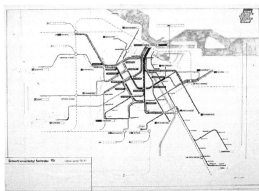

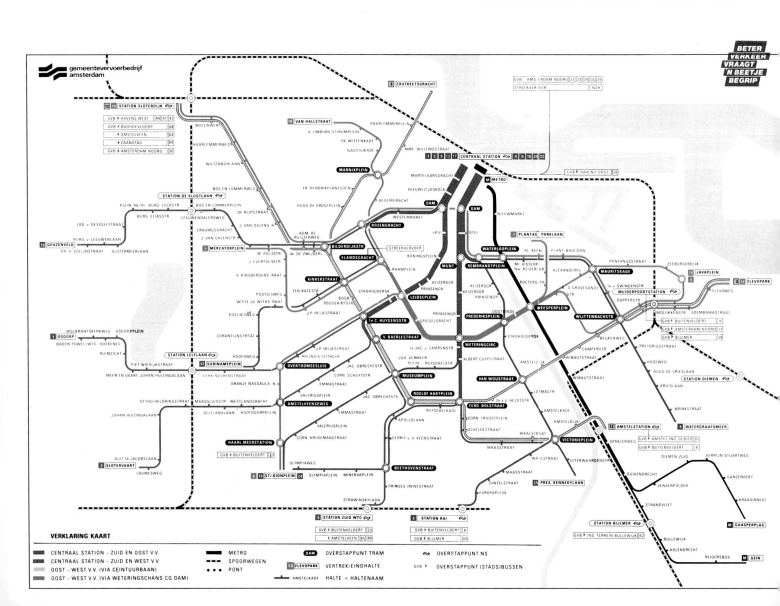

Right: First computer rendering of the pocket-sized map.

Below: The large map showing all public transport in Amsterdam including train, metro, tram, bus and regional transport. The ring of canals is clearly shown and acts as a series of reference points for the visitor.

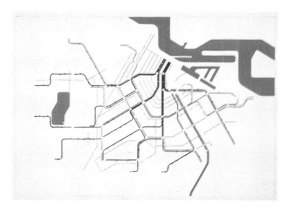

shown. Water, particularly the canals, is a strong visual element for finding one's bearings; the map presupposes some basic knowledge of the way in which the city is built up.

The thicknesses of the lines correspond with the number of tramlines following the same route; in the rail map the rail transport is shown from the Central Station in red (to the west) and blue (to the south and east) and these radial lines are emphasized. The trams crossing these lines and interconnecting with them are shown in yellow and green, the tangential and circle lines. All the names of the stops are given, the change-over stops are shown in white lettering on a black background, and the first and last stops are circled. Street names have been left out.

As a preliminary test the route finding behaviour of different people was studied with the use of a stopwatch and the time difference was measured between the use of the old map and the new small map. The time taken to find the fastest connection between two points became shorter as people learned to use the small map. With the old map time was not reduced and even went up because too much information was given.

This test was followed by the design of a map showing all the public transport in Amsterdam. This large map will be put up in the new shelters being erected everywhere in Amsterdam at the moment. This has determined the size of the map. Two smaller maps will be put up below to indicate the way in which tariff zones are divided up and to show the routes of night buses. In the large map we have also aimed at clarity and ease of use. However, this map gives much more information about different forms of traffic and covers a larger area. There is an attempt at a form of visual hierarchy in the representation of the traffic: train – metro – tram – bus – regional transport.

The colours are used in a slightly different way: all rail and bus transport to the Central Station is shown in red, the radial lines; the metro is marked with a blue line and this colour is also kept for the planned express train to Amstelveen; the circle and tangential lines are yellow and green, purple is used for lines in the suburbs and outer-circle lines and regional transport has just a black outline. There are also other changes in comparison with the tram map: the change-over stops are no longer represented with white letters on a black background but are circled. They were too prominent and predominated over the surrounding area. This time the terminals of the lines are shown with white letters on a black background.

To make it easier for people to get their bearings – as this map is not intended only for the people of Amsterdam – the city's main parks and several major roads into the city are also shown and the names of some of the main streets are marked.

In addition, we thought of including the names of some districts but after questioning the public we decided not to do so (the response was: 'It's not necessary – we know that already'). Personally I think it would be better at certain stops to replace not so well-known street names by the names of better known buildings such as a stadium, exhibition hall or theatre.

In June 1987 computer print-outs of this map were tested on 100 people, who were given in-depth ir terviews of half an hour to one hour. Again the responses were favourable; people quickly worked out on their own how the map was constructed and spontaneously recognized the difference between trains, trams and buses. When asked whether there was anything lacking, most people answered 'no, the less necessary information the map shows, the better' or 'better not to show too much – it'll just confuse the matter.'

The design process began with a felt tip pen. The decisions about what was and what was not shown on the map were taken at the sketching stage and at the drawing board. All the different parts of the map were knitted together at that stage – not on the computer screen, as that would have been too expensive.

The computer, an Aesthedes, was used later on because fairly major changes are made twice a year regarding the routes. The decisions on these are taken two to three weeks before the introduction of the new timetable. The computer than makes it possible to produce a new map in a short space of time. Every tram or bus route is separately recorded onto a floppy disc; they can be shown sliding over each other on the screen like a series of trans-

parencies. In addition, all the corrections can be stored electronically; in six hours a guillotine can cut all the lines in red foil which are used in the models; the text is inserted by hand. This leaves a week for printing and four days to put the new maps up in the shelters. The computer makes it possible to get everything ready a week before the route changes are introduced.

Work on the large map has influenced the first design and the two will be linked together, with, for example, the busiest bus routes being added to the tram map. When the small map is reprinted, the modifications on the large map will be changed; practical experience has shown, for example, that white lettering on a black-background cannot be reduced without adverse effects.

During the test of the large map the public has made it clear that the buslines and tramlines should not be distinguished only by their thickness. The tramlines now have small white transverse lines which provide a visual association with the sleepers under the rails; these are also familiar from the conventional method of indicating a railway line on a map.

The ring of canals is still clearly shown; water is the way the people of Amsterdam get their bearings and also our visitors.

The first print of the map is published and we hope that within four reprints we shall have solved all the remaining problems. We hope that this new approach will be accepted by the public and that it will help them to find their routes more easily and, not the least important, that this approach will raise the number of passengers using the Amsterdam public transport.

(Based on an interview with Kees Broos).

5   spatial and cartographic

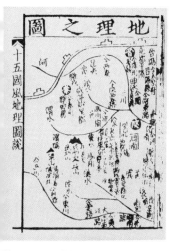

Above: one of the oldest known printed maps c 1155. It shows the west of China and part of the Great Wall is shown near the top edge.

Every designer who has created a map knows the amount of time and energy that goes into even the most elementary map. The jump from a freehand 'sketch' map to a map which purports to be accurate in terms of scale, shape and position of features is considerable and carries with it a responsibility to the user for its reliability. Each layer of added information such as contouring, road and rail networks adds complexity so that map making today tends to be a team effort supported by computers. However, the designer does play an important role in the concept and attention to detailing in general maps and to a greater extent in the design of networks which have fewer geographical constraints.

The designer's contribution is particularly important in the area of annotation, typographical choice and detailing and the selection and relation of colour and tone. Many examples of maps produced by the larger map makers have the most unadventurous graphic qualities and give every indication of being the outcome of committee decisions. When I use the word 'unadventurous' I am not using it to suggest that untried solutions should be adopted but that the graphics imput to maps is in many cases twenty or more years out of date.

Map making in its earliest period followed from the needs of travellers either over land or at sea. Maps were hardly necessary when one only travelled to the next village or town; all directions were by word of mouth and one still finds this to be the case in more remote country districts. Early travellers by foot or horse required information in units of a days travel and many early maps were a record of features or landmarks that the traveller could identify along the routes with little attempt at accuracy of scale. Many of these maps were intended for pilgrims, the first real mass tourists.

Sea navigation was the really great stimulus to map making on a continental scale. As ship design developed enabling them to leave the security of purely coastal routes their captains relied on the extensive and accurate charting of waters and land masses. Exploration and commerce pushed back the known frontiers, at least as far as coastal exploration was concerned and it was only much later that the more hostile interiors were fully explored.

Map projections

With increasing exactitude in map making in late medieval times the early map makers were faced with the dilemma of combining a number of desirable qualities into one map. Up to the middle of the 16th century these maps tended to be a compromise between establishing equality of area over the whole of the map with fidelity of angle which would enable the user to be certain that the cartographic readings would match his compass bearings.

Right: An early 13th century manuscript map showing important ecclesiastical centres in Europe (the map has been turned to show a conventional upper edge/north view). An interesting map drawn at a period of time when it was more important to show the relationship of centres to major rivers rather than roads. Ireland and Britain fill the left hand half of the map with the Orkney Islands shown as a pattern of dots above Scotland. Europe includes Flanders, France and Italy with Rome on the middle right hand edge. It has the simplicity and space distortion of some present day airline networks.
From the *Topographia Hiberniae* by Giraldus Cambrensis (1147 – 1223).

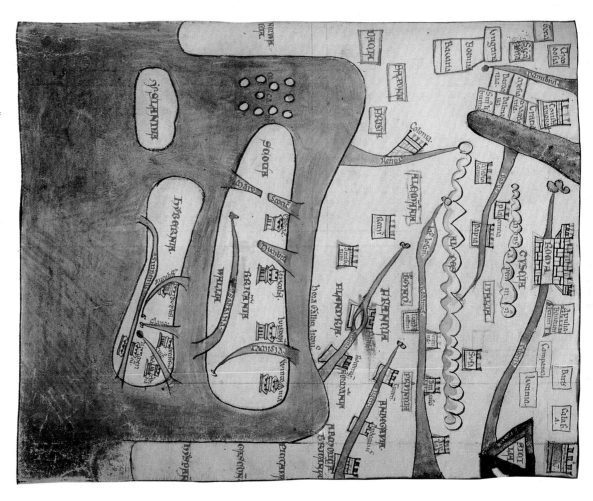

Examples of traditional map projections colour coded (see key) to show the degree of distortion in each case.

Below right: Mercator's projection which dates, in its original form, from 1569. Its great advantage in an age of exploration was that directions laid out on the map would agree with compass readings although at the expense of accuracy of shape and area over large areas of the map.

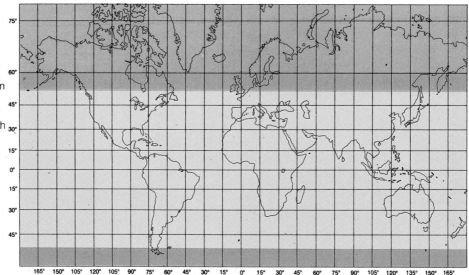

increasing distortion

Right: Sinusoidal (Sanson-Flamsteed) projection. An equal area projection although with considerable distortion on the outer edges.

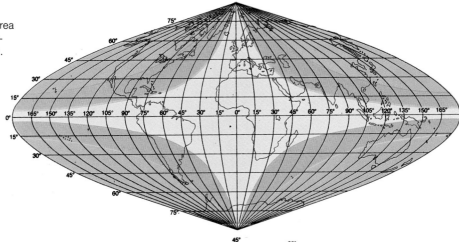

Right: Bartholomew's Nordic projection shows less distortion in northern latitudes, is also equal area and is closer to a global viewpoint.

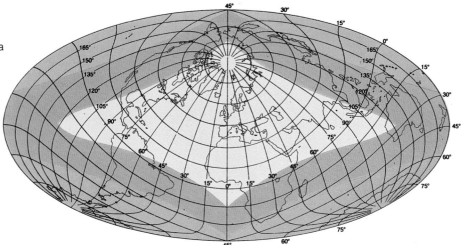

Right: Bartholomew's Regional projection. An 'interrupted' equal area projection split into three gores emphasising the north temperate zone of the earth. Although segmented it has the least distortion of the other projections shown.

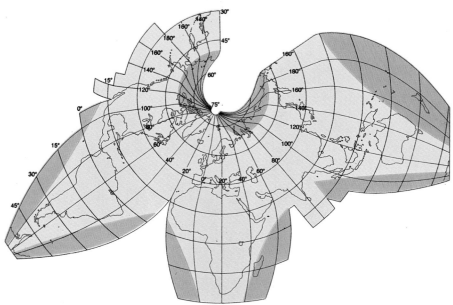

Left: An 18th century star map.
One of the earliest forms of pictorial
maps depicting the constellations as
mythological figures.

Right: Tactile navigational aids from
East Greenland. They were used by
Eskimo hunters to navigate the
coastal waters and date from the
late 19th century. The left hand map
measures 225×50 mm and the right
hand one 200×85 mm.

Above and right: The Buckminster
Fuller Dymaxion Air-Ocean map of
1943. It is composed of twenty
equilateral triangles which can be
placed together to form the solid
figure of an icosahedron, shown
above. It can also be laid out on a
flat plane in various 'interrupted'
configurations to show a variety of
geographical relationships without
any bias to one land mass or region.
The colouration shown relates to
mean low annual temperatures of
land and water.
Cartographers: Buckminster Fuller
and Shoji Sadas, USA.

ight: The Peters' projection used
s the basis for maps showing the
ensity of world population and the
ercentage of rural population in
eveloping countries with access to
ean water. Such information only
ecomes meaningful when shown
n an equal area projection.

elow: The Arno Peters' world map
rojection. It is a projection which
epresents countries accurately
ccording to their surface areas and
ves a true relationship between the
orthern hemisphere and the rest of
e world.

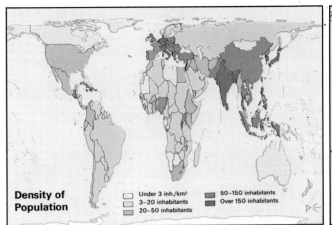

Density of Population

- ☐ Under 3 inh./km²
- ☐ 3–20 inhabitants
- ☐ 20–50 inhabitants
- ☐ 50–150 inhabitants
- ☐ Over 150 inhabitants

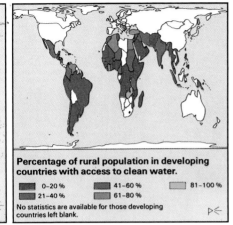

Percentage of rural population in developing countries with access to clean water.

- 0–20 %
- 21–40 %
- 41–60 %
- 61–80 %
- 81–100 %

No statistics are available for those developing countries left blank.

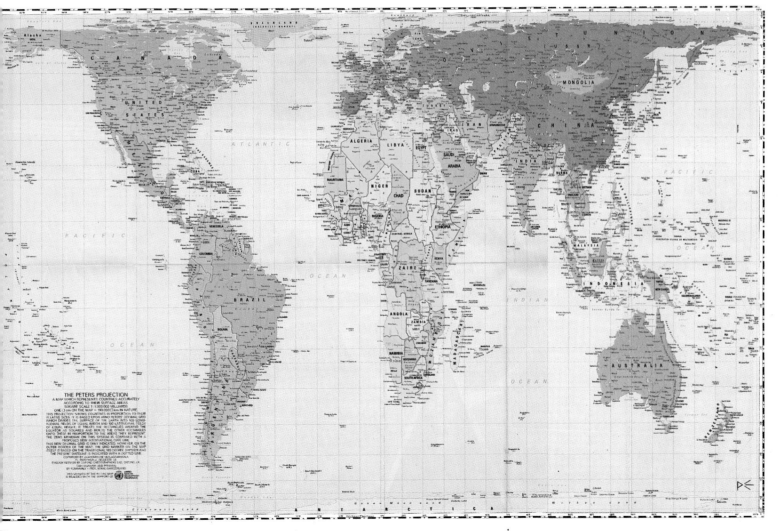

THE PETERS PROJECTION
A MAP WHICH REPRESENTS COUNTRIES ACCURATELY
ACCORDING TO THEIR SURFACE AREAS

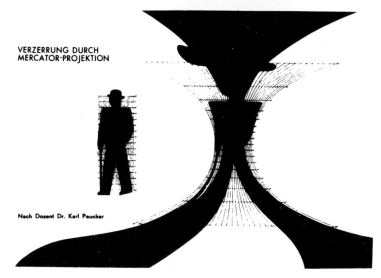

VERZERRUNG DURCH
MERCATOR-PROJEKTION

Nach Dozent Dr. Karl Peucker

Right: An Isotype diagram of 1933 which graphically portrays the nature of the distortion in Mercator's projection; in this case using a silhouette of a man.

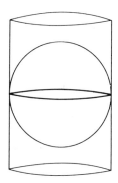

Above: Cylindrical projection as used for the original Mercator projection.

Opposite page: The Fuller Dymaxion projection uses spherical trigonometry dividing the surface of the earth into twenty equilateral spherical triangles radiating from the centre of the earth. When these triangles are projected onto a two-dimensional surface they give far less distortion than any of the traditional projections. They can also be arranged so that none of the land masses are divided.

In 1569, Gerhard Kremer Mercator, a Flemish born mapmaker from Duisburg, Germany, created a map with precisely calculated angular fidelity which meant that a direction laid out on his map would agree with a compass reading whether on land or at sea. This accuracy was gained at the expense of area equality so that areas to the north and south of his European based map became progressively more distorted in both size and shape. Mercator's map did not immediately find favour but thirty years after his death it became the standard world projection ('projection' signifying the attempt to render curved areas on the surface of the earth into two dimensions). Accuracy or fidelity of angle proved to be the most important quality during the Age of Discovery and world wide colonial acquisition (see page 78).

I am going to make a brief digression at this point to look at some of the problems involved in creating an accurate projection since they have a direct bearing on subsequent developments in map making. The problems arise in attempting to flatten the curved, spherical surface features of the earth in order to represent them on a flat two-dimensional surface. The most accurate way would be to take a series of very narrow vertical segments of the earth, each of which would be widest at the equator and tapering to points at the poles. Laid side by side these would have minimum distortion but would be so fragmented as to make the map useless for

practical purposes. A globe representing the earth was traditionally manufactured by sticking a series of similar pre-printed segments (known as gores) onto the surface of a hollow sphere. Many projections do use fragmented or 'interrupted' sections but, until recently, increasing accuracy in representation of either shape, angle, area or scale led to distortion in varying degrees in the other features. The result was a series of projections created for particular purposes but subject to limitations not always obvious to the user.

The Mercator map is based on the principle of cylindrical projection. If one imagines a sheet of translucent paper wrapped round a transparent world globe containing a light bulb then the resulting shadows of the continents projected onto the paper give a good idea of this type of projection. Where the paper in contact with the globe, along the equator, the image is accurately delineated but as we move up or down (north or south) of this contact area the image becomes increasingly distorted in size and shape and is almost unrecognisable at the poles.

Mercator's projection, was centred on Europe and the inaccuracies of shape which particularly affect northern Scandinavia and Greenland and the southern continents were not of particular concern at this period.

We should also remember that in Mercator's time, Australia and Antartica had not been discovered

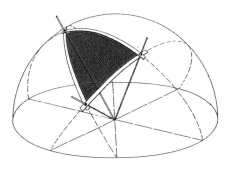

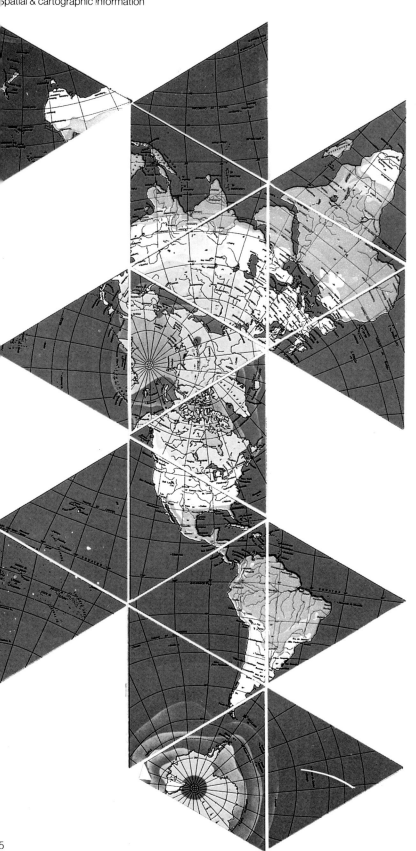

and that Greenland, Canada and northern Siberia were still unexplored. Mercator's projection has been the foundation for world maps for nearly four hundred years with continual reworking to show the newly discovered areas and more recently to overcome some of its limitations.

The need for change and improvement was high-lighted first by the development of long distance air travel during the 1920's and 1930's and more recently by space exploration.

The late Buckminster Fuller, best known for his 'geodesic' domes and constructions, published his Dymaxion Air-Ocean World Map in March 1943, although an earlier version dates from 1927. It was a considerable advance in reducing distortion over the whole map area and enjoys near equality of area and distance along Great Circle arc segments. It is made up of twenty equilateral triangles which can be joined together to form a solid figure (an icosahedron) or can be laid out as a series of triangles on a flat plane in various 'interrupted' configurations to bring out a variety of relationships without any over emphasis on one land mass or region (see page 82).

The Buckminster Fuller map had little effect on the public's perception of the world map although it was widely used by designers due to its flexibility of presentation. It seldom appeared in atlases and today seems almost to have been forgotten. The artificialness of the geometric 'globe' was soon to

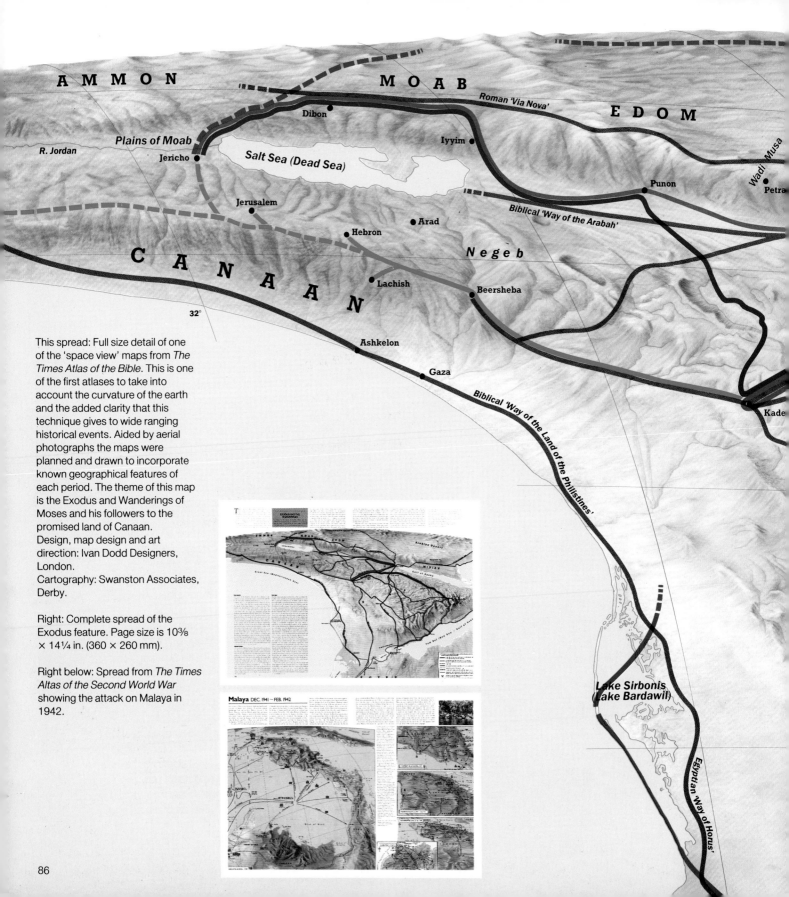

A M M O N

M O A B

E D O M

Roman 'Via Nova'

Dibon

Plains of Moab

Iyyim

R. Jordan

Jericho

Salt Sea (Dead Sea)

Wadi Musa

Punon

Petra

Jerusalem

Arad

Biblical 'Way of the Arabah'

Hebron

N e g e b

32°

Lachish

Beersheba

C A N A A N

This spread: Full size detail of one of the 'space view' maps from *The Times Atlas of the Bible*. This is one of the first atlases to take into account the curvature of the earth and the added clarity that this technique gives to wide ranging historical events. Aided by aerial photographs the maps were planned and drawn to incorporate known geographical features of each period. The theme of this map is the Exodus and Wanderings of Moses and his followers to the promised land of Canaan.
Design, map design and art direction: Ivan Dodd Designers, London.
Cartography: Swanston Associates, Derby.

Right: Complete spread of the Exodus feature. Page size is 10⅜ × 14¼ in. (360 × 260 mm).

Right below: Spread from *The Times Altas of the Second World War* showing the attack on Malaya in 1942.

Ashkelon

Gaza

Biblical 'Way of the Land of the Philistines'

Kade

Lake Sirbonis (Lake Bardawil)

Egyptian 'Way of Horus'

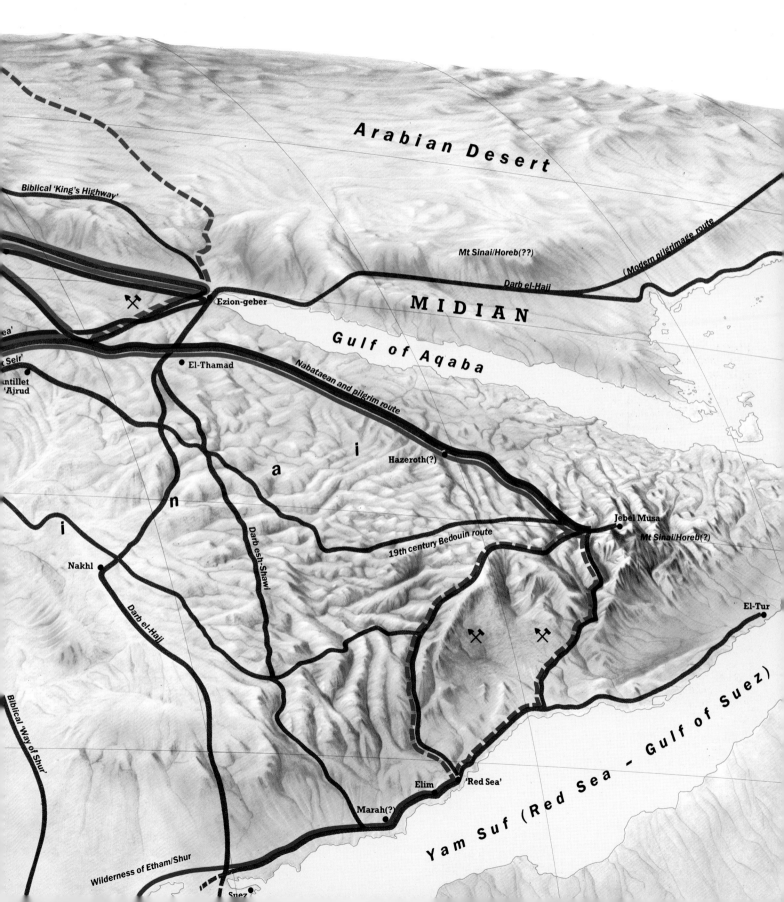

Arabian Desert

Biblical 'King's Highway'

✕ (mining symbol)

Ezion-geber

Mt Sinai/Horeb(??)

Darb el-Haji

(Modern pilgrimage route

MIDIAN

Gulf of Aqaba

El-Thamad

Nabataean and pilgrim route

Sea'

Seir'

ntillet
'Ajrud

i

a

n

i

Hazeroth(?)

19th century Bedouin route

Jebel Musa

Mt Sinai/Horeb(?)

Nakhl

Darb esh-Shawi

El-Tur

Darb el-Haji

✕ (mining)   ✕ (mining)

Biblical 'Way of Shur'

Elim   'Red Sea'

Yam Suf (Red Sea – Gulf of Suez)

Marah(?)

Wilderness of Etham/Shur

Suez

Right: Space map (detail) of the Mediterranean invasions of 1200 BC from *The Times Atlas of the Bible*. See credits on page 86.

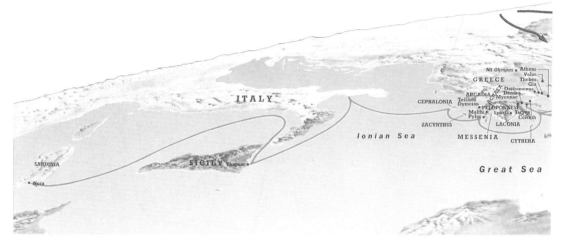

Above: The earth photographed from space.

Below: The Turnabout Map of the Americas produced in 1982. Designer: Jesse Levine

be overshadowed by the appearance of the first dramatic photographs of the earth taken from space. It was in 1948 that Fred Hoyle predicted that, 'Once a photograph of the earth, taken from outside, is available – once the sheer isolation of the earth becomes plain, a new idea as powerful as any in history will be let loose.' These space images dating from the first grainy, black and white photographs of 1966 to the first colour shots of the whole earth in November 1967 changed our perception as Hoyle had forseen. For the first time the veined and marbled globe could be seen against the blackness of space. Perhaps equally important were the oblique views of the earth taken in low orbit and showing the curvature of the horizon. These are now regularly used as the basis for weather forecast diagrams and maps reconstructing historical and world events (see pages 86–87).

An interesting reaction to the convention of north always appearing at the top of a map and the reduced symbolic importance felt by countries in the Southern hemisphere, particularly on the Mercator-type projections, is the project to invert the map. Turnabout Maps[2] have published a map of South America with south at the top giving us a new viewpoint of the continent and a similar map has been produced in Australia to remove the perceived stigma of being 'down under'. Peters' projection by restoring the equator to the exact half

depth of the map has also done much to restore the balance of north-south bias.

The most notable recent development in map making has been the world map projection developed by Professor Arno Peters, a West German historian and cartographer. Known as the Peters' projection, and carrying an identifying geometric monogram, it was launched in 1974 with the first English language version in 1983 (see page 83). It came about through Peters' historical dedication to the idea of evolving a world viewpoint of history to replace the traditional and outdated European centred one. This viewpoint inevitably led to questioning the continued use throughout most of the world, in classrooms and TV studios, of a global map which was centred on Europe. It was also biased towards the northern hemisphere and, in most cases, retained its traditional colouring of countries based on colonial influences.
Our school atlas has indeed conditioned most of us and strengthened our impression of being at the centre of the world and it comes as something of a cultural shock to see the true size and shape relationshp between the northern hemisphere and the rest of the world.
To illustrate the nature of some of the distortions in the Mercator type projections we can compare, for example, the size of Europe (9.7 million sq km) which is shown to be as large as South America (18 million sq km); Scandinavia (1.1 million sq km)

[2] The *Turnabout Map of the Americas* is published by Laguna Sales Inc. of San Jose, California, USA

Right: The Arno Peters' world map projection for comparison with the Mercator projections below.

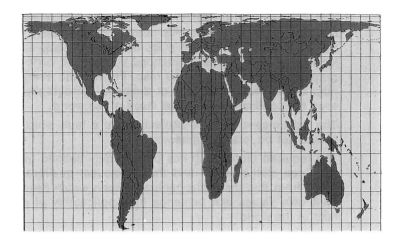

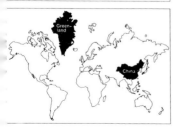

Above: Three comparisons of the distortions which occur on the Mercator projection (see text on page 88).

appears larger than India (3.3 million sq km) and Greenland (2.1 million sq km) appears llarger than China (9.5 million sq km).

Besides Arno Peters' search for fidelity to the true relative size of the continents lies a scientific quest to create a projection which no longer has to make large compromises between conflicting values. This is not to say that no compromises are necessary but that they have been distributed as evenly as possible over the whole surface of the earth. The three most important properties of the Peters' projection are fidelity of area with each country appearing in its true size in relation to its neighbours (this is not the same thing as fidelity of scale); fidelity of position so that north/south lines on the map always intersect east/west lines at right angles, as on a compass, and fidelity of axis which implies that north/south lines are shown as verticals and parallel to each other. There are a number of other desirable features of the Peters' projection some of which are aesthetic considerations.

Colour is one of the most striking aspects of the new map. In line with Peters' world view he has removed to a large extent any political or colonial overtones to the colouration of countries relying instead on one basic hue for each land mass with tonal variations within each to define separate states.

The United Nations Children's Fund (UNICEF) has made use of the Peters' projection in a series of maps comparing the relative world wide distribution

of such factors as density of population, schooling, medical care and nourishment in a way which would not have been meaningful with the old projections.

Arno Peters sums up his contribution to modern cartography, '. . . the comprehension of our earth and its topical reproduction on a map sheet and the expression and dominating basis of our view of the world is not a simple mathematical example but a mental task which had to be completed with regard to mathematical and aesthetic demands and also to the historic-politico-social considerations of our age'.[1]

Networks

Network design is probably the area of map making where the designers' imput is greatest. The delineation of the underlying terrain is very often minimal and the quality of the map lies in the consistency of its internal logic and aesthetic. The network or stages in a given route are more important than their relation to physical features of the area or countries covered and they forgo accuracy in respect of scale, compass orientation and geographical accuracy. They have proved to be very effective particularly for describing complex travel routes such as underground and overground railway systems and international airline routes. The advantages to the traveller of a network map is a considerably simplified route plan with regular

[1] *The Europe-Centred character of our Geographical View of the World and its Correction* by Arno Peters. Universum Verlag, Munich-Solln. 1979.

Right: The Reuter communications map showing their worldwide communications network, 1984. Designers: Mervyn Kurlansky, Robert Maude and illustrator Richard Clifton-Dey of Pentagram Design Ltd, London.

Below: The London Underground map showing the most recent version. Harry Beck's original network concept of 1931 has proved remarkably flexible in incorporating new stations and new lines over the past fifty years.

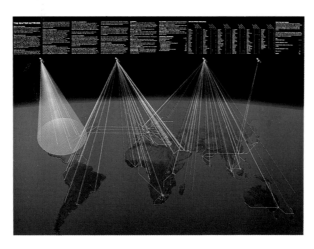

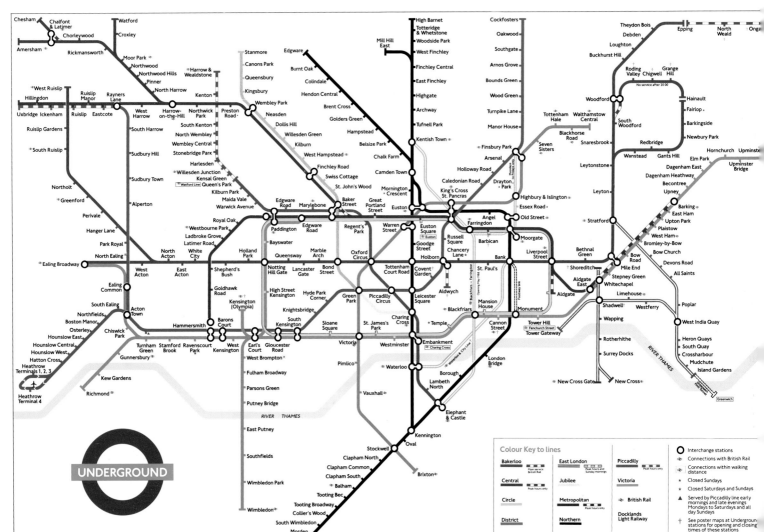

Right: Road network of the Los Angeles area for Pacific Bell's *Smart Yellow Pages Directory*.
Designer: Richard Saul Wurman, New York City, USA.

Below: Shenandoah Valley National Park. Road and trail network integrating river, mountains and wooded areas. From *Washington DC Access*.
Designer: Richard Saul Wurman, New York City, USA.

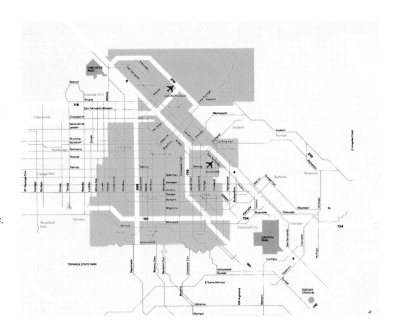

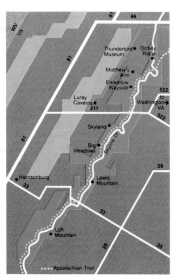

Right: Subway and commuter rail system in Philadelphia. An extremely lucid transport network design and, as with the London Underground network, the river pattern provides a topographical clue to the traveller's relative position within the city. See also the same designer's map of Philadelphia on page 94.
Designer: Richard Saul Wurman, New York City, USA.

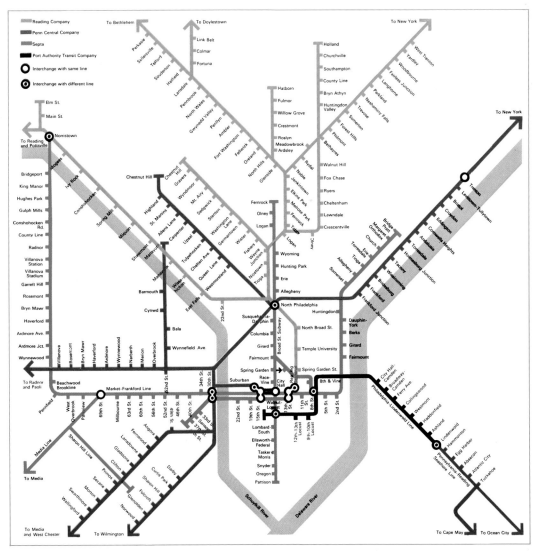

Right: Harry Beck's original drawing for the London Underground map. Beck's influence can be seen in the design of many rail and underground maps around the world.

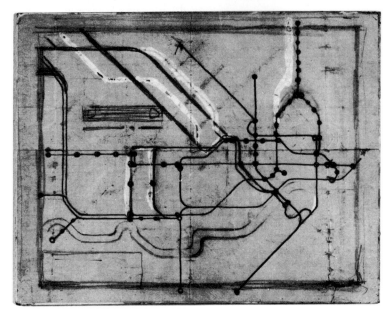

spacing of stops and intersections and their own logic of direction and scale. They enable different routes to be combined on one map by using colour coding to differentiate separate systems. If we take an underground (subway) map as an example, some of the design problems associated with networks can be demonstrated. Underground and airline network maps share a common feature in that in both cases the traveller sees very little of the terrain under or over which he travels.

I will use the London Underground map as an example simply because I am more familiar with it. It was designed in 1931 by Harry Beck, now probably better known than Frank Pick who was instrumental in raising the standard of design for the London Underground in the 1930's including its trains, station architecture, upholstery fabrics and printed matter. The map was not the work of a graphic designer but of an unknown twenty-nine-year-old engineering draughtsman. Beck designed it in his own time and it was initially rejected by London Transport as being too strange and revolutionary. Only after two years was it accepted for a trial run of 500 copies which proved immensely popular with the public. For the next twenty-six years Beck refined and updated it until his death in 1974, and the process continues as new lines and extensions are added to the system (see page 90).

Beck apparently had in mind the typical electrical circuit diagrams of his time and the sequence of stations and interchanges bear a close similarity to

the orderly crossing and interchange of coloured wires. The only direct connection with geography in Beck's map is the highly stylised length of the River Thames running through its lower half which gives the viewer a general sense of direction in relation to one of London's most prominent features.

Beck's most significant contribution was to convert a topographical map into a topological diagram by keeping to straight lines and limiting the choice of angles for his network to increments of 45°.

Within the flexible conventions of a network diagram the annotation of station names can be more easily arranged especially in the inner areas where stations are more densely packed. The lines running horizontally on the London Underground network, the Central Line (red), Circle Line (yellow), District Line (green) and the Metropolitan Line (violet) have their stations set well apart to provide sufficient width for each typeset entry and to help in this respect, the names are set alternatively above and below the line. On the lines running vertically and diagonally the stations names can be set much closer to each other as the typeset words are stacked in columns. As this is a non-linear diagram the varying station spacing does not indicate distance or time between stops (in fact there are two adjacent interchange stations shown on the map where it would be quicker to walk between them at street level than to take the train).

The detailing of interconnecting stations has varied considerably over a period of time and works well

Spatial & cartographic information

Right: Subways in Tokyo (English language version) designed for the Teito Rapid Transit Authority.
Designer: Hideya Kawakita, Japan Belier Art Center, Inc.

Below: Ferrovie Nord Milano rail map.
Designer: Giulio Cittato, Venice, Italy.

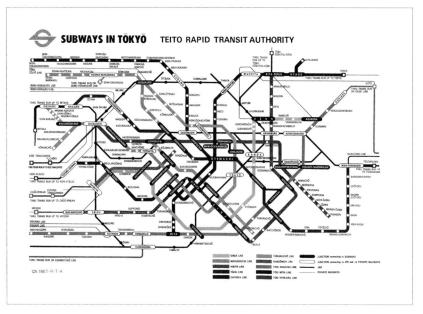

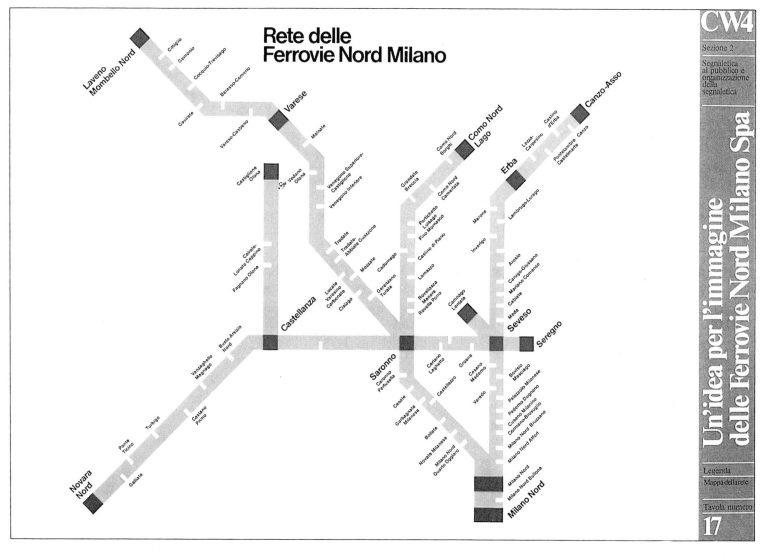

Right: an example of a *Starfold* map, one of several unique folding map systems developed by the West German cartographic publisher Falk-Verlag.

Below far right: An illustrated topo-graphical view of the southern part of Shikolen Island, Japan.
Designer: Ukei Tomori, Japan

Below right: One of a set of maps showing ski runs associated with an European winter sports centre. Colour coding is used to show the degree of difficulty of each run.

Below and below right: One of the first electronic maps to replace the paper map for the driver. The Etak *Navigator* is independant of external signalling systems and shows the driver's position at all times in relation to a map display. The vehicle position is shown at the centre of the screen and what is ahead in the windscreen is ahead on the screen no matter how often the vehicle turns. The map scale can be zoomed from an entire city area down to named streets. The map database is supplied by a series of map cassettes.

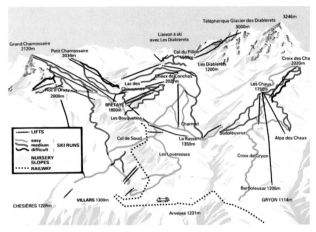

Far right: One of a series of maps from *Man-Made Philadelphia, A Guide to its Physical and Cultural Environment.*
Size: 8¾in. square (222 mm square).
Designer and co-author: Richard Saul Wurman, New York City, USA.

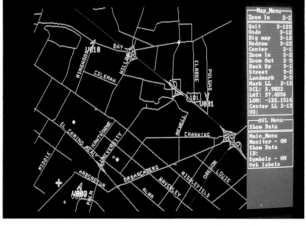

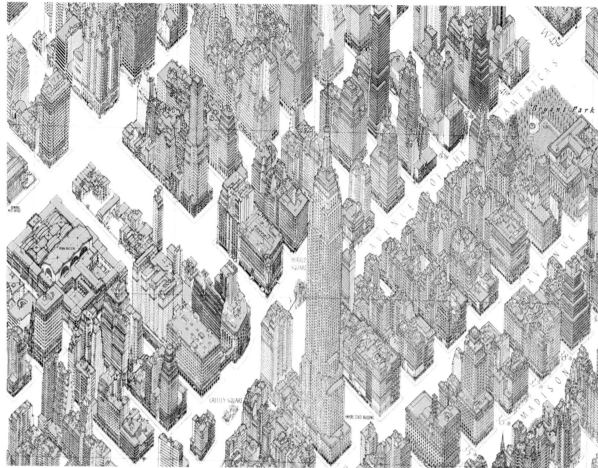

Above and right: The Bollmann map of New York complete and in full size detail. One of a series of city maps, mainly of European cities, based on a drawing technique used in Europe as early as the 15th century. The maps are hand drawn with considerable accuracy and are based on a large number of aerial photographs as well as photographs taken at street level. The numerical designation of New York streets overcomes a possible annotation problem with this type of projection. An intriguing and user-friendly guide.

Below and below right: Personal organiser maps of New York. One of a set of city information maps produced by Lefax.
Designer: Richard Saul Wurman, New York City, USA

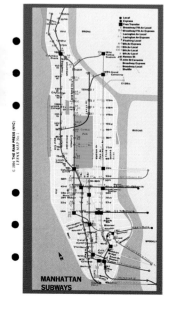

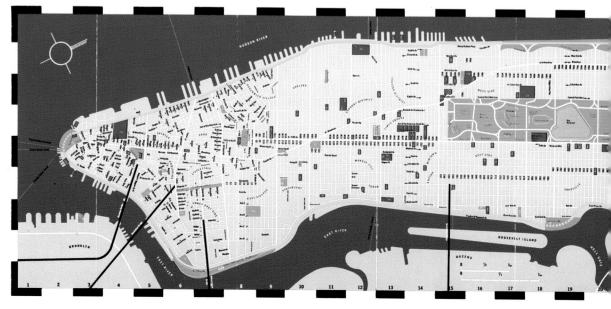

Information graphics

Right: A guide to bus routes from
Shibuya Station, Tokyo. The
numbers of buses starting from the
station are expressed in terms of the
widths of the route lines.
Designer: Nobuo Morishita, Japan.

Below: A map of bus routes serving
college towns.
Designer: Nobuo Morishita, Japan.

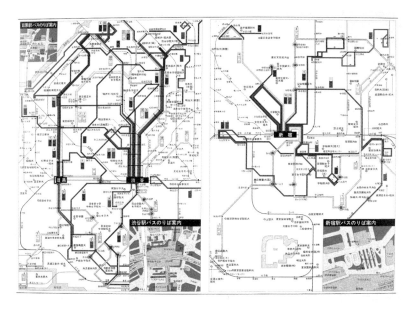

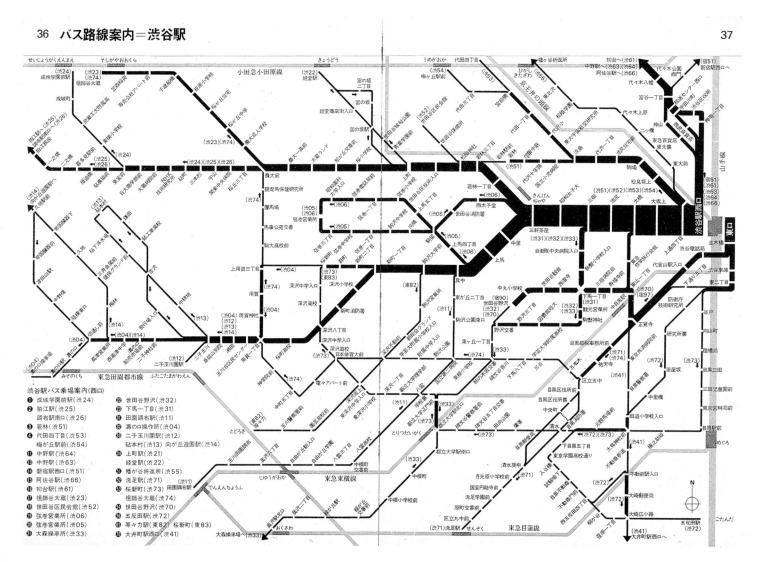

below: The Austrian rail network
987–8.

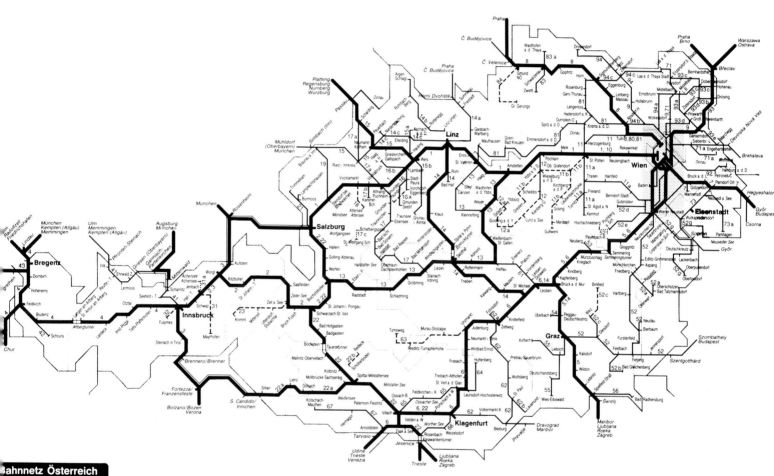

on the current version where two lines are involved but is less successful at triple junctions such as Paddington and Baker Street. The map has recently changed all capital set station names to upper lower case to good effect. Despite apparent simplicity the map has reconciled a number of technically difficult graphic problems and still shows itself capable of incorporating new additions. Not least of its virtues is that it works on both large wall map and pocket 'organiser' scales.

One of the most interesting, recent developments in London's transportation maps has been the unification of London's railway system into the network design of the London Underground following the same principles and treatment. For the first time the complete rail system can be seen as a whole. Harry Beck's influence can also be seen in the design of rail and underground maps around the world.

Right: Swiss rail network.

Map typography

Every map design which includes typeset annotation involves the designer in making a number of decisions about the typographic detailing. First is the choice of the type face or faces, range of weights of the faces available, the choice of upper case or upper lower case and the range of sizes deployed and finally the methods to be used for coping with the annotation of very small areas on the map and those areas with a high density of place names.

In general a network map involves fewer typographic compromises than one which is tied to geographic accuracy but there are still many general maps in which the typographic imput is at variance or in conflict with the cartographers' skills. While this was understandable in the days when each entry had to be pasted down by hand there does not seem to have been any noticeable improvement when computers have been used with their much greater flexibility in positioning and angling of entries.

The most legible faces are equal stroke thickness, sans serifs as these give good positive and reversal results without filling in. Sans serifs are also

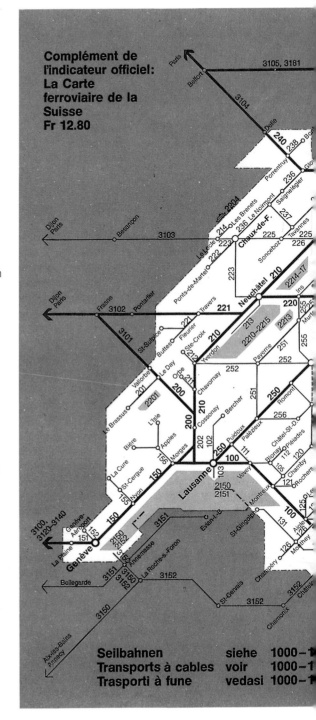

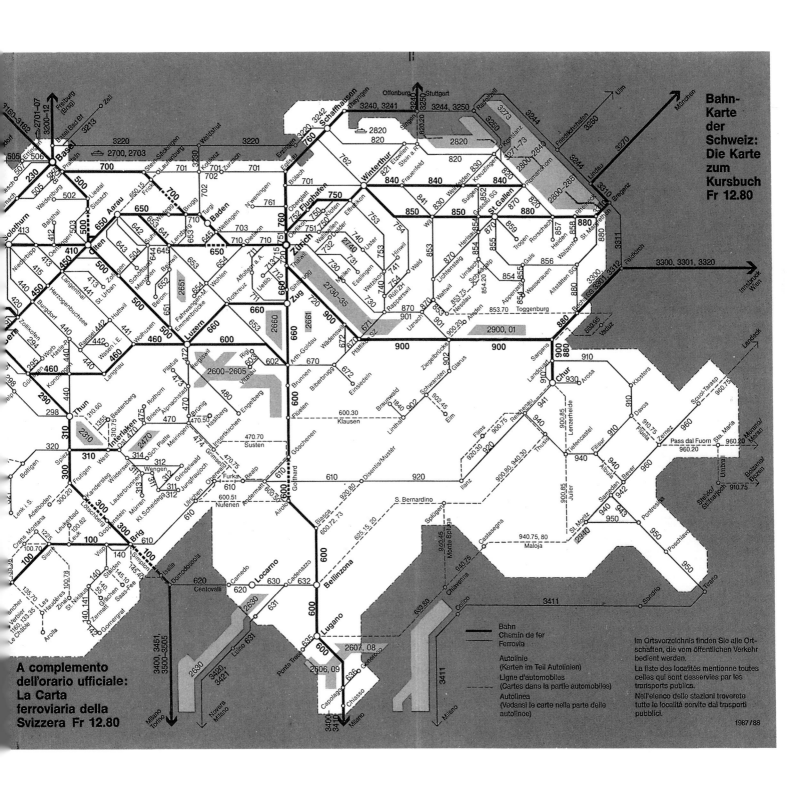

Bahn-Karte der Schweiz: Die Karte zum Kursbuch Fr 12.80

A complemento dell'orario ufficiale: La Carta ferroviaria della Svizzera Fr 12.80

	Bahn
	Chemin de fer
	Ferrovia

Autolinie
(Karten im Teil Autolinien)
Ligne d'automobiles
(Cartes dans la partie automobiles)
Autolinea
(Vedansi le carte nella parte delle autolinee)

Im Ortsverzeichnis finden Sie alle Ortschaften, die vom öffentlichen Verkehr bedient werden.

La liste des localités mentionne toutes celles qui sont desservies par les transports publics.

Nell'elenco delle stazioni troverete tutte le località servite dai trasporti pubblici.

1987/88

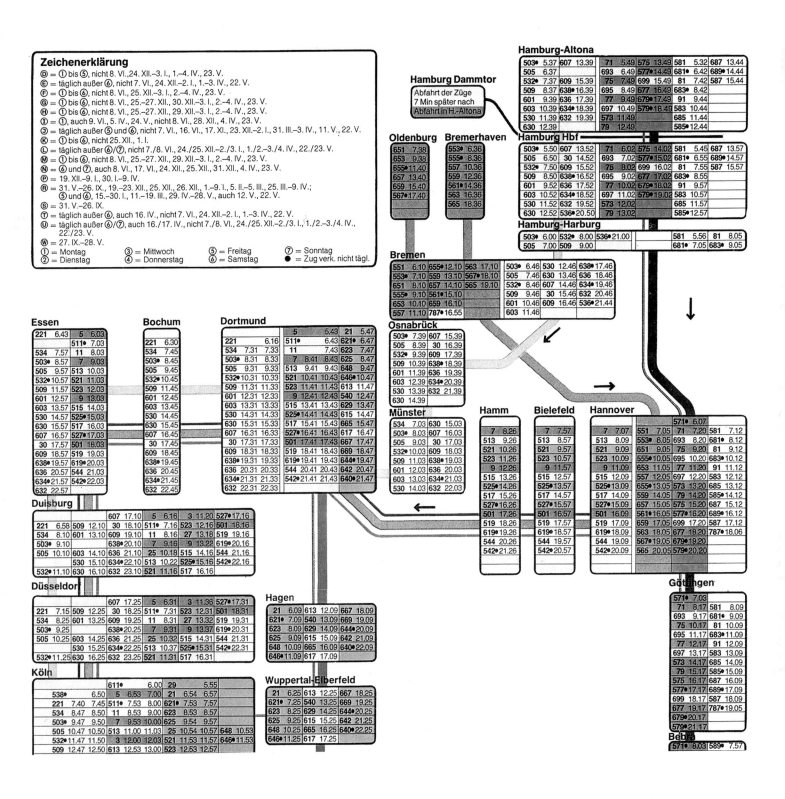

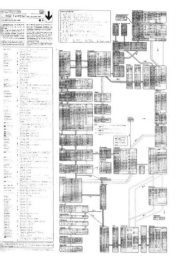

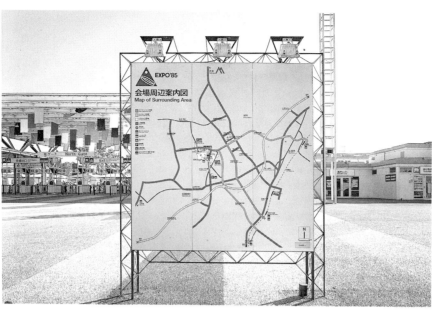

Above and left: German rail network 1987–8 combined with a time table. The full size detail is shown at left. The times shown are for the north-south direction with the south-north times shown on the reverse of the sheet.

Above right: Expo '85, map of surrounding area giving details of parking, bus routes and stations. Designer: GK Graphics Associates, Tokyo, Japan

Right: Plan 's-Gravenhage for the Dutch Postal Services PTT. Designer: Paul Mijksenaar, Amsterdam, Holland

Far right: Tourist city plan designed for the Dutch Tourist Organisation VVV. Designer: Total Design, Paul Mijksenaar/Rijk Boerma, Amsterdam, Holland

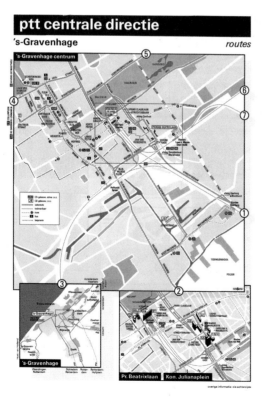

Below: Network of British Airways'
routes.

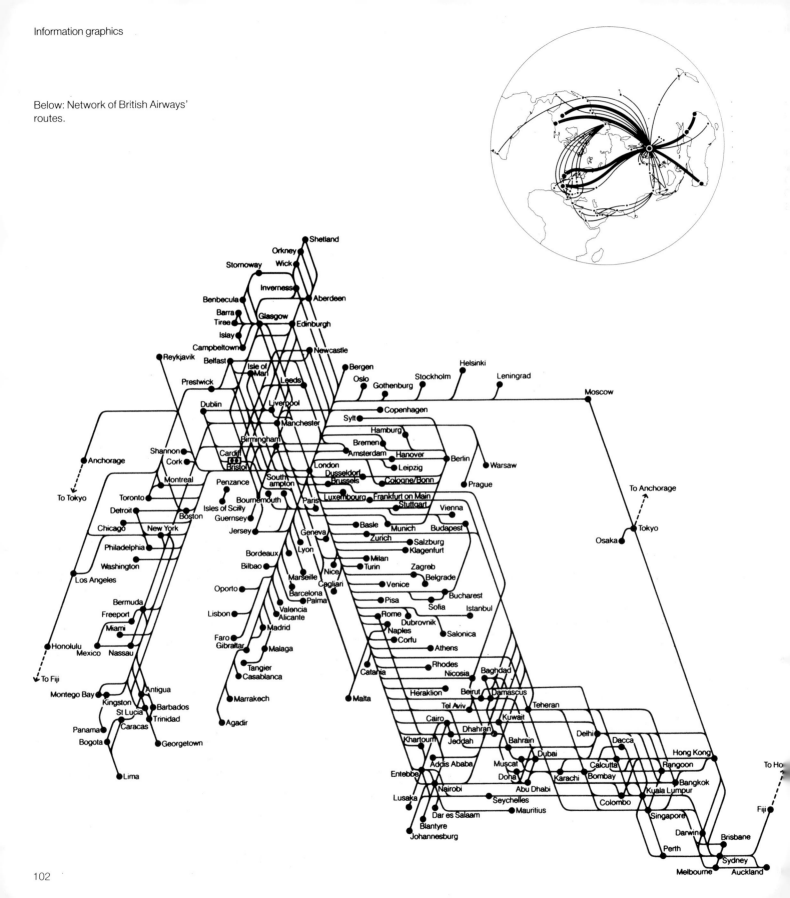

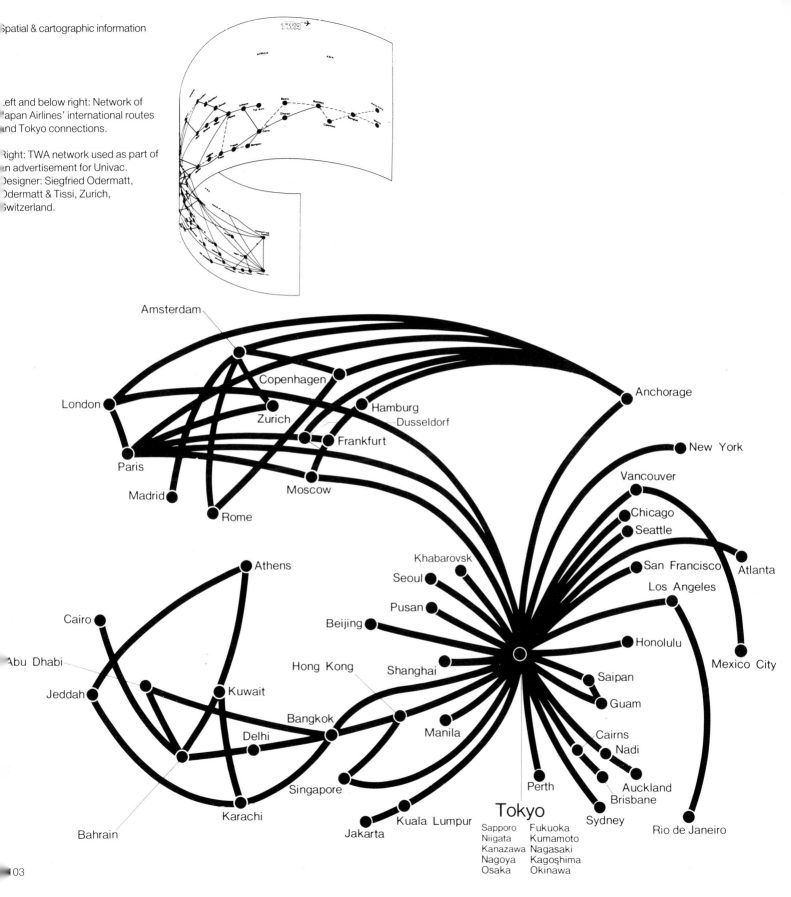

Left and below right: Network of
Japan Airlines' international routes
and Tokyo connections.

Right: TWA network used as part of
an advertisement for Univac.
Designer: Siegfried Odermatt,
Odermatt & Tissi, Zurich,
Switzerland.

TWA

Amsterdam
Copenhagen
Anchorage
London
Hamburg
Zurich
Dusseldorf
New York
Frankfurt
Vancouver
Paris
Chicago
Madrid
Moscow
Seattle
Rome
San Francisco
Atlanta
Los Angeles
Athens
Khabarovsk
Seoul
Cairo
Pusan
Honolulu
Abu Dhabi
Beijing
Mexico City
Jeddah
Kuwait
Hong Kong
Shanghai
Saipan
Bangkok
Guam
Delhi
Manila
Cairns
Singapore
Nadi
Bahrain
Karachi
Perth
Auckland
Kuala Lumpur
Brisbane
Jakarta
Sydney
Rio de Janeiro

Tokyo
Sapporo   Fukuoka
Niigata   Kumamoto
Kanazawa   Nagasaki
Nagoya   Kagoshima
Osaka   Okinawa

Right: Map of the USA in mono-
chrome for an advertisement.
Designer: Minoru Tomoda, Tokyo,
Japan

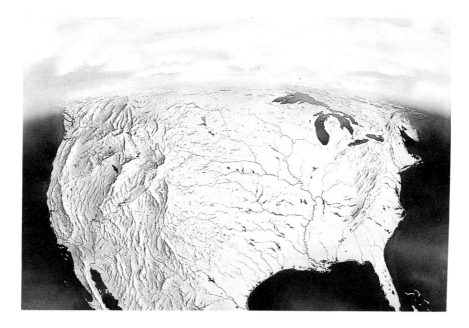

Right: Map showig the movement of
the surface platés and its effect on
the landscape for a magazine article.
Designer: Ukei Tomori, Japan

Far right: Map and geographic
diagram of oil bearing rock strata
under the North Sea from an Esso
Annual Report.
Designers: David Lock,
Lock/Pettersen Ltd, London.

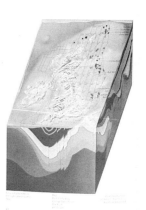

Right and far right: Map treatments
of the Mediterranean and Scandinavia in colour for Newton Magazine.
Designer: Minoru Tomoda, Tokyo,
Japan

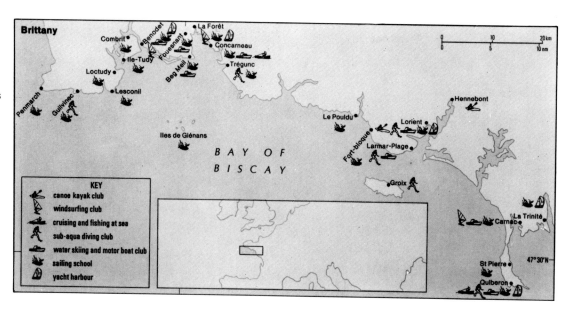

Right: Map of Brittany using symbols to show the type and distribution of water sports.

designed in a range of weights which means that a limited range of sizes can be used with changes of weight to provide degrees of importance to place names. A typeface that also provides condensed (narrow) versions within each weight is an advantage when place names have to be set closely together. It is quite common to have all the typographical annotation carried on the black printing plate so that revisions or foreign language editions can be prepared with changes to only one plate. The use of reversal (white out of colour) does however give more visual interest and can be used as an additional form of emphasis providing that the map's background colour tones are reasonably balanced.

For the reasons advanced in section 1, the need to use a mixture of upper and lower case and all upper case characters should be questioned at the beginning of the design and only in rare cases is it necessary to mix styles. An initial listing of the number of degrees of importance required for annotating any one map will produce a figure which can be broken down into a series of size/weight variations. For example: a requirement for twelve changes of emphasis in the annotation (disregarding reversal of names) could break down into three type sizes each in a range of two weights with each weight allowing a choice of normal or condensed versions.

The ideal map would be one in which the typeset place names remained horizontal for reading whichever way we turned the map (see page 94). This would enable us to point our map so that the map direction coincided with our direction over the ground. Computers have solved this problem but for all map users who still rely on printed maps it is necessary to compromise on the angles at which the place names are set. As a general rule we can say that all place names should be set horizontally for maximum consistency and legibility. Exceptions may be necessary for islands or regions which are narrow and which are inclined vertically on the map. Features which may also require annotations in this direction are rivers and mountains and in all these cases the most sympathetic treatment, and the one least likely to produce a set of discordant angles, is to curve the typesetting to follow the particular feature. The curved entry can also suggest that the name refers to a much larger area than covered by the typesetting and can be usefully employed for the names of countries especially those with short names but covering large areas of the map.

Symbols

Most maps carry out a geographic function but can be used as a base for specialised information when symbols are incorporated into their design. Symbols and pictograms can be used to denote such varied information as mineral deposits, historical sites, industrial processes or tourist facilities. A symbol is generally used to denote an area where

Below: Statistical map showing population density of New York. Designer: Richard Saul Wurman, New York City, USA.

the activity takes place rather than its size or intensity so that its exact positioning is not usually critical.

Symbols have two main limitations, the first of which is the type of information which they can sensibly convey. Where there is a clear visual equivalence between the activity and its representation, for example, a water skier representing water skiing or an aircraft representing an airfield there is no problem but where the activity is of an abstract or semi-abstract nature, such as a country park, an entertainment centre or a guided tour then an explanatory key will be required. A number of nationally and internationally known symbols and pictograms can and should be used where appro-

priate to limit the number of new symbols that have to be created and memorised. The second limitation relates to the smallest size to which the symbols will be reduced as this may curtail the legibility or cause confusion by filling in of the detail. Symbols are frequently used on maps with a maximum dimension of 2mm (1/16 in.) along the longest edge and this means that the design has to remain clear at this scale. A more interesting design approach is not to establish a fixed dimension for symbols but to create an optically even weighted series of symbols with the linear designs being made larger than solid area designs so that when viewed together they appear equal in weight and importance.

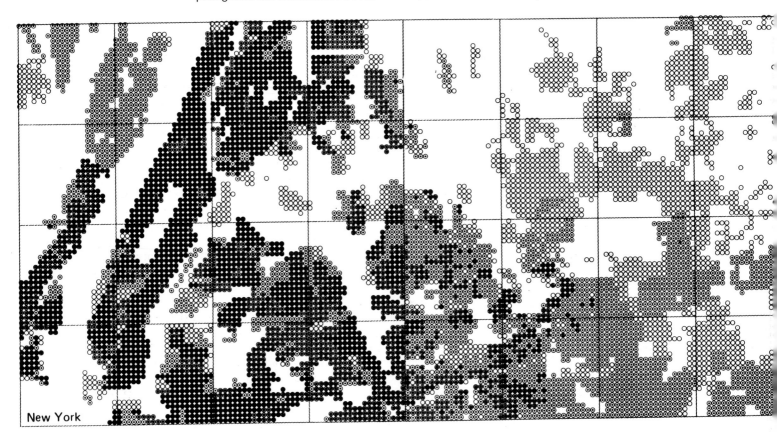

New York

comparative study

**The similarities and differences between the information graphics of print and television
George Daulby**

George Daulby was a freelance graphic designer in print before joining BBC TV. He has worked extensively with computer-aided graphic design since its introduction to television. Currently freelance, he is still unsure which medium he prefers. He questions whether the greater virtue is to be able to zoom or to turn back a page – but suspects the latter.

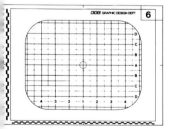

Above: One of a set of BBC TV field sizes. The gridded area (quartic shape) represents the 'safe' design area. This is the area in which the designer can work without risk of information being cut-off by the domestic receiver.

The two most powerful information systems are print and television. Print is an old and well-established system in which information is permanent, portable and easily retrievable. Print is inexpensive and its techniques of presenting information are widely understood. Television cannot as yet match these advantages; although it is developing rapidly, it is still in its infancy and it would be unwise to predict its development beyond the next five years.

The two systems differ radically in their methods of presenting information. Print does not dictate the pace at which it should be read; television does. With print, readers can make their own progress but with television, it is a conducted tour and to a fixed schedule.

Print packages information extremely efficiently. This page contains in the region of 500 words and the front page of a quality newspaper will carry far more words than an average news bulletin on the radio or television. In a television news programme, the commentary governs the length of an item as much as the visual images. This is based on the average rate for the spoken word of 3 words a second or 180 words a minute – a far less economic effect when compared with newspapers. Print gained part of its power from its ability to reach large audiences. However television measures its audiences in millions. Moreover it is an audience that has the power to turn the set off if it loses interest. Producers take great care that this

point is understood; it is emphasised that television is an intruder in the home of the viewer and that persuasion is essential if the attention of the audience is to be held. This is a subtle change of emphasis from that of print because its audience is already an interested party. The magazines we read have been paid for over the counter. Annual reports are sent to highly critical – but interested – readers. Each piece of print is aimed at a clearly defined audience not only of type but of age group.

Yet as an information system, television has tremendous power, for its ability to reach world-wide audiences gives it enormous potential. Television has its limitations; it is extremely easy to over-estimate its advantages by confusing its output with that of print. This is not surprising because the majority of the formulas that exist for conveying information were developed by the printing industry in the first instance. Since they are successful, it is only natural to attempt to duplicate them on television.

It is easy to be misled into assuming that print and television can handle identical information. Whilst most images that have originated in print can be reproduced on television, they may not work as well as in the original medium.

Television can use images, it can use colour, it can use type but it does not follow that print images shown on the screen will function as effectively. They may not work even if adapted for television. The apparent similarities between the two mediums are confusing; it often causes beginners in television to produce concepts that will be more suited to print and these may not translate into television. There are two reasons for this. The complexity of the editorial content will exclude some issues whilst the visual aspect will present difficulties because of the coarseness of the medium. Maps are a good example, a highly specialised newspaper such as the *Financial Times* is another. Packed with detailed information, the *FT* would be impossible to duplicate on television.

Yet the BBC TV 'Money Programme' enjoys great success but then it does not set out to compete with the *FT*. It avoids confrontation; it aims to present information more suited to its medium and has established its own territory. It sets a high standard in information design and this success is because it chooses simple issues that are easy to contrast. Histograms (bar charts) are used; these are easier to assimilate compared to graphs which require more detailed study. Issues must be distinct; otherwise it would reveal a major weakness of television. To be successful, television must concentrate the attention of the viewer; it cannot afford to let that attention wander.

In the case of the newspaper it is precisely the opposite; the *FT* thrives by allowing its readers to wander. Its success is not just its authority, it is because of the choice that it offers. Its readers are able to concentrate on a single page whilst standing in a swaying train or are free to take their time over it during breakfast. The reading process can be interrupted whilst passengers get off or when the marmalade is being spread; it is easy to regain concentration.

Television is closely related to the entertainment industry. One of the effects of this is that the flow of information in television (and therefore the amount) is conditioned by the pace of the items that surround it. A complex visual cannot be allowed to affect or slow down the overall pace of the story. Nor can there be a footnote. Many an otherwise excellent piece of work is thrown out because it cannot be shown without causing too great a diversion of attention from the story.

Despite this, the pace of television is accelerating. Whilst audiences must not be bombarded by unfamiliar concepts, our ability to accept information at a faster speed has increased and become sharpened by the advent of the faster story-telling of the commercials.

Print is still the yardstick by which information is disseminated. Throughout its evolution, a formula has been found to illustrate almost any piece of information that needs to be communicated. It is easy to assume that television is just as flexible. It is useful to compare the information contained in the sports pages of the Sunday papers with television coverage. The section dedicated to football not only contains the results but also a mass of

Below right and below: The section devoted to football in the *Sunday Times* compared with a single caption for television. The *Sunday Times* results panel measures 5½ × 13½ in. (140 × 343mm) and only a fraction of this information can be shown on a single caption (in this case Division 1 results). Even this would need to be on the screen for just under a minute if accompanied by a voice-over.

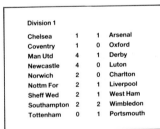

Division 1			
Chelsea	1	1	Arsenal
Coventry	1	0	Oxford
Man Utd	4	0	Derby
Newcastle	4	0	Luton
Norwich	2	0	Charlton
Nottm For	2	1	Liverpool
Sheff Wed	2	1	West Ham
Southampton	2	2	Wimbledon
Tottenham	0	1	Portsmouth

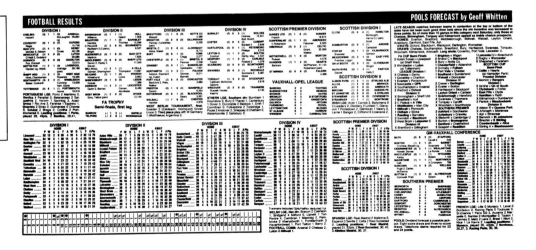

extremely detailed information that the papers regard as essential for the enthusiast. In print, this is contained within an area of about A4 landscape proportions yet this is about the size of a standard television caption (12×9 inches) that is unable to contain a fraction of that information.

To translate this information from print to television, radical copy-cutting would be necessary and the reason for omissions would fall into two categories: Some items would have had to be modified or ignored because their inclusion would interfere with the flow of the programme; other items would have to be omitted because of sheer quantity. It is essential to distinguish what cannot be physically accommodated on a television screen and what one should not attempt editorially.

Television appears to have many advantages. It can give the full results within minutes of the end of a game. It can even transmit a moving colour picture across the world, but, for a crisper image, then cinema cannot be surpassed. If a mass of detailed information is needed then print has the advantage. This is not just confined to sports coverage. Even with the resources of an Election programme, whilst the speed of obtaining the results is impressive then so is the amount of detail in the papers the next morning.

However the output from television sports departments provides a useful yardstick because they not only contain elegant design solutions, they

are close to the limits of what can be shown on a television screen in terms of physical quantities for general viewing. Yet despite the skill of the designer, they cannot overcome the handicap of both the transmission system and the method by which the image is displayed.

Most people have a basic understanding of printing techniques even if they are rudimentary concepts. In general, there is less understanding of television techniques and inevitably there is confusion with film because both mediums appear similar. Whilst television and cinema appear to have much in common, there is one significant difference.

A television programme cannot be shown directly in the cinema unless it has been transferred first onto film. On the other hand, it is relatively simple to transmit a film on television. However during this transition, the random-grain structure of the film becomes a highly-structured scanned image in which the picture is similar to a photograph created by a horizontal line screen.

In the cinema, a succession of single images (or frames) are shown at 24 frames per second. At this speed, the eye is deceived into accepting these single images as a moving picture. With television, to create the same illusion, each frame is projected upon the screen line by line. This building up of the picture by horizontal lines is the common principle that governs the various television systems throughout the world. In the UK, the PAL system is

Below right: The greatest challenge that faces television in terms of information design and real-time animation is with the coverage of a General Election. Only live television can react immediately and in such detail to the inflow of information and changes of direction that the event requires. Yet to achieve this effect smoothly, the computer is required for its manipulative powers and because the use of manual techniques is extremely cumbersome Designs have to be completed well in advance of an election as there may only be a three week warning. Every eventuality must be covered and this leads to the planning and designing of a number of graphic sequences each with their long and shortened routines.

The team that designed the graphic design content of the BBC TV 1987 General Election coverage was made up as follows:
Howard Moses, designer and project leader;
Jo Gibson; co-ordinating designer.
Rod Ellis, designer;
Laurie Russell, assistant designer;
George Daulby, consultant.
The internal information content was processed by the BBC TV Computer Graphic Workshop.

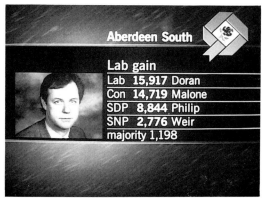

field a

first pass scans all odd lines in
1/50th second

field b

second pass scans all even lines in
1/50th second

field a + field b = composite frame

=1/25th second per frame
(lines not to scale)

Right: The television picture separates each frame into two passes. During the first pass, only odd-numbered lines are shown; during the second pass, the even-numbered lines. Each frame therefore consists of two fields with the picture constantly up-dating between odd and even fields at the speed of 50 fields per second (in UK). Known as 'interlace', this produces 25fps, close enough to the cinema industry's standard of 24fps. This enables films to be transmitted on television without difficulty.

Below: Lines of raster shown in relation to a capital E and a lower case g. A minimum of ten lines are required for the capital and an additional four lines for the descender of the lower case character.

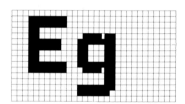

Modern 20
Plantin

standard which uses 625 scan lines (or lines of raster) to produce the picture. Actually, only 576 lines are visible since some lines are needed for engineering signals which drive and control the timing of the picture.

The effect of lines of raster upon fine horizontals and especially typefaces is far more serious. Horizontals must be thicker than 2 lines of raster otherwise they will flicker due to the effect of interlace. The capital E, for example requires a number of horizontal lines and since each line must be thicker than 2 lines of raster, a theoretical minimum of 14 lines is required if the essential form is to be retained. In practice a typesize with a cap height of less than 18 lines (the equivalent of 24pt) is rarely used. But the effect of this restriction upon serifed typefaces is equally serious. The fine serifs and fine horizontal bars of certain typefaces are notorious for the ease with which they can break up.

Modern no. 20 would be a far more risky choice than a sturdy face such as Plantin. In practice, designers tend to err on the generous side and this is a safe rule because one will only discover an error during transmission – and when it is too late to make a change of type.

One of the effects of the new technology is that type on television can now be originated by computers or from character generators (capgens). The individual characters are designed over a grid built up from lines of raster. Being electronic, there is no real need to integrate or even relate type sizes to the point system and sizes are specified by measuring the cap height in lines.

This emphasises the difficulty of placing a visual

reference upon the television system. The graphic designer working in print needs a typescale to establish a visible value whereas the essential tool for a graphic designer working in televison is the stop watch and the field size. This makes it difficult to conduct a dialogue between those trained in the discipline of accurately-dimensioned drawings or the point system for it is difficult to place a value on the thickness of a line of raster.

Since the size of screens differ, it would be pointless to lay a ruler over one to determine a size. Yet whatever their size, a screen will still contain 576 lines of raster. The 12×9 in. caption size is a useful reference point for with a television screen of approximately 9 inches in depth then a line of raster will be one point in thickness. Working to this standard, any horizontal that is finer than two points is in danger of breaking up because of the effect of interlace. Many typefaces designed for print have extremely fine serifs. However it must be stressed that this is a theoretical minimum and no substitute for experience.

This loss of definition is a considerable handicap for the graphic designer working in television for its resolution is not as refined as print or film. It is limited by its aerial analogue method of transmission and by the coarseness of the lines of raster. Whilst this latter standard is currently under discussion (High Definition Television), the cost of the change to the viewer will be considerable because each change of standard means that the viewers are faced with high capital expenditure.

informative and explanatory

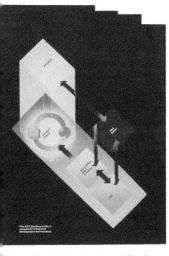

Above: Part of a set of graphics for
an artificial intelligence company,
nference Corporation Inc. Designed
on an Apple Macintosh and then fed
into a Quantel Paintbox for the
colouring and finish.
Designer: April Greiman, April Greiman Inc, Los Angeles, USA.

Most of this section concerns explanatory graphics used to inform and instruct the reader. The genre with which we are perhaps most familiar, and as a teenager is required reading, is the how-things-work book and the do-it-yourself instruction manual. The techniques for these types of presentation have been well developed over a period of time and, in the case of the DIY manuals, owe much to the compelling quality of the strip cartoon format using simple imagery with minimal captioning. They have also taken advantage of our ready acceptance of the action 'jumps' commonly used in TV and film commercials. The typical DIY presentation is so 'user friendly' that it can deceive the reader into believing that almost any repair or maintenance job is possible and can be carried out in a limited number of equally spaced out and painless operations. The reality is usually very different.

Unlike the professionalism of most of these manuals the quality of user's guides which are supplied with most new products are extremely variable and generally of a much lower equivalent quality than the product design itself. They often give the impression that they were an afterthought, hurriedly put together by a manufacturer with minimal regard to a potential user's previous experience of the product type. These guides are often poorly illustrated, sometimes using existing engineering drawings or poor quality photographs; the text often uses technical jargon and is not always updated to include the latest model variations. Not so long ago many products were

almost self explanatory starting off with a simple on/off switch and a limited number of operations but with the advent of the microchip the same products now sprout multi-functions and all the controls and lights to go with them. These controls and indicators are seldom self explanatory, even the captions are often in the form of abbreviations and so one has to learn the complete system.

The humble wrist watch is a good example of this transition from a user's guide of perhaps a hundred words to the multi-page booklet of programming instructions accompanying most of today's quartz watches. Many manufacturers seem determined to cram this information onto paper of airmail thickness using almost illegible type sizes.

The contrast between the brand new piece of technology sitting in its box and this mean looking document does little to bolster the buyer's morale in the efficiency of the product. At this point let me add a personal reaction to those first words that often open the introductory paragraph of a user's guide (and I quote from a recently purchased press button telephone guide), 'Congratulations, you are now the owner of a totally electronic auto dialling . . . plus much more'. Already I wonder if I have made the right choice of product. Any of these inadequacies of the user's guide are apt to colour our expectations of and confidence in the product.

Most of us soon learn to operate the new product but the guide can make the difference between just learning about the basic operations and getting the

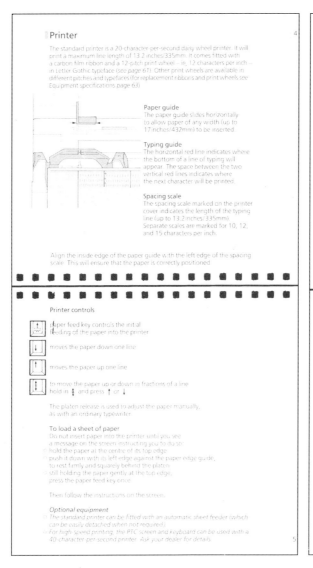

Manual for a small, inexpensive, dedicated wordprocessor and intended to be used as a quick reference guide. The copy was written using typists' terminology and computer terms were only used where screen messages could not be changed.

Tabs and an index direct the user to the relevant section; task/actions are described briefly and key presses indicated, alongside the illustrated screen confirmation. Help is available (to be switched on or off) on the screen; the manual is intended as a quick reference guide.

Designer: Gill Scott, London
Client: Panorama Office Systems, Milton Keynes, UK

Printer

4

The standard printer is a 20-character-per-second daisy wheel printer. It will print a maximum line length of 13.2 inches/335mm. It comes fitted with a carbon film ribbon and a 12-pitch print wheel – ie, 12 characters per inch – in Letter Gothic typeface (see page 61). Other print wheels are available in different pitches and typefaces (for replacement ribbons and print wheels see Equipment specifications page 63).

Paper guide
The paper guide slides horizontally to allow paper of any width (up to 17 inches/432mm) to be inserted.

Typing guide
The horizontal red line indicates where the bottom of a line of typing will appear. The space between the two vertical red lines indicates where the next character will be printed.

Spacing scale
The spacing scale marked on the printer cover indicates the length of the typing line (up to 13.2 inches/335mm). Separate scales are marked for 10, 12, and 15 characters per inch.

Align the inside edge of the paper guide with the left edge of the spacing scale. This will ensure that the paper is correctly positioned.

Printer controls

paper feed key controls the initial feeding of the paper into the printer.

moves the paper down one line

moves the paper up one line

to move the paper up or down in fractions of a line hold in ↕ and press ↑ or ↓

The platen release is used to adjust the paper manually, as with an ordinary typewriter.

To load a sheet of paper
Do not insert paper into the printer until you see a message on the screen instructing you to do so:
○ hold the paper at the centre of its top edge
○ push it down with its left edge against the paper edge guide, to rest firmly and squarely behind the platen
○ still holding the paper gently at the top edge, press the paper feed key once

Then follow the instructions on the screen.

Optional equipment
○ The standard printer can be fitted with an automatic sheet feeder (which can be easily detached when not required).
○ For high speed printing, the PTC screen and keyboard can be used with a 40-character-per-second printer. Ask your dealer for details.

5

Type

When you create a document in TYPE mode:
○ you type, correct and amend one line at a time
○ the printer moves as you type, so you can see just where you are on the page
○ your typing is printed as you work, line by line
○ you can store your work on a disk, and amend it or print more copies later.

Use TYPE mode to create documents when:
○ you have to position your typing very precisely on a page (eg, to fill in a form, where the details must be entered in pre-printed boxes)
○ you need an immediate print of your work.

Although you would normally store your typing on disk, you can use the PTC in TYPE mode without a disk, for example:
○ when you are typing short one-off items that you do not need to keep copies of (eg, typing an address on an envelope)
○ when you are short of disk space, or do not have a disk.

Starting to work in type mode

Press TYPE MODE.

Type mode instructions form
The PTC works to the standards specified in the current PERSONAL PREFERENCE SETTINGS.
○ The page format is the one selected for new documents; change it if you want to (see Specifying standards page 14).
○ Check that the keyboard and the printer instructions are as you want them; if not, change them.
○ If you are storing the document on disk, give it a name (see Housekeeping page 58).

NB   Do not put paper into the printer immediately. Wait until a message in the status zone tells you to do so.

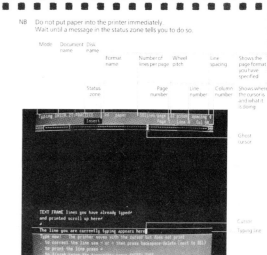

Mode   Document name   Disk name
Format name   Number of lines per page   Wheel pitch   Line spacing   Shows the page format you have specified
Status zone   Page number   Line number   Column number   Shows where the cursor is and what it is doing
Ghost cursor
Cursor
Typing line

TEXT FRAME lines you have already typed scroll up here
The line you are currently typing appears here

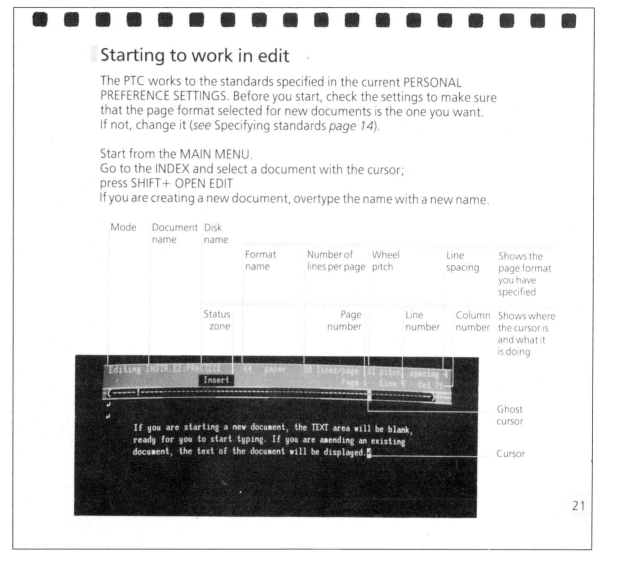

Starting to work in edit

The PTC works to the standards specified in the current PERSONAL PREFERENCE SETTINGS. Before you start, check the settings to make sure that the page format selected for new documents is the one you want. If not, change it (*see* Specifying standards *page 14*).

Start from the MAIN MENU.
Go to the INDEX and select a document with the cursor; press SHIFT+ OPEN EDIT
If you are creating a new document, overtype the name with a new name.

Mode   Document   Disk
        name   name

Format   Number of   Wheel   Line   Shows the
name   lines per page   pitch   spacing   page format
                                                             you have
                                                             specified

Status   Page   Line   Column   Shows where
zone   number   number number   the cursor is
                                                               and what it
                                                               is doing

Editing INSTR.EZ:PRACTICE   A4   paper   50 lines/page 12 pitch spacing 4
                    Insert   Page 1 Line 5   Col 71

If you are starting a new document, the TEXT area will be blank,
ready for you to start typing. If you are amending an existing
document, the text of the document will be displayed.

Ghost
cursor

Cursor

eft and right: double page spreads
nd single page (actual size) from
e wordprocessor manual. Page 25
iows a photograph of the monitor
creen and labels screen areas in
II, offering more than the abbrevi-
ions of the screen and indicates
e connections between screen
arks and data.

21

The rapid technological development of desk top publishing has not been accompanied by a greater awareness of how to prepare and design information on the part of the typical user, usually a typist. Consequently much of the work being produced is of a low design standard. This experimental desk top publishing manual, produced by a designer, aims to give the user an insight into the design process. It sets out to examine the nature of the problems involved in dealing with the major elements of a publication such as the choice of format, page structure and selection of type faces as well as the numerous smaller scale problems produced by such items as lists, tables and footnotes. It guides the user through the process stage by stage and illustrates the principles which underlie each design solution.

Top right: The sheet shows in diagrammatic form the stages covered by the manual. The user is led through an interrogative algorithm (software or paper-based) starting with the equipment available for output, reproduction and binding and then goes on to deal with the makeup of the publication. At each stage the user is directed to groups of sheets which cover both the methods of preparing the electronic copy and organising the pages in the page composition program.

Right: One of the sheets dealing with type size, inter-character, inter-word and inter-linear spacing.

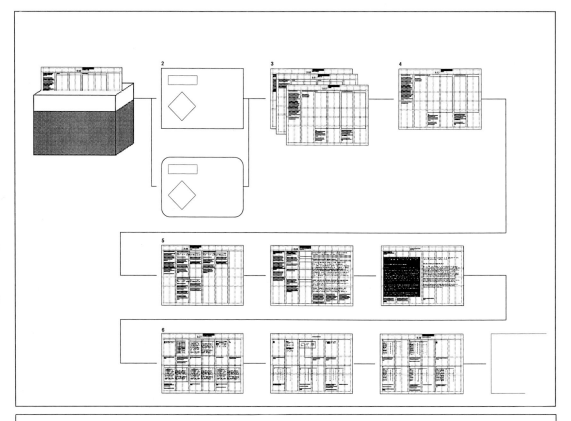

General principles of visual communication

The elements of good text typography

The combination of type size, optimum inter-character, inter-word and inter-linear space with a reasonable line length contributes to the reader's comfort and ability to continue reading for lengthy periods of time.

responsible

The spaces between the letters that make up a word should appear even. The type designer carefully determines the balance of white space around each letter, taking into consideration the weight of the strokes, the width of the character and the size of the counters.

The fashion for very tight inter-letter spacing has developed because it is *possible* for computer based systems to move the letters closer together, rather than through any sound typographic principle. Generally output from laser printers is too tight which makes a typeface less discernible.

A documents' sole purpose in life is as a paper vehicle for information, in transit from one person's head into another's. The person who is responsible for shaping the document on paper (we'll call him or her the designer for convenience), making decisions about how it should look, what it is printed on, how it is bound together, can have a profound effect on the ease with which the

nation, in transit from one person's head into anc rson who is responsible for shaping the documer we'll call him or her the designer for convenienc g decisions about how it should look, what it is p is bound together, can have a profound effect on hich the information goes into other people's hea

call him or her the ions about how it

The inter-word space is related to the type size and should be of a fixed and unchanging dimension. Such practice contributes to an even reading pattern.

a profound effect to other people's

The inter-linear space should always be larger than the inter-word space. This helps form the text into clear lines which aids the eye as it scans along from left to right. In addition such practice ensures that descenders in one line do not clash with the ascenders in the line below it.

Main text

Organising the main text

Continuous text and extracts

To prepare the word processed text see sheet **2.02** and **2.09**.

To organise the page in PageMaker see sheet **3.27—3.29**.

Listed information

To prepare the word processed text see sheet **2.20**

To organise the page in PageMaker see sheet **3.25**

Illustrations and captions

To prepare the word processed text see sheet **2.20—2.22**

To organise the page in PageMaker see sheet **3.60**

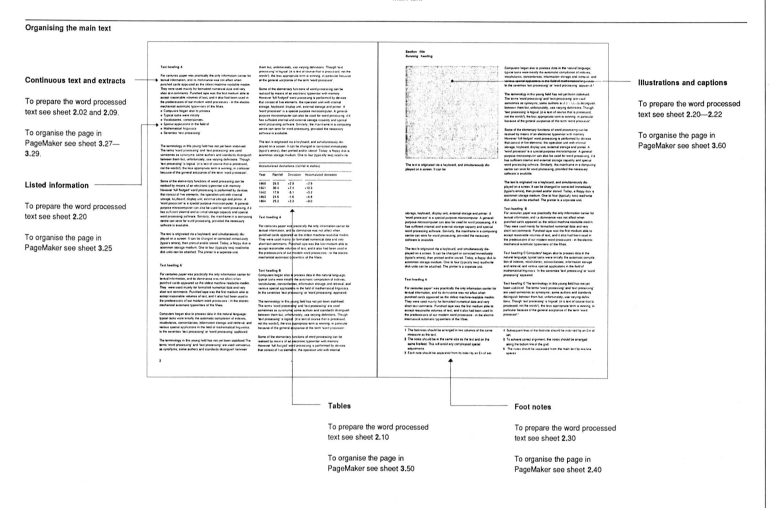

Tables

To prepare the word processed text see sheet **2.10**

To organise the page in PageMaker see sheet **3.50**

Foot notes

To prepare the word processed text see sheet **2.30**

To organise the page in PageMaker see sheet **2.40**

Above: A sheet dealing with the organisation of the main text with references to further sheets containing information on word processing and page composition. All sheets are A4 horizontal format.

Right: The user's initial task is to prepare the electronic copy and illustrations. The sheets that deal with these problems do not address particular word processing or drawing software, but deal with the generic aspects of the problem. This is possible because software packages that run on the Apple Macintosh share many interface characteristics.

Right below and opposite page: Finally the user imports the prepared text and illustrations into the selected layout. The instructions are very specific at this point and deal step by step with the procedures that are applicable when using PageMaker 2.0 (with PageMaker 3.0 it would be possible to speed up the decision process by utilizing the program 'style sheets'). This allows controllable and predictable results provided the instructions are followed carefully.

This project has been jointly supported by the Department of Education and Science and Ravensbourne College of Design and Communication. The project was undertaken by Paul Leadbitter and supervised by Graham Stevens.

Text word processed using Microsoft Word 3.0.
Pages composed using Aldus PageMaker 2.0.
System: Apple Macintosh SEHD.
Page output on Apple LaserWriter Plus.

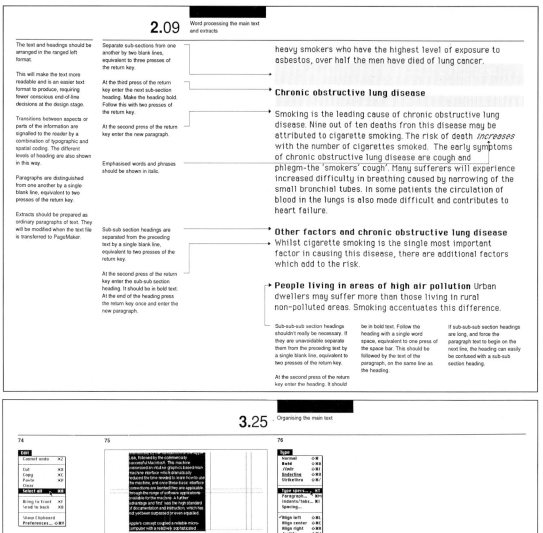

2.09 Word processing the main text and extracts

The text and headings should be arranged in the ranged left format.

This will make the text more readable and is an easier text format to produce, requiring fewer conscious end-of-line decisions at the design stage.

Transitions between aspects or parts of the information are signalled to the reader by a combination of typographic and spatial coding. The different levels of heading are also shown in this way.

Paragraphs are distinguished from one another by a single blank line, equivalent to two presses of the return key.

Extracts should be prepared as ordinary paragraphs of text. They will be modified when the text file is transferred to PageMaker.

Separate sub-sections from one another by two blank lines, equivalent to three presses of the return key.

At the third press of the return key enter the next sub-section heading. Make the heading bold. Follow this with two presses of the return key.

At the second press of the return key enter the new paragraph.

Emphasised words and phrases should be shown in italic.

Sub-sub section headings are separated from the preceding text by a single blank line, equivalent to two presses of the return key.

At the second press of the return key enter the sub-sub section heading. It should be in bold text. At the end of the heading press the return key once and enter the new paragraph.

heavy smokers who have the highest level of exposure to asbestos, over half the men have died of lung cancer.

Chronic obstructive lung disease

Smoking is the leading cause of chronic obstructive lung disease. Nine out of ten deaths fron this disease may be attributed to cigarette smoking. The risk of death *increases* with the number of cigarettes smoked. The early symptoms of chronic obstructive lung disease are cough and phlegm-the 'smokers' cough'. Many sufferers will experience increased difficulty in breathing caused by narrowing of the small bronchial tubes. In some patients the circulation of blood in the lungs is also made difficult and contributes to heart failure.

Other factors and chronic obstructive lung disease Whilst cigarette smoking is the single most important factor in causing this disease, there are additional factors which add to the risk.

People living in areas of high air pollution Urban dwellers may suffer more than those living in rural non-polluted areas. Smoking accentuates this difference.

Sub-sub-sub section headings shouldn't really be necessary. If they are unavoidable separate them from the preceding text by a single blank line, equivalent to two presses of the return key.

At the second press of the return key enter the heading. It should

be in bold text. Follow the heading with a single word space, equivalent to one press of the space bar. This should be followed by the text of the paragraph, on the same line as the heading.

If sub-sub-sub section headings are long, and force the paragraph text to begin on the next line, the heading can easily be confused with a sub-sub section heading.

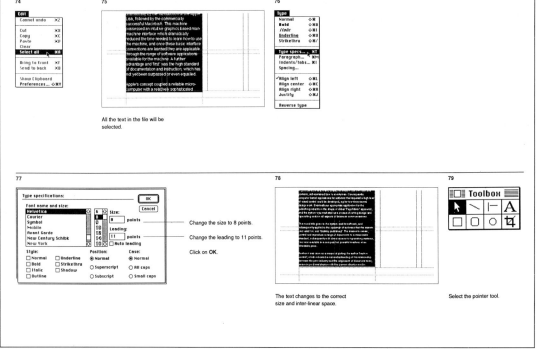

3.25 Organising the main text

74

Edit
Cannot undo ⌘Z
Cut ⌘X
Copy ⌘C
Paste ⌘V
Clear
Select all ⌘A
Bring to front ⌘F
Send to back ⌘B
Show Clipboard
Preferences... ⇧⌘Y

75

All the text in the file will be selected.

76

Type
Normal ⇧⌘N
Bold ⇧⌘B
Italic ⇧⌘I
Underline ⇧⌘U
Strikethru ⇧⌘/
Type specs... ⌘T
Paragraph... ⇧⌘M
Indents/tabs... ⌘I
Spacing...
Align left ⇧⌘L
Align center ⇧⌘C
Align right ⇧⌘R
Justify ⇧⌘J
Reverse type

77

Type specifications:

Font name and size:
Helvetica
Courier
Symbol
Mobile
Avant Garde
New Century Schlbk
New York

Size:
6
7
8
9
10
12
14
Size: 8 points
Leading: 11 points
☐ Auto leading

Style:
☐ Normal ☐ Underline
☐ Bold ☐ Strikethru
☐ Italic ☐ Shadow
☐ Outline

Position:
◉ Normal
○ Superscript
○ Subscript

Case:
◉ Normal
○ All caps
○ Small caps

OK
Cancel

Change the size to 8 points.

Change the leading to 11 points.

Click on OK.

78

The text changes to the correct size and inter-linear space.

79

Toolbox

Select the pointer tool.

3.26   Organising the main text

88

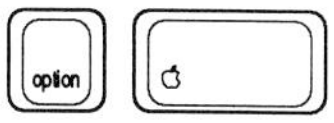

Hold down together the keys shown.

Click the mouse button **once**.

89

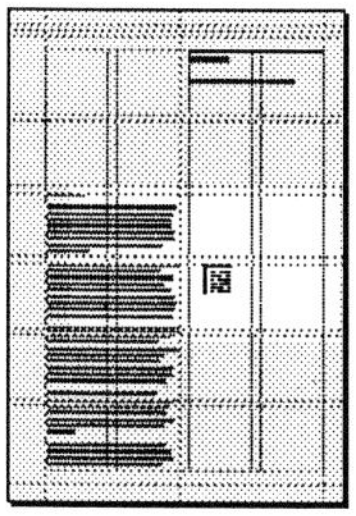

The untinted area will be enlarged.

90

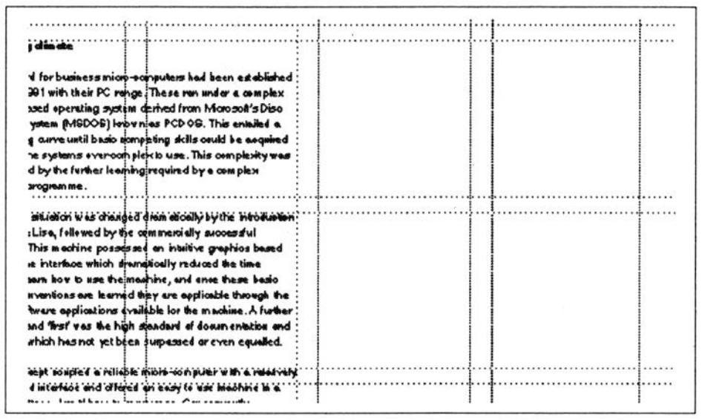

The page is enlarged as shown.

91

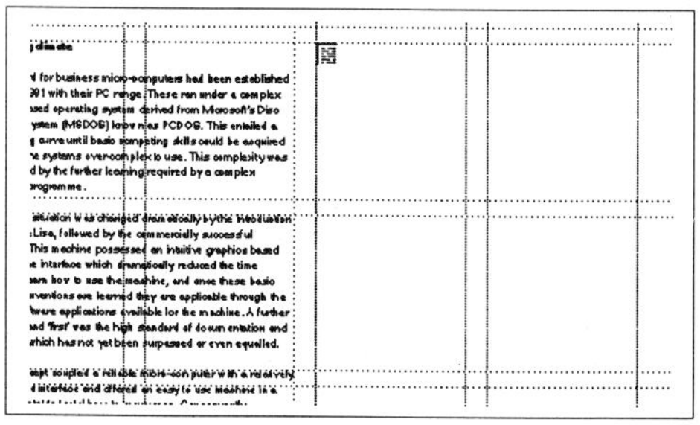

Position the text icon as shown. It will automatically 'snap' to the column guide.

Click the mouse button and **hold it down**.

92

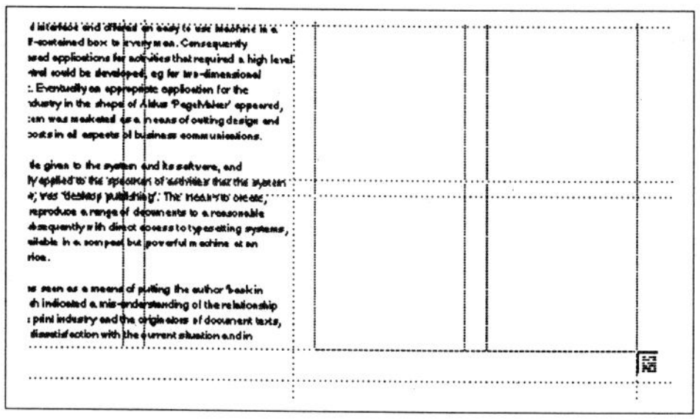

Still holding the mouse button down, drag the text icon to the bottom of the column and position as shown.

The page will automatically scroll downwards.

93

Release the mouse button.

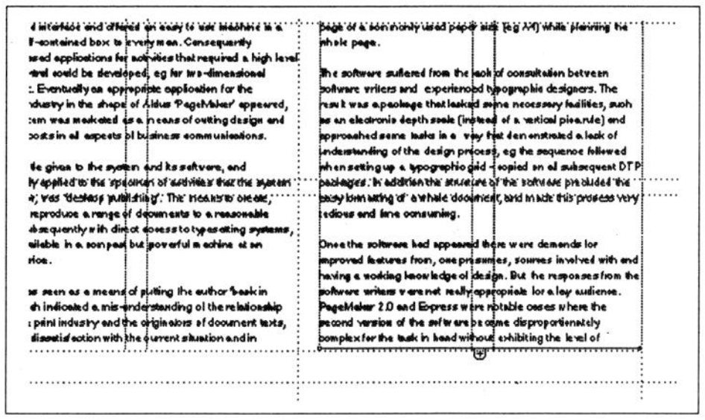

The text will appear as shown.

94

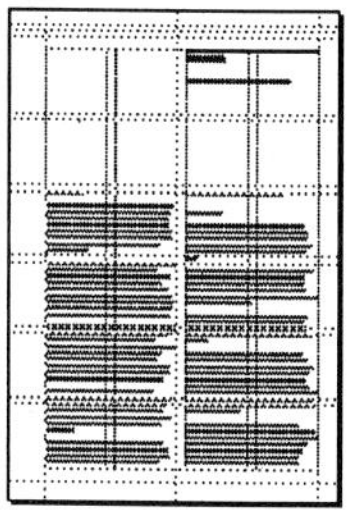

The section opening page with the text in position.

If there are other information elements, eg lists, tables illustrationes etc, to go on the section opening page go to sheet 3.02 step 3.

If there are no more information elements to go on the section opening page go to sheets 3.30 to 3.31

Right: Part of a sequence for the General Election results using computer generated graphics. Shown on the giant Maiden Spectacolor display screen in Piccadilly Circus in London's West End. This wide, curved screen measures 15 × 30ft and is illuminated by an array of 64 × 128 coloured lights made up in groups of red, blue, green and white bulbs. Each bulb switches on and off eight times a second and the screen works on the same colour principle as a television image containing, in this case, the equivalent of 8,192 pixels. When mixed this produces up to 80 different colours and is capable of animation sequences as well as topical news items and sports results. The visual texture of the coloured light mosaic is a new addition to the night city landscape. Art Director: Ann Hughes. Designer/animator: Tony Watson, Arthur Maiden Ltd.

Right: Computer generated illustrations from *Thinking Machines, the search for artificial intelligence* by Igor Aleksander and Piers Burnett, a book about the nature and limitations of artificial intelligence. The illustrations were designed in close collaboration with the book's authors and produced in a modular form so that some visual concepts could be carried over to other groups of illustrations. Designer: Mark Norton of 4i Design Partnership and Imagine, London and produced on an Arton PC 2000. Publishers: Oxford University Press, UK and Alfred A Knopf Inc, USA.

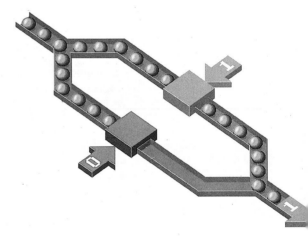

most out of the equipment. A good guide could also be used in the promotional material for the product and there is a good case to be made out for supplying either a second copy of the guide or a simplified version of it attached to the product at the point of sale so that the buyer can assess the quality and accessibility of the instructions.

We can establish a number of desirable qualities that a user's guide should possess despite the wide variety of products that they relate to.

The format should be of such a size that type and illustrations can be read easily. Formats that have to be folded or rolled up to accompany the product should be avoided. If there is an annotated drawing or photograph showing all the main features of the product then it is useful if this can be printed on a fold-out page so that it can be seen in relation to any spread of the guide. The paper should be opaque and durable and, in the case of guides likely to be used out of doors or in garages, should be printed on untearable paper and be washable.

Text and illustrations should be thought of as an entity, one supporting the other, with the illustrations either incorporated at the appropriate point in the text or in an adjoining column. Avoid asking the reader to turn backwards or forwards to consult an illustration mentioned in the text (repeat the same illustration if necessary). Ensure that captions/annotations use the same words as in the text and the master diagram. The writing itself should avoid jargon and technical terms unless they are defined on their first appearance. Explain the general plan and sequence of the guide at the beginning and provide a contents list and, if necessary, tabbing or colour coding of sections. A glossary of technical terms is a useful contribution and an index is essential if the guide runs to more than about twelve pages. Page numbering and/or paragraph numbering is useful for cross-referencing and updating material. Paragraph numbering is to be preferred if other language versions are to be used which may take up more pages Reference should be made at the beginning as to the date of issue and which model numbers the guide refers to. The differences between model versions should be highlighted wherever they appear in the text and also collated together for general reference. Space should be provided for any updated material to be

inserted and the readers' attention drawn to any facility for further information or a 'hot line'. Manufacturers prefer, for economic reasons, to produce a single multi-language booklet rather than a separate edition for each language. Most users find this annoying, both for easy reference and in disappointment that of, say, sixteen pages only two of these may turn out to be in their own language. Translations must use equivalent levels of technical vocabulary and failings in this area can prove misleading or even dangerous.

Next, I want to take a look at the various types of graphic treatments used for explanatory purposes. They cover the whole spectrum of visual effects but they can be narrowed down to three main categories and a few 'special effects' which, although very attractive, are of limited use. Many graphics, use a combination of effects but it is useful to look first at the strengths and weaknesses of each of these treatments.

Photography is widely used for explanatory graphics but usually requires special lighting if it is to provide really clear informative images. Photographs taken of a product for promotion purposes are seldom suitable as they are designed to bring out some quality of the product, such as shape or texture, which often hides or obscures the parts or controls requiring explanation in the guide or manual. Most explanatory photographs are used in black and white and, ideally, each should be set up and lit to give the optimum legibility to the particular part to be described. Lighting can be used to reveal and emphasise, say, the control knobs and captions, reduce unwanted reflections and play down irrelevant detail and texture. The control of tone values so that adjacent areas of tonal contrast do not detract from the required detail is often difficult to achieve and usually time consuming. This type of photography calls for even lighting rather than dramatic lighting and has the effect of producing rather flat images. A further limitation is that details of products requiring greater than life size enlargement may reveal an unacceptable degree of finish or texture especially in black and white and require retouching.

Most photographic images contain a range of tones which makes it difficult to superimpose the annotation on the image with an equal degree of

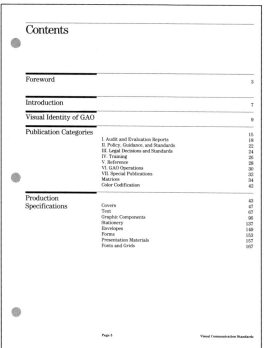

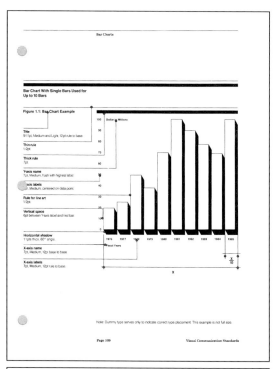

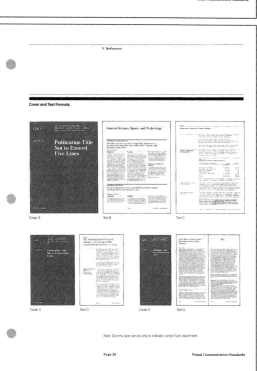

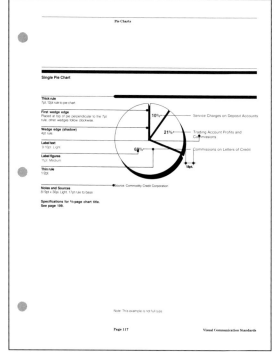

Above and right: A visual Communication System for the United States Accounting Office. The manual (above) covers all the key graphic elements for the organisation's diverse publications and communications including stationery, forms and reports. Sample manual sheets are shown on the right and include the treatment of text pages, barcharts and pie charts.
Designer: Robert P Gersin Associates Inc, New York

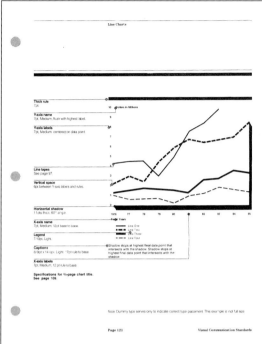

Right: Further sheets from the manual showing visual treatments for line charts, organisation and flow charts, illustrations and maps and photographs and captions. All sheets are 11 × 8½ in.

used to inscribe the names on the granite, and locating a contractor who could inscribe the names. The architect also utilized a number of other architects and engineers to deal with specific technical issues regarding the design. Actual costs for Cooper-Lecky have exceeded the original estimates. We reviewed the billings from them and determined costs incurred were proper. The additional costs were due, in part, to:

--Changes to the design required by the various groups responsible for review and approval.

--Additional review and changes required by the design controversy.

--Engineering changes required by soil and other conditions.

Costs were also increased by the nature of the design itself. The design required engineering to tolerances of 1/100th of an inch as opposed to the 1/8 of an inch used in normal construction. It was determined that the length of the walls had to be increased from 200 feet to 246 feet to adequately display the names. Difficulties were also experienced in locating suitable granite, identifying and developing a methodology to inscribe the names, and arranging for data processing and photographic enlarging of the names to prepare them for typesetting. Details of the inscriptions are shown below.

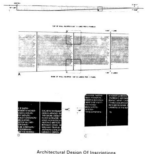

Architectural Design Of Inscriptions

30

The disbursements to architects and engineers for this work were as follows:

Architects and Engineers

Firm	Services	Amount
Cooper-Lecky, Partnership	Architect of Record	$ 422,052
EDAW, Inc.	landscape design	87,493
Schnabel Engineering	soil and concrete testing	20,195
Arthur C. Mosley	consulting architect	14,117
Other firms	misc. engineering	11,975
Total		$ 555,832

We reviewed the billings from these firms and individuals and determined they were for services performed in connection with the Memorial design effort. Billings from Cooper-Lecky were supported by detailed time incurred by employee. Total professional time to March 31, 1984, totaled 9,328 hours at a $32 average rate per hour. These billings were also reviewed by the Fund Project Director who was responsible for oversight of both the architects and the engineers.

Construction

Through March 31, 1984, our analysis of disbursements showed the following had been expended for construction of the Memorial.

Construction

Description	Amount	Percent
Materials and supplies	$ 963,283	38.6
Subcontractors	1,381,174	55.4
Supervisory payroll	66,764	2.7
Profit (Gilbane's fee)	83,043	3.3
Total	$ 2,494,264	100.0

The construction of the Memorial was done by a general contractor, Gilbane Building Company, and subcontractors selected by the general contractor and approved by the Fund. The general contractor was selected by the Board of Directors after review of proposals submitted by three contruction firms. The general contractor was awarded the contract based on size and experience. The contractor selected was also the lowest bidder. We reviewed the contract for construction and all billings from the contractor and subcontractors for support. Our review disclosed no unsupported charges to the Fund. All billings were also reviewed and approved by the independent architect and by the Fund's Project Director.

31

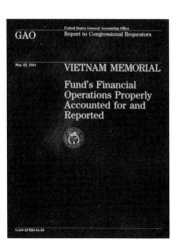

REPORT BY THE
Comptroller General
OF THE UNITED STATES

The Vietnam Veterans Memorial Fund's Financial Operations Were Properly Accounted For And Reported

GAO/AFMD-84-59
MAY 22, 1984

GAO
United States General Accounting Office
Report to Congressional Requestors

May 22, 1984

VIETNAM MEMORIAL

Fund's Financial Operations Properly Accounted for and Reported

GAO/AFMD-84-59

Figure 4.2: Architectural Design of Inscriptions

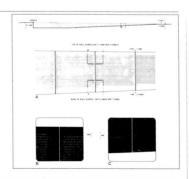

Table 4.5: Architects and Engineers

Firm	Services	Amount
Cooper-Lecky, Partnership	Architect of Record	$422,052
EDAW, Inc.	landscape design	87,493
Schnabel Engineering	soil and concrete testing	20,195
Arthur C. Mosley	consulting architect	14,117
Other firms	misc. engineering	11,975
Total		**$555,832**

Construction

Through March 31, 1984, our analysis of disbursements showed the following had been expended for construction of the Memorial.

The construction of the Memorial was done by a general contractor, Gilbane Building Company, and subcontractors selected by the general contractor and approved by the Fund. The general contractor was selected by the Board of Directors after review of proposals submitted

Table 4.6: Construction

Description	Amount	Percent
Materials and supplies	$963,283	38.6
Subcontractors	1,381,174	55.4
Supervisory payroll	66,764	2.7
Profit (Gilbane's fee)	83,043	3.3
Total	**$2,494,264**	**100.0**

by three contruction firms. The general contractor was awarded the contract based on size and experience. The contractor selected was also the lowest bidder. We reviewed the contract for construction and all billings from the contractor and subcontractors for support. Our review disclosed no unsupported charges to the Fund. All billings were also reviewed and approved by the independent architect and by the Fund's Project Director.

The chart on the following page lists the major contractors and subcontractors on the project. All billings to the Fund were submitted through the general contractor and payments were made to the general contractor. As a result, the subcontractors shown on this chart are not included in the list of payees in app. VI. The review of billings, which was made by the architects and by the Fund Project Director, disclosed only one major error in billing by the general contractor in the amount of approximately $49,000. This error and a small number of minor errors were subsequently corrected. Our review of billings disclosed no errors which had not been identified by the architect and the Project Director.

As part of our work, we obtained the progress reports which were prepared by the general contractor and determined by discussion with Fund personnel and the general contractor that they accurately reflected the Memorial construction. Included in these reports were photographs taken during the construction. Shown below is a photo as of April 1982. The extensive excavation work necessary to build the wall below ground level has been completed by this point. The 140 concrete pilings have been installed to support the wall. Several of the pilings are shown in the photograph, as is the fence which was erected around the construction site. While construction began, work to finish the granite panels and begin the inscription process was proceeding.

During May 1982, work began on the storm water drains, some up to 18 inches in diameter, which were to be laid and connected to the storm water system around the site. Forms were also constructed for the concrete foundation and the foundation was poured.

122

Left: Covers and double spreads from two associated publications for the United States General Accounting Office showing before and after design treatments. The lower illustrations show the application of the visual communication system set out in the manual shown on the previous spread.

Right: Shown at larger scale is a single page from the redesigned report illustrated opposite. It shows the strong organisation of the text and tabular matter and the positive use of space.

Chapter 3
Receipts and Fundraising Disbursements

The fundraising firms were responsible for assisting in developing the fundraising plans, designing the mail solicitation materials, providing mailing lists, arranging for printing of the solicitation materials, addressing and mailing the materials and eventually, maintaining the list of donors to the Fund. The Fundraising Campaign Director was responsible for overall direction and coordination of the plan and for arranging visits to potential corporate and other organizational donors.

We reviewed the contractor selection process and related documentation, including contracts finally issued, and conclude that a reasonable and thorough effort was made by the Fund to select competent mail solicitation firms. Further, we reviewed all billings from these firms and found that the charges were properly supported and within the terms of the contracts. Our analysis shows that disbursements for fundraising were made to the following firms for professional services and reimbursement of costs, such as postage.

Table 3.3: Fundraising Disbursements by Vendor

Firm	Purpose	Amount
Creative Mailing Consultants of America	mailings	$1,138,610
Mattera Litho, Inc.	printing material	282,443
Tri-State Envelope Corp.	envelopes	186,897
Epsilon Data Management	mailings	176,082
Carol Enters List Co.	list rental	106,412
J. J. Mailing, Inc.	mailing services	102,480
Smith Lithograph Corp.	printing	89,043
U. S. Postmaster	postage	87,104
Robert F. Semple & Associates	planning campaign	60,636
Bond Office Services	mailing services	59,792
Oram International Group	consulting	51,394
Berlin & Jones	printing	39,251
Diversified Mail	mailing services	23,380
Printers II	printing	22,560
UARCO	printing	11,584
Techna-Graphics, Inc.	graphics	8,722
Constituency Builders, Inc.	mailing	7,809
Other	payroll and other	125,835
Total		**$2,580,034**

These disbursements were made based on billings from the vendors which did not separate costs between fundraising and education. While the Fund, in accordance with generally accepted accounting principles, allocated billings between fundraising and education in its financial reports, we have presented these disbursements by vendor. See chapter 5 for a further discussion of the allocation process used by the Fund.

23

Slalom

Competitors in the slalom follow twisting courses defined by pairs of flags (known as gates). A competition is decided by two runs down different courses. The winner is the competitor with the fastest aggregate time for the two runs.

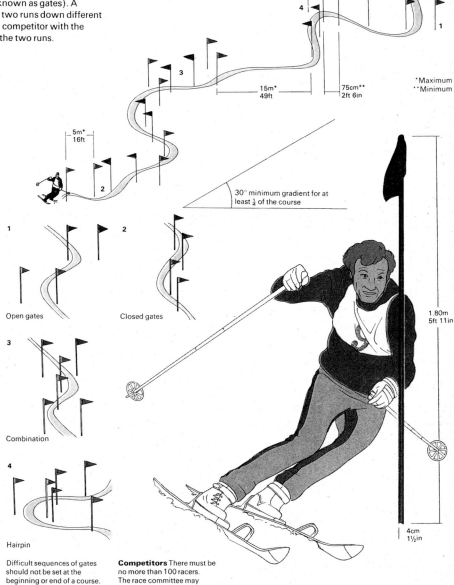

Courses should test a wide variety of ski techniques. Traverses across the slope are interspersed with runs down it, and courses must include turns that allow maximum speed, precision, and neat execution. The snow must be as hard as possible.
In world and Olympic championships at least a quarter of each course must be on slopes exceeding a gradient of 30°.
Vertical drop World and Olympic championships: men 180–220m; women 130–180m.
Other international races: men 140–200m; women 120–160m.

Gates Slalom gates consist of two solid, uniform poles, which must be 3–4cm in diameter and extend 1.8m above the snow.
The gates must be alternately blue or red, with flags of the same color.
The distance between any two gates must be at least 0.75m, and not more than 15m.
Each gate must be between 4m and 5m wide.
In a hairpin gate the distance between the two verticals must be 0.75m.
The course must contain open and vertical gates, and two or three vertical combinations (consisting of between three and five gates) and at least four hairpin combinations.
For men's courses there are between 55 and 75 gates; for women's courses between 40 and 60 gates.
Except for the starting and finishing gates, the gates are numbered down the course, with the numbers on the outside of the poles.
Gates must not be set in monotonous combinations; nor must they spoil the fluency of a run by forcing sudden braking.

Difficult sequences of gates should not be set at the beginning or end of a course. The last gates should be fast, to enable a racer to finish at good speed.
The last gate should not be too near the finishing line (to avoid danger to officials), and should direct racers toward the middle of the finishing line.

Competitors There must be no more than 100 racers.
The race committee may reduce the number for the second run, provided competitors have been told beforehand.
Courses may not be used simultaneously by two groups of competitors.

5m*
16ft

15m*
49ft

75cm**
2ft 6in

*Maximum
**Minimum

30° minimum gradient for at least ¼ of the course

1.80m
5ft 11in

4cm
1½in

1

2

Open gates

Closed gates

3

Combination

4

Hairpin

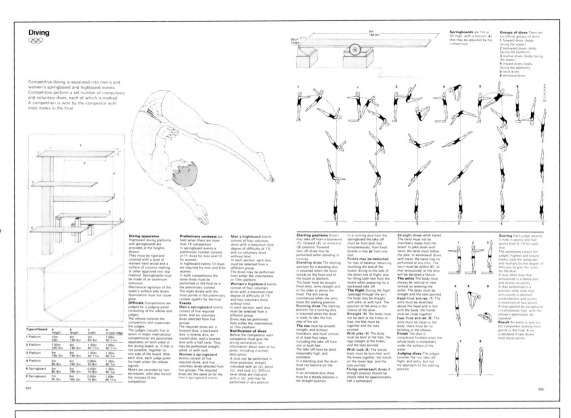

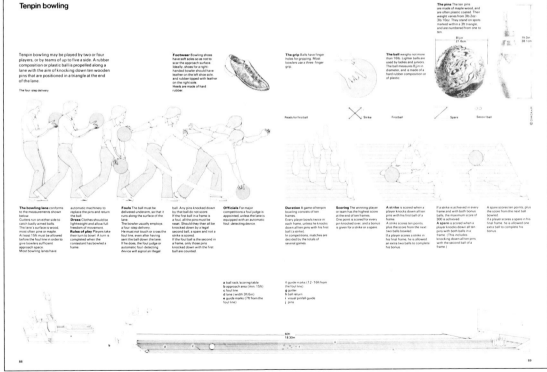

Left and this page: Single page and double spreads from *Rules of the Game*. A predominantly visual presentation of over 200 sports in which the major objectives, playing area and equipment, timing and scoring, rules and regulations, participants and officials, playing procedure and misconduct and its consequences are all set out. Those sports that appear in the Olympic calendar carry a symbol beneath their title.

The technique of multiple imagery is used to good effect in showing fast moving, complex manoeuvres as in the diving spread. Page size: 305 × 225mm.

Designers: Diagram Visual Information Ltd, London

Publisher: Bantam Books/Corgi

Diving

Competitive diving is separated into men's and women's springboard and highboard events. Competitors perform a set number of compulsory and voluntary dives, each of which is marked. A competition is won by the competitor with most marks in the final.

Tenpin bowling

Tenpin bowling may be played by two or four players, or by teams of up to five a side. A rubber composition or plastic ball is propelled along a lane with the aim of knocking down ten wooden pins that are positioned in a triangle at the end of the lane.

The four-step delivery.

Right: Graphic analysis of the 100 metres final in the World Championships held in Rome in 1987 when Ben Johnson beat the existing world record and beat the previous Olympic champion Carl Lewis.
Illustration: Phil Green for The Sunday Times Magazine, Times Newspapers Ltd.

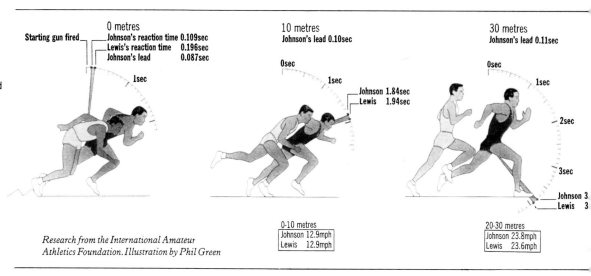

Research from the International Amateur Athletics Foundation. Illustration by Phil Green

legibility over the whole image. An alternative method of annotation is to position the type outside the image area with rules (leaders) pinpointing the desired features. The use of a second colour is the best solution which also enables updating to be carried out or other language editions to be prepared without changing the image plate. A technique which can be very effective on photographs is to reduce the overall tone of those parts of the image which are not important to the area being explained leaving only the key area in full tone. The background can be reduced to fifty per cent of the full tone or less, sufficient to give context to the key area but not enough to distract from it. Although an old technique used in the early days of half tone reproduction it is still very effective. The strengths of the photographic image are that they relate directly to the viewer's perception of the product and appear less technical to the user than drawings or diagrams.

As a half way stage between photographs and line drawings as a method of presentation is the tone or colour rendered image in which planes and surfaces are rendered in even or gradated tones. Being completely under the designer's control every aspect of the product from the initial selection of viewpoint to finished tone and colour contrast can be used to give maximum value to the parts or processes requiring explanation. The rendering can also be modified to provide a degree of transparency to reveal parts below the surface and can integrate arrows and other symbols to show direction of movement or flow. They

can be used to simulate the realism of photography or ignore the laws of lighting and shadows completely and use their own conventions of showing changes of plane or curvature. Because of the time involved in analysing the most effective ways of treating the subject and the preparation of finished artwork the costs may be equal to or higher than photography. It is a technique seen at its best in the communication of complex technical or electronic processes such as the working of the internal combustion engine or an explanation of colour television.

The third major method is the linear approach, perhaps the most commonly used of all techniques. Line drawings are easy to produce and to reproduce and integrate well with type. Being schematic in nature they do not need tone or the effects of light and shade and can be selectively detailed as required. By means of the addition of mechanical tints they can approach the effectiveness of fully rendered images. Repair manuals are a good example of the use of simple key line drawings with a limited range of applied tints in black and, usually, one other colour.

The adaptability of the technique is considerable; besides the drafting conventions of plan and elevation; the realistic conventions of perspective, axonometric and isometric projections they can be used to show highly artificial exploded views in which each part of an assembly is shown in complete detail as well as in relation to the other parts. It can thus show the order of assembly as well as the compon-

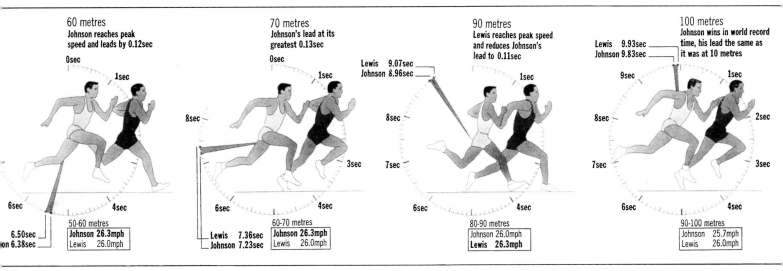

60 metres
Johnson reaches peak
speed and leads by 0.12sec

50-60 metres
Johnson 26.3mph
Lewis 26.0mph

6.50sec
on 6.38sec

70 metres
Johnson's lead at its
greatest 0.13sec

Lewis 9.07sec
Johnson 8.96sec

60-70 metres
Johnson 26.3mph
Lewis 26.0mph

Lewis 7.36sec
Johnson 7.23sec

90 metres
Lewis reaches peak speed
and reduces Johnson's
lead to 0.11sec

80-90 metres
Johnson 26.0mph
Lewis 26.3mph

100 metres
Johnson wins in world record
time, his lead the same as
it was at 10 metres

Lewis 9.93sec
Johnson 9.83sec

90-100 metres
Johnson 25.7mph
Lewis 26.0mph

ents. Any of these treatments can also include a degree of transparency so that details below or behind the main components can be shown in their true position.

Amongst the more unusual types of graphic treatments are those concerned with the slowing down of rapid motion and the presentation of objects in simulated or true three dimensions.

Sports activities lend themselves to the multiple image technique which shows a sequence of actions in one drawing so that, for example, an athlete's high jump can be studied stage by stage. In most cases these drawings are based on high speed photographs and the drawing is able to isolate and define only the key movements at each stage of the action. In some cases, such as showing swimming techniques, part of the action is normally out of sight beneath the water and a drawing is able to show the action more clearly than an underwater camera. When different viewpoints of the same activity are shown side by side this technique forms a powerful teaching aid.

There are a few cases where stereo illustrations can clarify the relationship between objects and actions and, again, the stereo version of the line drawing can be more effective than a stereo photograph. I have seen it used to good purpose in a text book on geometrical constructions and some examples of its use appear in a book by R L Gregory.[1] The limitations to its more widespread use is the two colour printing requirement and the availability of appropriate filter spectacles. There is also a short time delay in viewing the images before stereo vision occurs. A further factor in its limited use at present is that there is no simple method of 3D image generation which would allow stereo drawings to be produced simply and economically.

The last of the three dimensional techniques is the pop-up illustration which is mainly confined to children's books. It has been effectively used to show three dimensional bar charts but so far, and perhaps this is also the case with holograms, it has not found the most appropriate type of subject matter or theme to be widely used.

[1] *The Intelligent Eye* by R L Gregory. Weidenfeld and Nicolson, London 1970.

Conkers

Right and opposite page: Page and double spreads from *The Way to Play*. It covers all the well known family and social games, as well as little known ones from foreign countries and includes some dating back many centuries. It sets out the rules of each game, the number of players and equipment required. Conkers (right) is described in a single page, Backgammon and Baccarat (opposite page) are each described in four pages.
Designers: Diagram Visual Information Ltd, London.
Publisher: Paddington Press Ltd.

Conkers is a popular game with British children. Two players each have a "conker" threaded on a knotted string. Players take alternate hits at their opponent's conker and the game is won when one player destroys the other's conker.

The conkers The game is usually played with nuts from the horsechestnut tree, but is sometimes played with hazelnuts (often called "cobnuts").

When preparing their conkers, players make a hole through the center with a sharp instrument such as a meat skewer, or a compass or a pair of geometry dividers. Many players then harden their conkers by soaking them in vinegar or salt and water and/or baking them for about half an hour. Excellent conkers are obtained by storing them in the dark for a year.

When the conker is ready, a strong piece of string or a bootlace is threaded through the hole and knotted at one end. The string should be long enough for about 9in to hang down after it is wrapped once or twice around the hand.

The game Players take alternate hits at their opponent's conker.

The player whose conker is to be hit first, holds his conker as shown (**a**)—with the string wrapped around his hand. He must adjust the height of his hand to suit his opponent, and must then keep his conker perfectly still for the hit.

The striker takes his conker in one hand and holds the opposite end of his string in the other hand (**b**). For the strike, he first draws the conker back and then releases it in a fast swinging motion in the direction of his opponent's conker (**c**).

If the striker misses his opponent's conker he is allowed a maximum of two further attempts to make a hit. If the players' strings tangle, the first player to call "strings" can claim an extra shot.

Play continues until one of the conkers is destroyed—ie until no part of it remains on the string.

Scoring Conkers are usually described according to the number of victories won with them—eg a "oner," "fiver," "seventy-fiver."

A conker adds one to its title each time it destroys a conker that has never won a game. A conker that defeats a conker with previous wins claims one for defeating it plus all the defeated conker's wins—so a "fiver" that defeats another "fiver" becomes an "elevener."

CONQUERORS

This is a similar game to conkers and seems to have been very popular in the eighteenth and nineteenth centuries.

Two players press empty snail shells tip to tip until one of them breaks.

Scoring is the same as for conkers.

SOLDIERS

This game is now usually played with lollipop, or ice cream, sticks.

One player holds his stick with both hands, one at each end. The other holds his stick in one hand and gives his opponent's stick a sharp blow. Turns at striking alternate as in conkers, and the game continues until one of the sticks breaks. Scoring is as for conkers.

The game used to be played with stalks from the ribwort plantain—the winner being the first player to knock the head off his opponent's stalk.

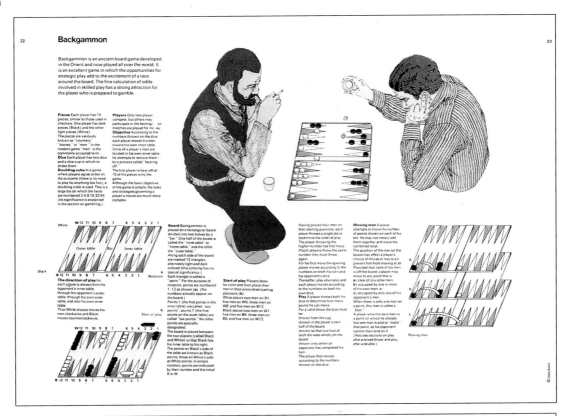

Backgammon

Backgammon is an ancient board game developed in the Orient and now played all over the world. It is an excellent game in which the opportunities for strategic play add to the excitement of a race around the board. The fine calculation of odds involved in skilled play has a strong attraction for the player who is prepared to gamble.

Pieces Each player has 15 pieces, similar to those used in checkers. One player has dark pieces (Black) and the other light pieces (White). The pieces are variously known as "counters," "stones," or "men." In the modern game "men" is the commonly accepted term.
Dice Each player has two dice and a dice cup in which to shake them.
Doubling cube In a game where players agree to bet on the outcome (there is no need to play for anything but fun), a doubling cube is used. This is a large die on which the faces are numbered 2:4:8:16:32:64. (Its significance is explained in the section on gambling.)

Players Only two player compete, but others may participate in the betting when matches are played for mc 'ey.
Objective According to the numbers thrown with the dice, each player moves his men toward his own inner table. Once all a player's men are located in his own inner table he attempts to remove them—by a process called "bearing off."
The first player to bear off all 15 of his pieces wins the game.
Although the basic objective of the game is simple, the rules and strategies governing a player's moves are much more complex.

Board Backgammon is played on a rectangular board divided into two halves by a "bar." One half of the board is called the "inner table" or "home table," and the other the "outer table."
Along each side of the board are marked 12 triangles, alternately light and dark colored (this coloring has no special significance.)
Each triangle is called a "point." For the purpose of notation, points are numbered 1-12 as shown (a). (No numbers actually appear on the board.)
Points 1 (the first points in the inner table) are called "ace points"; points 7 (the first points on the outer table) are called "bar points." No other points are specially designated.
The board is placed between the two players (called Black and White) so that Black has his inner table to his right. The points on Black's side of the table are known as Black points, those on White's side as White points. In simple notation, points are indicated by their number and the initial B or W.

The direction of play for each player is always from his opponent's inner table, through his opponent's outer table, through his own outer table, and into his own inner table.
Thus White always moves his men clockwise and Black moves counterclockwise.

Start of play Players draw for color and then place their men in their prescribed starting positions (b).
White places two men on B1; five men on W6; three men on W8; and five men on B12.
Black places two men on W1; five men on B6; three men on B8; and five men on W12.

Having placed their men on their starting positions, each player throws a single die to determine the order of play. The player throwing the higher number has first move. If both players throw the same number they must throw again.
For his first move the opening player moves according to the numbers on both his own and his opponent's dice.
Thereafter, play alternates and each player moves according to the numbers on both his own dice.
Play A player throws both his dice to determine how many points he can move.
For a valid throw the dice must be:
thrown from the cup;
thrown in the player's own half of the board;
thrown so that one face of each die rests wholly on the board;
thrown only when an opponent has completed his turn.
The player then moves according to the numbers thrown on the dice.

Moving men A player attempts to move the number of points shown on each of his dice. He may not merely add them together and move the combined total.
The position of the men on the board may affect a player's choice of moves or may even prevent him from moving at all. Provided that none of his men is off the board, a player may move to any point that is:
a) clear of any other men;
b) occupied by one or more of his own men; or
c) occupied by only one of his opponent's men.
When a player throws both dice to determine how many points he can move, he moves each in turn.
When there is only one man on a point, this man is called a "blot."
A player who moves a man to a point on which he already has one man is said to "make" that point, as his opponent cannot then land on it.
(Also see sections on play after a mixed throw and play after a double.)

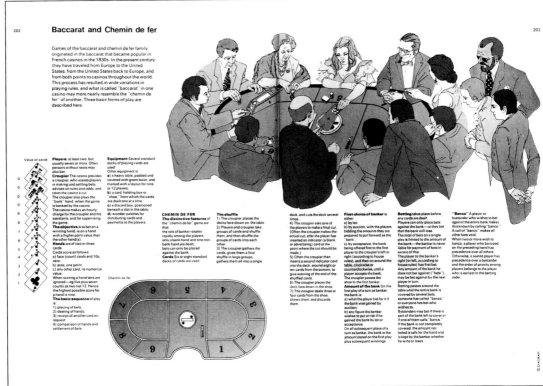

Baccarat and Chemin de fer

Games of the baccarat and chemin de fer family originated in the baccarat that became popular in French casinos in the 1830s. In the present century they have traveled from Europe to the United States, from the United States back to Europe, and from both points to casinos throughout the world. This process has resulted in wide variations in playing rules, and what is called "baccarat" in one casino may more nearly resemble the "chemin de fer" of another. Three basic forms of play are described here.

Value of cards

Players: at least two, but usually seven or more. Often persons without seats may also bet.
Croupier The casino provides a croupier, who assists players in making and settling bets, advises on rules and odds, and takes the casino's cut.
The croupier also plays the "bank" hand when the game is banked by the casino.
The casino makes an hourly charge for the croupier and his assistants, and for supervising the game.
The objective is to bet on a winning hand—a hand with a higher point value than the other hand(s).
Hands are of one or two or three cards.
Cards score as follows:
a) face (court) cards and 10s, zero;
b) aces, one point;
c) any other card, its numerical value.
When scoring a hand tens are ignored—so that any seven counts as two not 12. Hence the highest possible score for a hand is nine.
The basic sequence of play is:
1) placing of bets;
2) dealing of hands;
3) receipt of another card on request;
4) comparison of hands and settlement of bets.

Equipment Several standard decks of playing cards are used.
Other equipment is:
a) a heavy table, padded and covered with green baize, and marked with a layout for nine or 12 players;
b) a card-holding box or "shoe," from which the cards are dealt one at a time;
c) a discard box, positioned beneath a slit in the table;
d) wooden palettes for distributing cards and payments to the players.

CHEMIN DE FER
The distinctive features of the "chemin de fer" game are that:
the role of banker rotates rapidly among the players, only a bank hand and non-bank hand are dealt, bets can only be placed against the bank.
Cards Six or eight standard decks of cards are used

Chemin de fer

The shuffle
1) The croupier places the decks face down on the table.
2) Players and croupier take groups of cards and shuffle them, and then shuffle the groups of cards into each other.
3) The croupier gathers the cards, gives them a final shuffle in large groups, gathers them all into a single

deck, and cuts the deck several times.
4) The croupier asks one of the players to make a final cut. (Often the croupier makes the actual cut, after a player has inserted an indicator (a blank or advertising) card at the point where the cut should be made.)
5) Often the croupier then inserts a second indicator card into the deck, around eight or ten cards from the bottom, to give warning of the end of the shuffled cards.
6) The croupier places the deck face down in the shoe.
7) The croupier deals three or four cards from the shoe, shows them, and discards them.

First choice of banker is either:
a) by lot;
b) by auction, with the players bidding the amounts they are prepared to put forward as the "bank."
c) by acceptance, the bank being offered first to the first player (according to house rules), and then on around the table, clockwise or counterclockwise, until a player accepts the bank.
The croupier passes the shoe to the first banker.
Amount of the bank On the first play of a turn as banker, the bank is:
a) what the player bid for it if the bank was gained by auction;
b) any figure the banker wishes to put at risk if he gained the bank by lot or acceptance.
On all subsequent plays of a turn as banker, the bank is the amount stated on the first play plus subsequent winnings.

Betting takes place before any cards are dealt.
Players can only place bets against the bank—ie they bet that the bank will lose.
The total of bets on a single play is limited to the amount of the bank—the banker is never liable for payment of bets in excess of this.
The player to the banker's right (or left, according to house rules) has first bet.
Any amount of the bank he does not bet against ("fade") may be bet against by the next player in turn.
Betting passes around the table until the entire bank is covered by several bets, someone has called "banco," or everyone has bet who wishes to.
Bystanders may bet if there is part of the bank left to cover or if one of them calls "banco."
If the bank is not completely covered, the amount not faded is safe for the hand and is kept by the banker whether he wins or loses.

"Banco" A player or bystander who wishes to bet against the entire bank makes this known by calling "banco." A call of "banco" makes all other bets void.
When two or more wish to banco, a player who bancoed on the preceding hand has precedence over all others.
Otherwise, a seated player has precedence over a bystander and the order of priority among players belongs to the player who is earliest in the betting order.

Right and opposite page: Page and double spread from *Weapons, an international encyclopedia from 5000 BC to 2000 AD*. It is arguable as to whether there will not be new forms of weapons by the year 2000 but it covers chemical, nuclear and biological warfare and the whole range of weaponry from neolithic times onwards.
Designers: Diagram Visual Information Ltd, London.
Publisher: St Martins' Press Inc, New York.

Devices to assist throwing

Here we survey ways that have been used to enhance the power of the thrower's own arm. In some cases the device is an integral part of the missile or simply an aspect of its shape; in others the device is separate from the missile and can be reused. The more important and widely used of these devices are covered in greater depth later in this chapter.

Exploiting gravity (left)
The simplest means of adding to the power of a thrown missile is to have the advantage in height over the enemy, as in this detail after a medieval illustration of a siege. Stones are being hurled from the walls onto attackers who are climbing scaling ladders.

Integral devices (right)
1 A rigid handle can extend the thrower's arm and act as a lever to increase the momentum of the heavy head (e.g. throwing-club).
2 A flexible handle, such as a cord, allows a weight to be swung at speed before release (e.g. *bolas*).
3 A thin cross-sectional shape allows a missile to skim through the air with minimum drag (e.g. quoit or *chakram, shuriken*).
4 An aerodynamic cross-sectional shape can help sustain the missile in flight (e.g. *boomerang*).
5 A loop of cord fixed to a spear can give added leverage to the hand at the moment of release (e.g. Roman *amentum*).

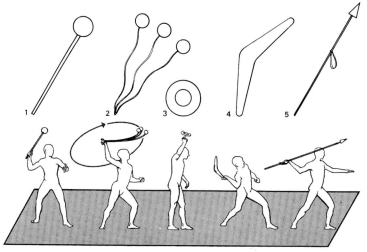

Separate devices (right)
A A sling allows a stone to be swung at high speed, then released (see opposite page).
B A staff-sling combines the leverage of a rigid handle with the release mechanism of a sling (e.g. medieval *fustibal*).
C A launching stick can be used as a lever to fling a perforated stone. If the stick has a forked end, a thin, flat stone can be thrown (e.g. as used by the Peruvians against the Spanish Conquistadores).
D A spear-thrower is a lever adapted to increase the momentum given to a throwing-spear (e.g. the Australian *woomera*).
E A separate, knotted cord, looped in a "half hitch" round a spear-shaft can be used to give added leverage at the moment of release.

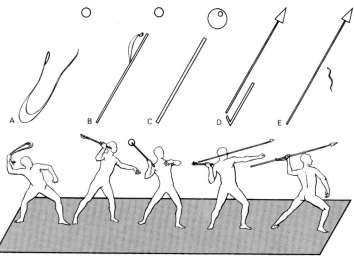

76

Semi-automatic pistols

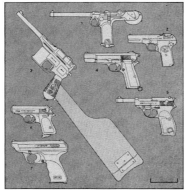

Semi-automatic pistols (left)
1 Borchardt pistol of 1893. One of the first successful pistols of the type, and a forerunner of the Luger. Caliber 7.63mm.
2 Browning Modèle 1900 The first of Browning's pistol designs, made by Fabrique Nationale in Belgium. Caliber 7.65mm.
3 "Broomhandle" Mauser pistol, shown here fitted with the optional shoulder-stock. Produced in many versions from 1896. This is the Model 1916, in 9mm caliber.
4 Browning High Power pistol, or the GP35. Originally made in Belgium in 1935. Shown is the No.2 Mk1 version made in Canada for the British Army. 13-round magazine. Caliber 9mm.
5 Walther P38 Used by Germany in WW2, and still made in modified form. Double-action hammer. Caliber. 9mm.
6 Walther PPK The initials stand for Polizei Pistole Kriminal, which indicates its intended use. A blowback design. Caliber 7.65mm and 9mm.
7 Heckler and Koch VP70 A recent innovation, able to fire three-shot bursts when fitted with a shoulder-stock. 18-round magazine. Caliber 9mm.

Locked breech systems (below) In order to use more powerful ammunition than is possible with blowback designs, many semi-auto pistols have barrel and breech-block locked together at the moment of firing. Here we examine two famous designs of pistol unlock and open by using recoil.

Cartridges (right) The two calibers most widely used in semi-auto pistols. Shown here are:
a 7.65mm Parabellum. This caliber is not particularly popular in Europe.
b The 9mm ACP. The design is used by the United States Colt Pistol which introduced this caliber. Later variants of the caliber increased the power.

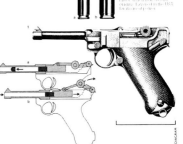

Luger P'08 (right) This well-known German pistol (1) uses a "toggle" action. A series of joints, like the joints of a finger, lock the breech-block to the barrel as long as the center joint is below the other two (a). On firing, barrel and breech-block are thrust back by recoil, sliding in grooves on the frame of the pistol. After a short distance, the toggle is knocked upward (b) by sloping projections on the frame. This unlocks the breech-block, which continues to the rear to eject the spent case. The barrel moves no further back.
Many variations of Luger exist, differing chiefly in the length of barrel. Eight-shot magazine. Caliber 7.65mm Parabellum or 9mm Parabellum.

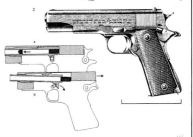

Colt 1911 A1 (right) The most popular of US semi-autos, this design (2) uses a variety of "short recoil" system. Before firing (a), the barrel is locked, by ribs on its upper surface, to the slide. A short flexible link attaches the barrel to the lower body of the pistol. On firing, barrel and slide recoil together until the link swings the barrel down (b), freeing it from the locking recesses on the slide. The slide then continues to the rear to eject the spent case and complete the operating cycle.
The 1911 A1 was produced in 1923 as a result of improvements to the original 1911 design. The 1911 A1 is still in production and in use in many parts of the world. Caliber .45in ACP.

These pistols, often called "automatics," are more correctly called autoloaders or semi-automatic pistols, as they do not fire in bursts. Before use, a full magazine must be inserted and the mechanism "cocked" by hand to feed a cartridge into the breech. Thereafter, they fire a shot each time the trigger is pressed. Most designs date from before WW1.

Position of the magazine (right) Several early designs of semi-auto pistol had the magazine placed in front of the trigger-guard (a), as on a rifle. Far more common and compact are pistols with the magazine placed inside the grip (b). As well as being neater, this solution improves the balance of the weapon.

Blowback system (right) This is the simplest of the semi-auto systems, but it can only be used with weaker types of ammunition. The essential point is that barrel and breech are not locked together on firing (A). The mass of the slide (or breech-block) and the strength of the return-spring delay opening (B) until the bullet has left the barrel and bore pressure is low. In addition, the cartridge has a case with parallel sides. The detail (C) shows how this continues to seal the breech during opening until the whole length of the case is clear of the barrel.
As with all semi-auto designs, the return-spring pushes the slide forward again, feeding the next cartridge into the breech.

116 117

Solid fuel rocket propulsion

Solid fuels were used to power the earliest known rockets, and they still find wider use than liquid fuels. Here we illustrate a variety of 19th century war-rockets that used solid fuel, and go on to explain the ways in which solid fuels are applied in modern rocketry.

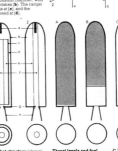

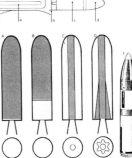

Rocket-propelled "fire-arrows," such as those held by the warrior (left), were fired by lighting the closed end of the container, and were developed and used by the Chinese from the 10th century. Rocket-launched explosive grenades existed by the 13th century. By 1250 the rocket had been introduced, mainly through the Arabs, to Europe.

Combinations (right) of solid fuel motors with other forms of propulsion.
1 Solid fuel boosters are sometimes fitted to ramjet and liquid-fueled missiles.
2 Integrated rocket/ramjet missiles exist, where the rocket motor (a) becomes, after burning out, the ramjet combustion chamber, with air-intakes (b), the ramjet fuel is at (c), and the warhead at (d).

Congreve's rockets (above) were the first to be used by Western armies. They were made in ten sizes and with three main kinds of warhead. Shown are the complete 12-pounder size with shell warhead (1), and the head and motor of the 8in (203mm) 'carcass' or bombardment type (2). The launching ramp for the larger versions is shown (below).

The Hale rocket (above), used, in several versions, in the American Civil War and by Britain. It had no stick, being stabilized instead by the spinning action of the propellant gas, acting on three vanes as it escaped at the rear. Shown in side (A) and rear (B) views, is the British 24-pounder model of the 1880s. The launcher is shown (below).

French artillery rockets of the 1870s (above) were fitted with three types of warhead: explosive (1), incendiary (2), or solid shot (3). They weighed 15.43lb (7kg). Stabilization was achieved by the grooved stick (a). The end view (b) shows the exhaust vents and the corresponding grooves in the stick. The launcher is shown (below).

A basic two-stage solid-propellant ICBM (above) The first and second stages (A and B) of a two-stage rocket each contain a solid propellant charge (a), the exhaust nozzle system (b), and the thrust termination system (c), which shuts off the engine when the desired velocity has been reached. The re-entry body (C) contains the guidance and control systems that keep the missile on course, the auxiliary power supply, arming systems, safety systems, fuzes, and the warhead (d). Most contemporary re-entry bodies are termed re-entry vehicles, and are classed either as Multiple Independently-targetable Re-entry Vehicles (MIRVs), or Maneuverable Alternative target Re-entry Vehicles (MARVs) (see p.274).

Rocket structure (above) Solid propellant rockets consist mainly of a solid propellant charge or 'grain' contained within a case. The grain contains all the elements necessary for complete, smooth burning. It can either be contained within a separate case (1), or be bonded to the case—case-bonded (2)—which can reduce size and weight. The shape of the central conduit determines the surface area exposed to burning at any one time. Both those illustrated have a tubular grain type of configuration.
a Igniter
b Outer casing
c Insulation
d Inhibitor
e Charge
f Central conduit
g Throat insert
h Nozzle

Thrust levels and fuel configurations (above) The larger the surface area of the burning propellant, the greater is the motor's thrust. Thrust levels can therefore be controlled by the design of the charge shape. We show four examples
A An end-burning grain burns only in one direction (like a cigarette) and gives a constant level of thrust.
B An end-burning configuration with two grains of different burning rates varies the thrust level, giving, for instance, initial high-level thrust followed by a lower-level thrust for sustained flight.

C Tubular-grain configuration produces a progressive thrust. As the period of burning continues the area of the burning grain and the resultant thrust progressively increase.
D This single-grain configuration will give an initial boost with the large star-shaped area and sustain the flight with the smaller burning area.

Nozzle protection (left) To prevent the nozzle being damaged by the heat of the escaping exhaust gases (a), complex inserts of heat-resistant materials (b) are used. A ring of cool burning propellant (c) inserted just above the nozzle provides a protective layer of cool gas (d) next to the nozzle.

Solid-propellant missiles (above)
1 US Poseidon C3 two-stage submarine-launched ballistic missile. Targets 3230mi (5200km) away can be hit by fitting a Mk3 MIRV with ten 50KT warheads.
2 US Minuteman III three-stage intercontinental ballistic missile. Range over 8080mi (13,000km). It carries a Mk12 MIRV with three 170KT warheads.

244 245

Right and opposite page: Double
spreads and page from *Musik-
instrumente der Welt*. An illustrated
encyclopedia of musical instruments
from all countries and periods. The
page illustrating the organ (opposite
page) is from a five page section
describing this instrument while the
two spreads are complete on their
own.
Designers: Diagram Visual Information Ltd, London.
Publisher: Orbis, Munich, West
Germany.

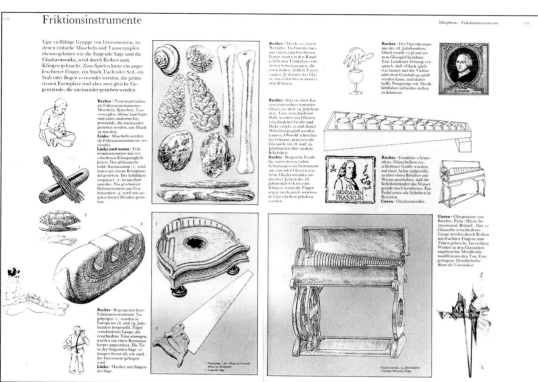

Friktionsinstrumente

Mechanische Musikinstrumente

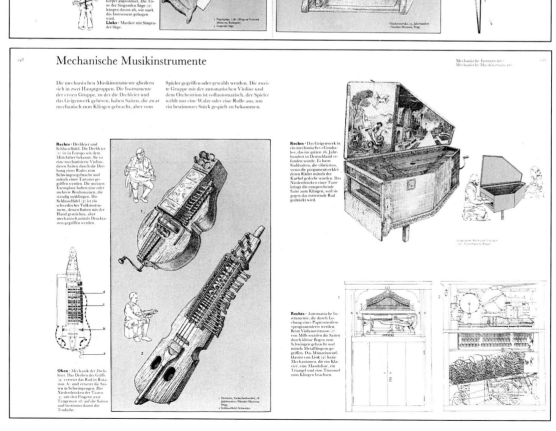

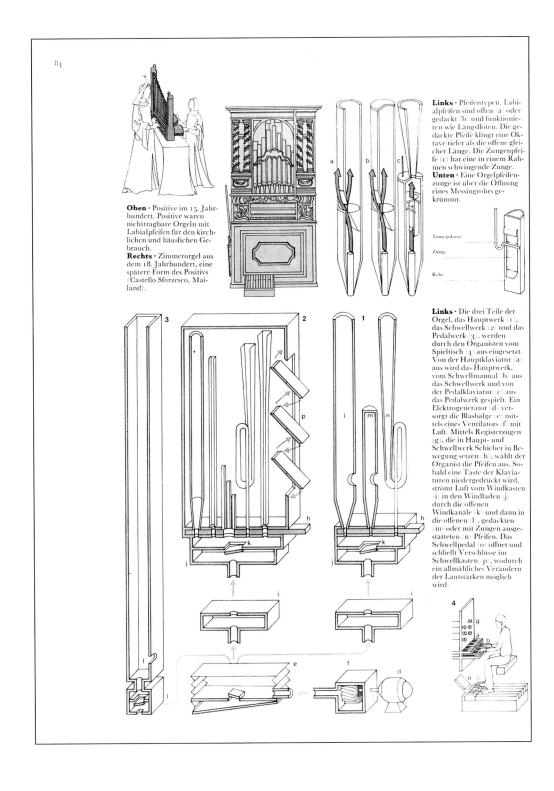

81

Oben · Positive im 15. Jahrhundert. Positive waren nichttragbare Orgeln mit Labialpfeifen für den kirchlichen und häuslichen Gebrauch.
Rechts · Zimmerorgel aus dem 18. Jahrhundert, eine spätere Form des Positivs (Castello Sforzesco, Mailand).

Links · Pfeifentypen. Labialpfeifen sind offen (a) oder gedackt (b) und funktionieren wie Längsflöten. Die gedackte Pfeife klingt eine Oktave tiefer als die offene gleicher Länge. Die Zungenpfeife (c) hat eine in einem Rahmen schwingende Zunge.
Unten · Eine Orgelpfeifenzunge ist über die Öffnung eines Messingrohrs gekrümmt.

Tonregulator

Zunge

Rohr

Links · Die drei Teile der Orgel, das Hauptwerk (1), das Schwellwerk (2) und das Pedalwerk (3), werden durch den Organisten vom Spieltisch (4) aus eingesetzt. Von der Hauptklaviatur (a) aus wird das Hauptwerk, vom Schwellmanual (b) aus das Schwellwerk und von der Pedalklaviatur (c) aus das Pedalwerk gespielt. Ein Elektrogenerator (d) versorgt die Blasbälge (e) mittels eines Ventilators (f) mit Luft. Mittels Registerzügen (g), die in Haupt- und Schwellwerk Schieber in Bewegung setzen (h), wählt der Organist die Pfeifen aus. Sobald eine Taste der Klaviaturen niedergedrückt wird, strömt Luft vom Windkasten (i) in den Windladen (j) durch die offenen Windkanäle (k) und dann in die offenen (l), gedackten (m) oder mit Zungen ausgestatteten (n) Pfeifen. Das Schwellpedal (o) öffnet und schließt Verschlüsse im Schwellkasten (p), wodurch ein allmähliches Verändern der Lautstärken möglich wird.

Right and opposite page: Single pages and double spreads from *Reader's Digest Repair Manual.* First produced in 1972 this guide to home maintenance runs to 704 pages and covers repairs to almost every conceivable part of the house, garden and garage and its equipment. The storyboard is meticulously prepared to explain a sequence of actions in the minimum amount of space and, on average, with only a three line caption under each illustration. Equally interesting is the variety of colour/tonal effects achieved with black and one other printing colour, with the exception of part of the electrical section where extra colours are used to show the colour coding of electrical flex and connections. Page size is 190 × 265mm.

Edited and designed by The Readers' Digest Association Ltd, London.

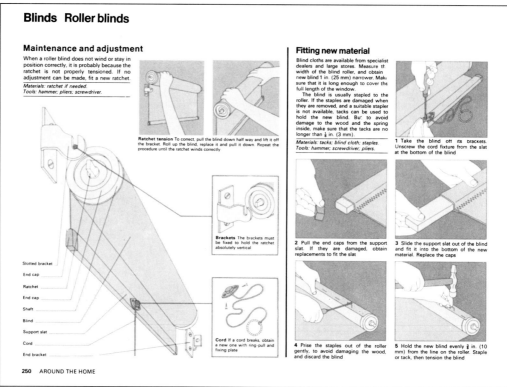

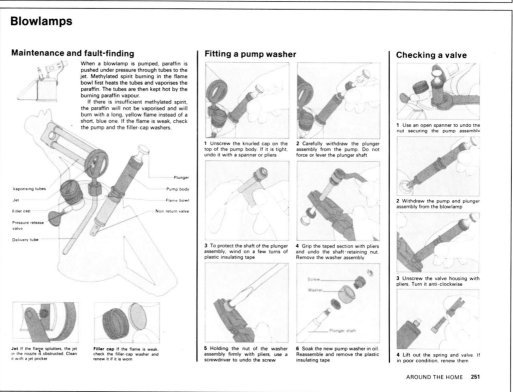

Plumbing Traps and waste fittings

Fitting new washers on a waste trap

Every basin, sink and bath has a waste trap which retains a quantity of water to ensure that smells cannot enter the house from the waste pipe; it also collects waste which may block the pipe.

Traps are of lead, copper or plastic. Blockages can be dealt with in all types by the householder, but repairs to lead traps require the skill of a plumber.

Place a bucket under a leaking trap, unscrew the connections and remove the washers. Take the washers to an ironmonger or builders' merchant and buy new ones to match. After refitting a trap, run the water to check for leaks.

U-shaped trap   **Bottle trap**

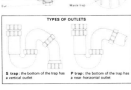

TYPES OF OUTLETS

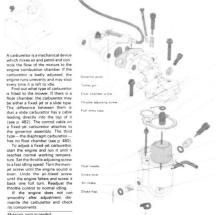

S trap: the bottom of the trap has a vertical outlet

P trap: the bottom of the trap has a near-horizontal outlet

Sealing a waste fitting

A waste fitting is a short pipe connecting the sink or bath outlet to the trap and the waste pipe.

The flange which sits on the sink outlet and the back nut below the sink should both be sealed with a linseed oil or mastic putty. If they leak, remove and clean the fitting. Replace with new putty.

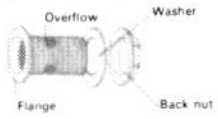

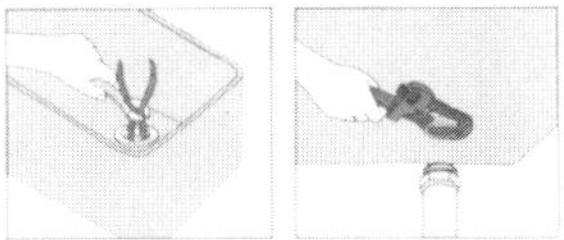

1 Disconnect the trap below the sink (see p. 151). Fit pliers into the grating and grip with a spanner

2 Hold the grating steady with the pliers. Unscrew the back nut below the sink with an adjustable spanner

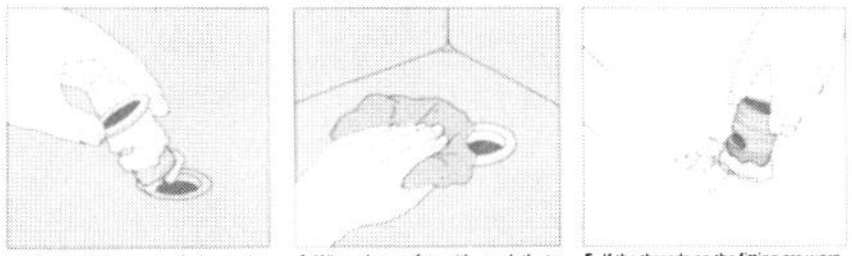

3 Lift the fitting out of the outlet. Strip off the old washer and brush the fitting clean

4 Wipe the outlet with a cloth to remove dirt and putty. Dry it thoroughly to ensure that new putty sticks

5 If the threads on the fitting are worn, buy a new one. Knead putty under the flange

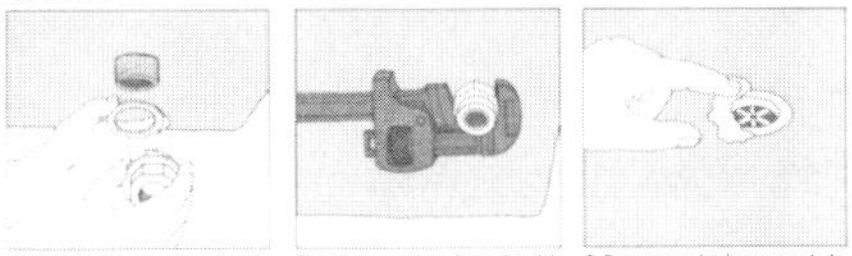

6 Insert the fitting in the outlet. Put putty on washer and fit the washer and the back nut underneath the sink

7 Hold the grating above the sink with pliers. Tighten the back nut with an adjustable spanner

8 Remove surplus putty round the flange and press the back nut with the fingers. Check for leaks

Plumbing Taps and stop valves

Maintenance and repair

Wash and polish all taps regularly to prevent corrosion. Do not use abrasives: they destroy the chrome finish.

Maintenance and repair for ordinary taps and stop valves is the same: some others—for example, the Supatap or one with a pull-off head—need slightly different adjustments (see pp. 144, 145).

Use replacement washers that match the size of the existing ones and before fitting them make sure

there are no pieces of the old washer left in place. If the old washers are leather or fibre, use rubber or nylon replacements.

Materials: washers as required—⅜ in. (13 mm) for sinks and basins, ¾ in. (20 mm) for baths, or washer plate (Supataps); mixer unit seals; rubber O rings.
Tools: adjustable spanner; screwdriver; small spanner for jumper nut, pliers.

STOP VALVES AND SUPATAPS

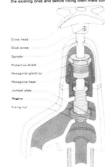

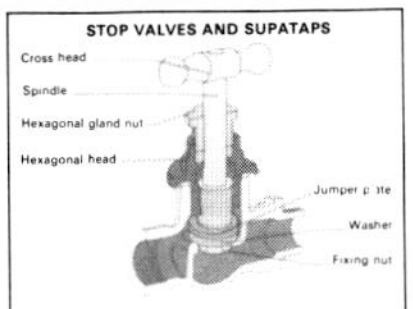

Cross head
Grub screw
Spindle
Protective shield
Hexagonal gland nut
Hexagonal head
Jumper plate
Washer
Fixing nut

Stop valves are used to control the flow of water in pipework and are often found near cold-water tanks, hot-water cylinders and lavatory fittings.

Cross head
Spindle
Hexagonal gland nut
Hexagonal head

Jumper plate

Washer

Fixing nut

Spindle
Hexagonal gland nut
Protective shield

Automatic check valve
Combined jumper and check valve
Flow straightener

Supataps prevent water vibration noises in pipework. The washers can be changed without turning off the water supply

Fitting a new washer

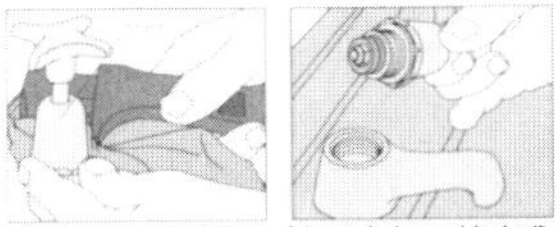

1 Shut off the water supply and open the tap or valve fully. Fit waste plug in sink. Protect shield with rag and remove it with a spanner

2 Loosen the hexagonal head with an adjustable spanner. Unscrew the loosened nut by hand and lift the top of the tap away from the body

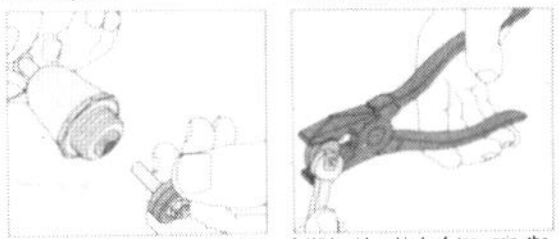

3 On some taps the jumper can be removed; on others it fits loosely. The washer is usually held against the jumper plate with a small nut

4 With either kind of tap, grip the edge of the jumper plate with pliers. If the washer is held by a nut, undo it with a small spanner

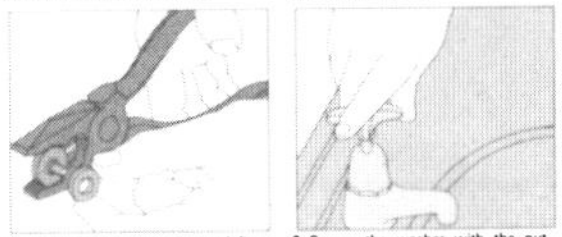

5 Remove the old washer and fit a matching new one. Fit the side of the washer bearing the maker's name so that it faces downwards

6 Secure the washer with the nut. Reassemble the tap. Turn on the water supply. Turn the tap on and off to check that it does not drip

---

Lawn mowers Carburettors

Adjusting and maintaining a fixed-jet carburettor

A carburettor is a mechanical device which mixes air and petrol and controls the flow of them to the engine combustion chamber. If the carburettor is badly adjusted, the engine runs unevenly and may stop every time it is left to idle.

Find out what type of carburettor is fitted to the mower. If there is a float chamber, the carburettor may be either a fixed-jet or a slide type. The difference between them is that a slide carburettor has a cable leading directly into the top of it (see p. 482). The control cable on a fixed-jet carburettor attaches to the governor assembly. The third type—the diaphragm carburettor—has no float chamber (see p. 480).

To adjust a fixed-jet carburettor, start the engine and run it until it reaches normal working temperature. Set the throttle adjusting screw to a fast idling speed. Turn the main-jet screw until the engine sound is even. Undo the air-bleed screw until the engine falters and screw it back one full turn. Readjust the throttle control to normal idling.

If the engine does not run smoothly after adjustment, dismantle the carburettor and check its components.

Materials: parts as needed.
Tools: screwdriver; spanners; pliers.

Governor pivot
Tickler pin
Float chamber screw
Throttle adjusting screw
Fuel entry tube

Float needle
Choke lever
Air intake
Choke flap

Air-bleed screw Fit a new one if the tapered point is grooved. Blow through the drilling, where the screw fits, to make sure it is clear

Gasket Always fit new gaskets at the inlet manifold and carburettor flange when the carburettor is dismantled

Needle seating Unscrew the assembly from the body of the carburettor. If the needle is pitted or grooved, fit a complete new assembly

Slow-running tube Never push wire into it. If a blockage cannot be cleared with an air line, obtain and fit a new tube

Jet-adjusting screw Screw right in. Count the number of turns. Remove it and check the needle point. If it is grooved or worn, fit a new screw

Float-chamber bowl Clean out sediment. If the varnish on the float itself is worn or cracked, renew the float

Vent hole Make sure that the vent hole in the side of the float-chamber bowl is clear to allow air to leave the chamber

Bore hole Make sure the small bore hole inside the base of the float chamber is clean and that the float spigot fits in it

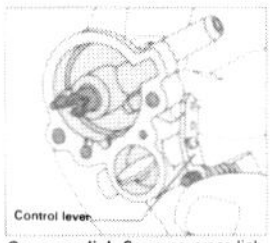

Control lever.

Governor link Some governor linkages have more than one possible position. Note the hole in the control lever in which the governor link fits. Replace the link in the same hole to give correct governor speeds

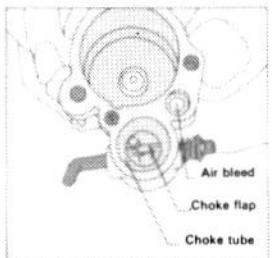

Air bleed
Choke flap
Choke tube

Choke flap Check that the choke tube and air-bleed screw are clear. Make sure the flap opens and closes fully when the lever is operated

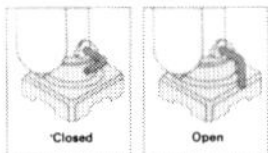

'Closed'   Open

Choke lever To close the choke, turn the lever horizontal to the carburettor body. To open, turn it downwards

Dismantling a fixed-jet carburettor

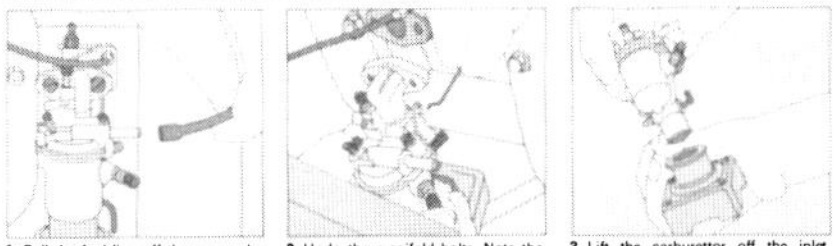

1 Pull the fuel line off the entry tube at the side of the carburettor above or beside the float chamber

2 Undo the manifold bolts. Note the governor linkage or spring position and remove it from the carburettor

3 Lift the carburettor off the inlet manifold. Pull the air-filter assembly from the carburettor air intake

  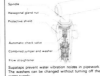

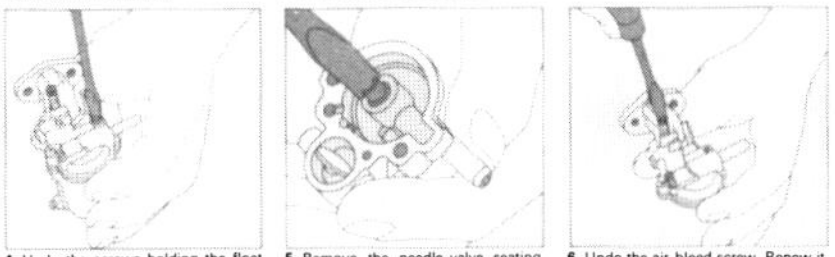

4 Undo the screws holding the float chamber. Note their correct positions if they differ in length

5 Remove the needle-valve seating from the top of the carburettor with a screwdriver wider than the slot

6 Undo the air-bleed screw. Renew it if it is worn or grooved. Screw it in fully. Turn it back three-quarters of a turn

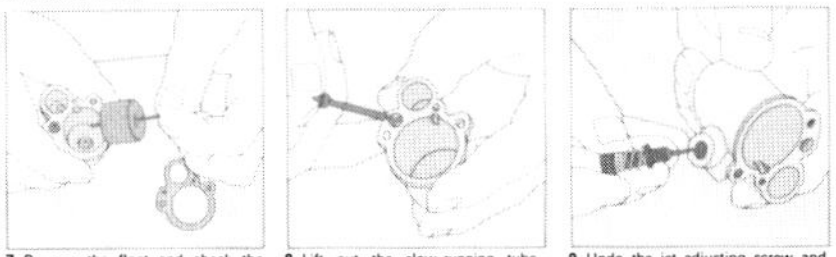

7 Remove the float and check the needle seat. If it is worn, or if the float is damaged, renew it

8 Lift out the slow-running tube. Blow through it to clear the bore. Use an air line if possible. Do not use wire

9 Undo the jet-adjusting screw and check that the needle is not bent or grooved. If damaged, fit a new one

Reassembling the carburettor

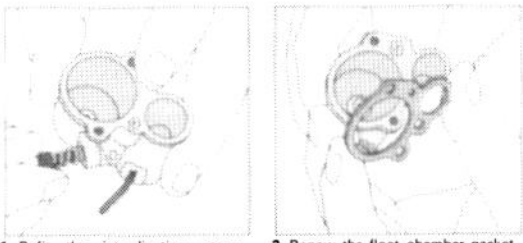

1 Refit the jet-adjusting screw. Screw it fully into the body, then unscrew it one-and-a-quarter turns

2 Renew the float-chamber gasket. Make sure that it fits over the head of the slow-running tube

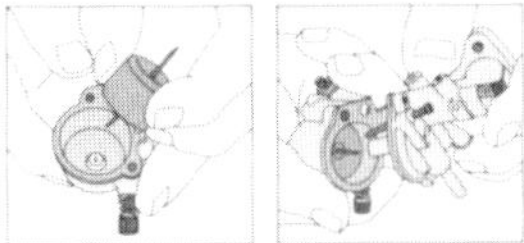

3 Fit the float assembly. Make sure that the square shaft of the needle fits correctly into the housing hole

4 Fit the top of the carburettor. Make sure the float needle enters the needle seat. Tighten the bolts

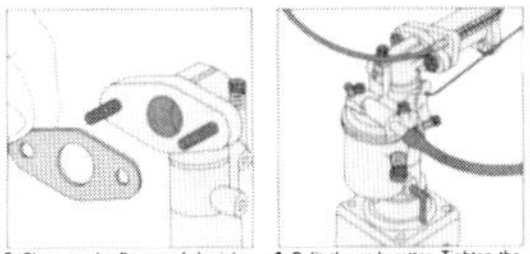

5 Clean up the flanges of the inlet manifold and the carburettor. Obtain and fit a new flange gasket

6 Refit the carburettor. Tighten the flange bolts, then refit the air cleaner, governor link and fuel line

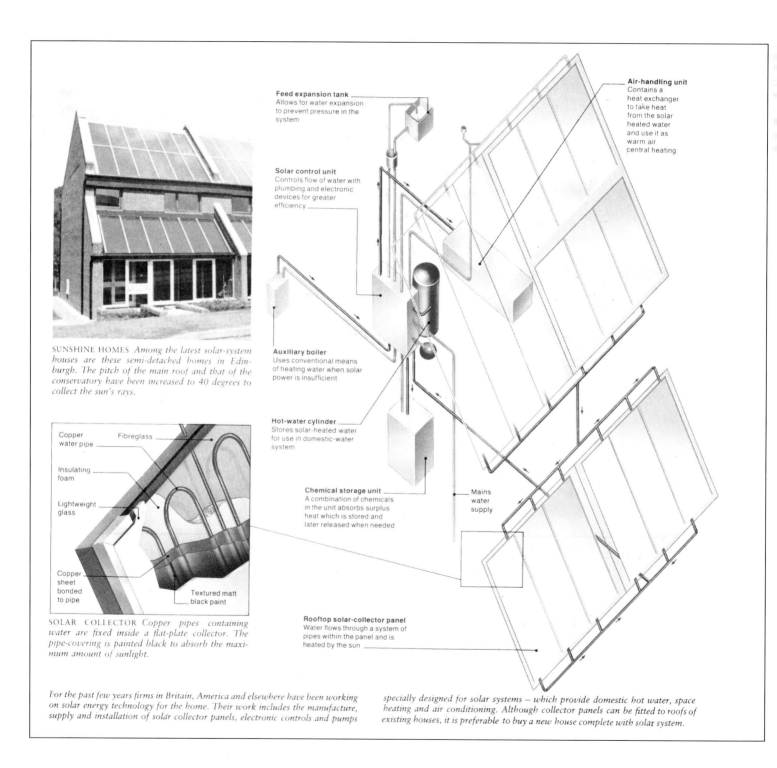

Feed expansion tank
Allows for water expansion to prevent pressure in the system

Solar control unit
Controls flow of water with plumbing and electronic devices for greater efficiency

Air-handling unit
Contains a heat exchanger to take heat from the solar heated water and use it as warm air central heating

SUNSHINE HOMES *Among the latest solar-system houses are these semi-detached homes in Edinburgh. The pitch of the main roof and that of the conservatory have been increased to 40 degrees to collect the sun's rays.*

Auxiliary boiler
Uses conventional means of heating water when solar power is insufficient

Hot-water cylinder
Stores solar-heated water for use in domestic-water system

Copper water pipe

Fibreglass

Insulating foam

Lightweight glass

Copper sheet bonded to pipe

Textured matt black paint

Chemical storage unit
A combination of chemicals in the unit absorbs surplus heat which is stored and later released when needed

Mains water supply

SOLAR COLLECTOR *Copper pipes containing water are fixed inside a flat-plate collector. The pipe-covering is painted black to absorb the maximum amount of sunlight.*

Rooftop solar-collector panel
Water flows through a system of pipes within the panel and is heated by the sun

For the past few years firms in Britain, America and elsewhere have been working on solar energy technology for the home. Their work includes the manufacture, supply and installation of solar collector panels, electronic controls and pumps specially designed for solar systems – which provide domestic hot water, space heating and air conditioning. Although collector panels can be fitted to roofs of existing houses, it is preferable to buy a new house complete with solar system.

Left: Heating a house from the sun, explanatory graphics from *'The inventions that changed the world'*, published by The Reader's Digest Association Ltd, London.

Right: Bringing a TV picture to the screen in colour, explanatory graphics from the same book as above.

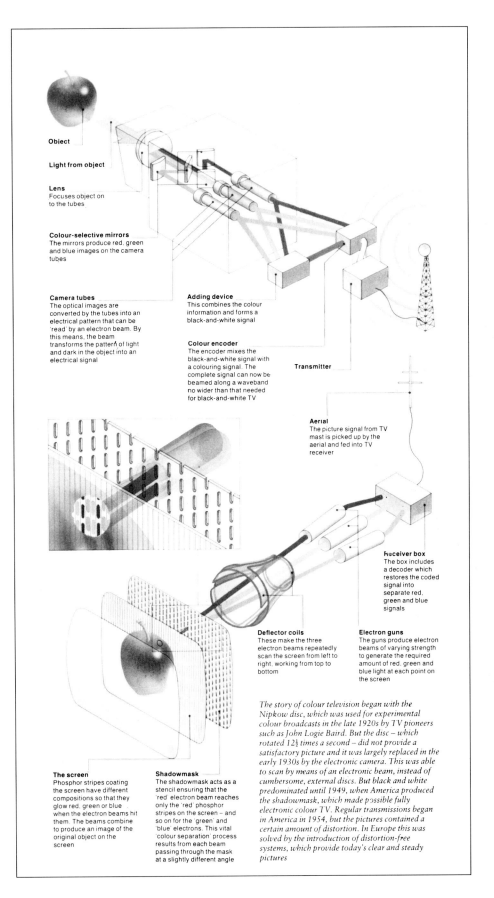

Object

Light from object

Lens
Focuses object on to the tubes

Colour-selective mirrors
The mirrors produce red, green and blue images on the camera tubes

Camera tubes
The optical images are converted by the tubes into an electrical pattern that can be 'read' by an electron beam. By this means, the beam transforms the pattern of light and dark in the object into an electrical signal

Adding device
This combines the colour information and forms a black-and-white signal

Colour encoder
The encoder mixes the black-and-white signal with a colouring signal. The complete signal can now be beamed along a waveband no wider than that needed for black-and-white TV

Transmitter

Aerial
The picture signal from TV mast is picked up by the aerial and fed into TV receiver

Receiver box
The box includes a decoder which restores the coded signal into separate red, green and blue signals

Deflector coils
These make the three electron beams repeatedly scan the screen from left to right, working from top to bottom

Electron guns
The guns produce electron beams of varying strength to generate the required amount of red, green and blue light at each point on the screen

The screen
Phosphor stripes coating the screen have different compositions so that they glow red, green or blue when the electron beams hit them. The beams combine to produce an image of the original object on the screen

Shadowmask
The shadowmask acts as a stencil ensuring that the 'red' electron beam reaches only the 'red' phosphor stripes on the screen – and so on for the 'green' and 'blue' electrons. This vital 'colour separation' process results from each beam passing through the mask at a slightly different angle

The story of colour television began with the Nipkow disc, which was used for experimental colour broadcasts in the late 1920s by TV pioneers such as John Logie Baird. But the disc – which rotated 12½ times a second – did not provide a satisfactory picture and it was largely replaced in the early 1930s by the electronic camera. This was able to scan by means of an electronic beam, instead of cumbersome, external discs. But black and white predominated until 1949, when America produced the shadowmask, which made possible fully electronic colour TV. Regular transmissions began in America in 1954, but the pictures contained a certain amount of distortion. In Europe this was solved by the introduction of distortion-free systems, which provide today's clear and steady pictures

Right: Honda Ballade cutaway drawing showing mechanical details.
Designer: Mamoru Watanabe.
Illustrator: Hisashi Saitoh.
Art Director: Shizuo Tonooka.
Project Team: Tokyo Graphic Designers.

Right: Cutaway drawing of Yamaha YZ 125.
Designer: Makoto Ouchi, Japan.

Far right: Cutaway drawing of a TDK video cassette.
Illustrator: Hisashi Saitoh, Japan.
Project Team: TDK Design Corporation.

case study

Designing the users' manual for Longines' new portable sports timer
Gill Scott

Gill Scott studied graphic design at the Central School of Art and Design, London. She worked as a research assistant at the Department of Applied Psychology, University of Aston (Birmingham) and as a design assistant with Ernest Hoch, Ken Garland and Dick Negus. She formed her own design consultancy practice in 1983.

Above: The Longines TL 3000, portable sports timer which can be operated by one timekeeper.

Longines, of Switzerland, have made watches since 1867. They started sports timing in 1912, using sports events to publicise and advertise their name and their watches. With the backing of research, design and engineering teams from Longines' Laboratories, they have continued to provide precision apparatus for timing at major sports events from Olympic to club level. As events required more sophisticated timing the number of pieces of equipment increased and teams of professional timekeepers were created to carry out the complicated procedures.

The TL3000, a microprocessor based, portable sports timer, was initiated, developed and designed by Patscentre UK and PA Design Unit for Longines. The anlaysis of the user's need (both the timing team and the club timekeeper) and potential sales were combined in presenting a new idea to the client.

The design of this sports timer brought all the timing facilities into one small box operatable by one person. The timer could be sold to clubs (as opposed to hired) and operated by amateurs (as opposed to professional Longines' teams). Sports clubs, training centres and sports associations could be offered timing facilities to standards prescribed by international sporting bodies, which they could operate themselves.

This machine has eighteen timing programs of which two are devoted to alpine events and two are for bob and luge; between them they take the majority of the microprocessor's capacity. Other timing programs can be applied to athletic track events, cycling, canoeing, equestrian, motor racing and match events.

The professional equipment and the system of timing was seen, by the sports organisers, to be complicated. The portable timer with its new technology made timing procedures less complicated; but, on the other hand, the organisers were in charge of the equipment for the first time.

The sale of expensive equipment which incorporates new technology is often supported by 'teaching courses' or 'telephone help'. Neither of these could be provided; the machine had to stand alone following a sale. As sales were expected to develop from user recommendation it was imperative that users learnt to operate the machine quickly and easily. The only 'help' that the machine could provide was by acknowledging a key press with an audible bleep via the lights on the keys, a one line numeric display and the paper printout. A short introductory 'teaching program' was designed in the machine software, to help operators become familiar with machine functions but a printed operator's manual was still required.

The writing and design of the manual began when the 'machine' consisted of a mass of components, secured to a 600 × 400 mm sheet of plywood, driven by a main frame computer. At this stage the machine software had not been completed and as it is seldom possible for the user instructions to be

Right: The TL 3000 showing the
keyboard layout, LC display and
paper print-out.

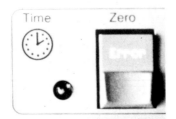

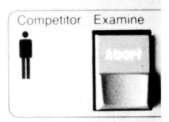

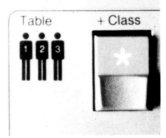

Above: Detail of part of the keyboard.

organised and written before this takes place it was
sheer luxury for me to work alongside the software
designer to carry out this task.

I acted out the part of the näive user as the
operator's ease of use was always considered
paramount. The number of hand movements, key
presses and the amount of explanation involved in
carrying out a procedure were all considered. If the
length of procedure was considered excessive a
polite request was made for the software to be
changed.

Task patterns evolved; the same task being carried
out in exactly the same way in each sport. It was
ensured that visual machine confirmation was given
in the same form each time and it followed that the
manual design would echo these structures in its
visual and written layout.

In collaboration with Longines' marketing staff
descriptions of the tasks were worked out. The use
of language was carefully considered and care was
taken to exclude electronic and technical terms.

In all cases descriptions were sought for tasks in
relation to the actual sports events.

Some tasks were common to each program but
it was possible that different sports would produce
different operators. It was decided that such tasks
would not be described separately but that each
sport should have all operating information required
to start the machine and run a timing programme
in one place; a search should not have to be made
through several sections to find the information.

The assumption was made that a new operator
would need to run through all the procedures at
least once. The manual copy provides key push-by-
push instructions with confirmation in the picture
column. Once the procedure has become relatively
familiar the picture column alone can be used as a
quick reference guide.

Longines publish all their literature and information
in French, German and English. Manuals had
previously been produced with all languages in the
same book requiring a search through three languages to find the relevant information.

It was considered desirable for a separate manual
to be produced for each language with the user
language in the machine and the manual. The
translation to French and German was carefully
supervised to ensure that precise use of language
was maintained. The manual was designed using
the same pagination and the same position for
diagrams in each language edition.

To summarise:

The software structured the tasks logically;
The manual described tasks in terms of the job
being done;
The transition of sport's organisers from being näive
to being competent equipment users was accom-
plished in hours.
The Longines' sales team regarded the manual as
a sales aid in itself and the print run was extended.

right: pages from the users' manual
showing stage by stage operating
details and examples of the print outs
from four of the programs.

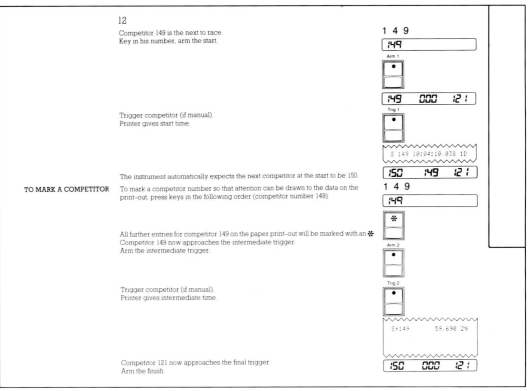

12

Competitor 149 is the next to race.
Key in his number, arm the start.

1 4 9

Trigger competitor (if manual).
Printer gives start time.

The instrument automatically expects the next competitor at the start to be 150.

TO MARK A COMPETITOR

To mark a competitor number so that attention can be drawn to the data on the print–out, press keys in the following order (competitor number 149).

1 4 9

All further entries for competitor 149 on the paper print–out will be marked with an ✻
Competitor 149 now approaches the intermediate trigger.
Arm the intermediate trigger.

Trigger competitor (if manual).
Printer gives intermediate time.

Competitor 121 now approaches the final trigger.
Arm the finish.

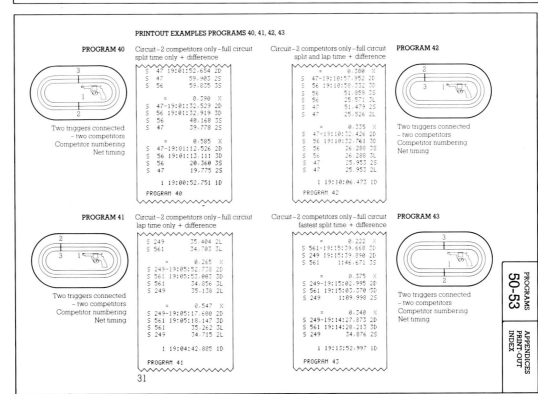

PRINTOUT EXAMPLES PROGRAMS 40, 41, 42, 43

PROGRAM 40

Circuit – 2 competitors only – full circuit
split time only + difference

Two triggers connected
– two competitors
Competitor numbering
Net timing

Circuit – 2 competitors only – full circuit
split and lap time + difference

PROGRAM 42

Two triggers connected
– two competitors
Competitor numbering
Net timing

PROGRAM 41

Circuit – 2 competitors only – full circuit
lap time only + difference

Two triggers connected
– two competitors
Competitor numbering
Net timing

Circuit – 2 competitors only – full circuit
fastest split time + difference

PROGRAM 43

Two triggers connected
– two competitors
Competitor numbering
Net timing

31

Right: A typical double spread from the user's manual describing programs for timing circuit events such as cycling or speed skating. Each language has its own edition and a finger index appears on the lower right hand side for easy access. Manual pages are shown slightly smaller than actual size.

The Longines TL 3000 software design and electronic hardware are by Dr Bob Crichton, the product design by Laurence Gunzi and the graphic design of manual and product by Gill Scott.

Programs 40, 41, 42, 43

Four programs are provided for the separate timing of two competitors in circuit events such as cycling, and speed skating or in parallel ski races. One trigger point is established for each competitor. Split and lap times are recorded and the instrument calculates the difference between the two competitors. Numbers 1–999 can be assigned to each competitor. All times subsequently recorded will be marked with the appropriate competitor number.

Program 40	Split time only of both competitors, and the difference between the two.
41	Lap time only of both competitors, and the difference between the two.
42	Split and lap times of both competitors, and the difference between the two.
43	Fastest competitor's split time and the difference between the two.

A lap is defined as successive passes of the *same* trigger.

SET INSTRUMENT — Set up instrument using the instructions on page 4.
Connect external trigger cables to appropriate channels at the back of the instrument.

Channel 1 – relates to the start.
Channel 2 – relates to competitor 1.
Channel 3 – relates to competitor 2.

Manual triggers are accepted by the instrument at all times
Ensure that the required external trigger channels are open.
REMOTE keys should be in the green / ● open position
REMOTE and MODE keys have to be pressed simultaneously to set each
REMOTE key in the required position. They may be closed and opened during or between races to avoid unwanted triggers being recorded.

SET PROGRAM — The TIME, NUMBER and TABLE keys have now to be set in association with the program selected.

TIME: Times must be recorded as net times and the key must be in the green / 2 position.

NUMBER: The number key must be in the green / ● on position. The numbers 1 and 2 will be automatically assigned, by the instrument, to the two channels. Competitor numbers can be assigned at the beginning of the race thereby overriding the system.

TABLE: Table facilities used in other programs, are not used here and the key should be in the red / 1 off position.

All three keys have each to be set simultaneously with the MODE key.
Set program, pressing keys in the following order.

TIME: green / 2

NUMBER: green / ● on

TABLE: red / 1 off

Check all keys are in the correct positions.
Press selected program numbers 40, 41, 42, 43 as appropriate.
If an error is made when typing a number, type number again using three digits (041).

4 1

4 1

Printer confirms the program number.

29

PROGRAMS 40-43

PROGRAMS 50-53

APPENDICES PRINT-OUT INDEX

book list

Alphanumeric

Herbert Spencer, *The Visible Word, Problems of Legibility.* Lund Humphries in association with the Royal College of Art (London 1968)

Patricia Wright, Informed Design for Forms, *Information Design.* John Wiley & Sons Ltd (Chichester 1984).

Pictogrammic

Symbol Signs, the Development of Passenger/Pedestrian Oriented Symbols for use in Transportation related Facilities. American Institute of Graphic Arts; prepared for the Department of Transportation. National Technical Information Service (Springfield, Virginia 1974).

Product interface

Tomás Maldonadó and Gui Bonsiepe, Sign System Design for Operative Communication, *Uppercase* no.5. Whitefriars (London 1976).

Diagrammatic

Diagraphics. Japan Creators' Association (Tokyo 1986).

Walter Herdeg (editor), *Graphis Diagrams, the Graphic Visualisation of Abstract Data.* The Graphics Press (Zurich 1974).

Robin Kinross, On the Influence of Isotype, *Information Design Journal,* volume 2/2 (Milton Keynes, UK 1981).

Arthur Lockwood, *Diagrams.* Studio Vista (London 1969).

Otto Neurath, *International Picture Language.* Kegan Paul (London 1936).

Edward R Tufte, *The Visual Display of Quantitative Information.* Graphics Press (Cheshire, Connecticut 1983).

Spatial and cartographic

Michael Burke and Ian McLaren, London's Public Transport Diagrams – Visual Comparisons of some Graphic Conventions, *Information Design Journal,* volume 2/2 (Milton Keynes, UK 1981).

Arno Peters, *The Europe Centred Character of our Geographical View of the World and its Correction.* Universum Verlag, (Munich-Solln 1979).

General

Ronald Easterby and Harn Zwaga (editors), *Information Design, the design and evaluation of signs and printed material.* John Wiley & Sons Ltd (Chichester 1984).